False profits of ethical capital

Manchester University Press

PROGRESS IN POLITICAL ECONOMY

Series editors: Andreas Bieler (School of Politics and International Relations, University of Nottingham), Gareth Bryant (Department of Political Economy at the University of Sydney), Mònica Clua-Losada (Department of Political Science, University of Texas Rio Grande Valley), Adam David Morton (Department of Political Economy, University of Sydney), and Angela Wigger (Department of Political Science, Radboud University, The Netherlands).

Since its launch in 2014, the blog Progress in Political Economy (PPE) – available at www.ppesydney.net/ – has become a central forum for the dissemination and debate of political economy research published in book and journal article forms with crossover appeal to academic, activist and public policy related audiences.

Now the Progress in Political Economy book series with Manchester University Press provides a new space for innovative and radical thinking in political economy, covering interdisciplinary scholarship from the perspectives of critical political economy, historical materialism, feminism, political ecology, critical geography, heterodox economics, decolonialism and racial capitalism.

The PPE book series combines the reputations and reach of the PPE blog and MUP as a publisher to launch critical political economy research and debates. We welcome manuscripts that realise the very best new research from established scholars and early-career scholars alike.

To buy or to find out more about the books currently available in this series, please go to: https://manchesteruniversitypress.co.uk/series/progress-in-political-economy/

False profits of ethical capital

Finance, labour and the politics of risk

Claire Parfitt

MANCHESTER UNIVERSITY PRESS

Copyright © Claire Parfitt 2024

The right of Claire Parfitt to be identified as the author of this work has been asserted in accordance with the Copyright, Designs and Patents Act 1988.

Published by Manchester University Press
Oxford Road, Manchester, M13 9PL

www.manchesteruniversitypress.co.uk

British Library Cataloguing-in-Publication Data
A catalogue record for this book is available from the British Library

ISBN   978 1 5261 7424 6 hardback

First published 2024

The publisher has no responsibility for the persistence or accuracy of URLs for any external or third-party internet websites referred to in this book, and does not guarantee that any content on such websites is, or will remain, accurate or appropriate.

Typeset
by New Best-set Typesetters Ltd

For Aziza

Contents

Acknowledgements	*page* viii
List of abbreviations	ix
Introduction: a more responsible and resilient capitalism?	1

Part I Moral economies

1 A history of capital's moral economies and speculation	17
2 A speculative moral economy	40

Part II Risk and value

3 Ethics, risk and value: the derivative logic in action	67
4 Accounting for ethics: SASB and Integrated Reporting	94

Part III Producing ethical capital

5 Brands and the (re)production of ethics	119
6 ESG information as an ethical capital asset	139
Conclusion: risky politics	158
References	163
Index	192

Acknowledgements

Life has brought many challenges during the production of this book, some global and collective, and some local and personal. From COVID-19 and climate chaos to the more mundane ups and downs of daily life, I feel fortunate to be embedded in several supportive, and often overlapping, communities of colleagues, comrades, friends and loved ones.

Dick Bryan and Gareth Bryant have been a constant source of invaluable guidance as my work has developed over the last few years. I am ever grateful for all that I learn from and with you both.

Many thanks to the staff at Manchester University Press who shepherded this manuscript to publication.

I am thankful to be a part of a community of scholars within and beyond the University of Sydney. My colleagues in political economy are always a refreshing relief from the ruthlessness of the corporate university. Generous and inclusive colleagues elsewhere have opened doors and created spaces for me to share ideas, as well as providing support and advice, especially Ben Spies-Butcher, Elizabeth Humphrys and Eve Vincent. Rachel Rowe and Leanne Stevenson read chapters, offered valuable feedback and moral support.

Friends and comrades who help me make sense of and navigate the world: Shane Reside, Katie Hepworth, Julie Macken, Kirsty McCully, Jacqui Housden, Iona Flett and Tanya Hardy (who also helps me navigate the ocean!).

My beloved family is spread out across the planet, which can be challenging but never lessens the love and support that binds us together: Auntie Ali, Auntie Marilyn and all my cousins, my brother Gareth, my sister (not only in-law) Melissa, and my niblings Rhys and Keira. Mum and Dad, who never waiver. Last, my daughter Aziza, whose exuberance, joy and determination bring me hope every day. My darling, this book is for you (even though it's not a kids' book!).

Some of the material in Chapter 4 has been reprinted from *Critical Perspectives on Accounting*, 'A foundation for "ethical capital": the Sustainability Accounting Standards Board and Integrated Reporting', 2022, 102477, ISSN 1045-2354, https://doi.org/10.1016/j.cpa.2022.102477 with permission from Elsevier.

Abbreviations

ACCR	Australasian Centre for Corporate Responsibility
ASIC	Australian Securities and Investments Commission
AUM	assets under management
BIS	Bank of International Settlements
CFA	Chartered Financial Analysts
CSR	corporate social responsibility
ESG	environmental, social and governance
ETFs	exchange traded funds
FCA	Financial Conduct Authority
FDIC	Federal Deposit Insurance Corporation
GRI	Global Reporting Initiative
ICT	information and communications technology
IFRS	International Financial Reporting Standards
IIRC	International Integrated Reporting Council
ILO	International Labour Organization
IOSCO	International Organization of Securities Commissions
ISO	International Organization for Standardization
ISS	Institutional Shareholder Services
ISSB	International Sustainability Standards Board
LSEG	London Stock Exchange Group
NGO	non-government organisation
ONS	Office for National Statistics
SASB	Sustainability Accounting Standards Board
SEA	social and environmental accounting
SEC	Securities and Exchange Commission
SFDR	Sustainable Finance Disclosure Regulation
UNEP FI	United Nations Environment Programme Finance Initiative
UNPRI	United Nations Principles for Responsible Investment
US BRT	United States Business Roundtable
WBCSD	World Business Council for Sustainable Development
WEF	World Economic Forum

Introduction: a more responsible and resilient capitalism?

Crisis is a recurrent state for capital. Economists and social scientists of many stripes have long recognised the inherent instability of this economic system. For Karl Marx and Friedrich Engels (2018), writing in 1848, the contradictions embedded in capital's relations of production condemned it to instability and crisis. According to Joseph Schumpeter (1943), the logic of accumulation depends on an on-going process of creative destruction. James O'Connor (1998) recognised that capitalism tends to undermine its own social and ecological conditions of production, also leading to crisis. Charles Kindleberger showed in his monetary history that 'the last four hundred years has been replete with financial crises' (Kindleberger and Aliber, 2005: 239).

Advocates of responsible investment argue that this need not be the case. During the COVID-19 pandemic, the head of the United Nations Principles for Responsible Investment (UNPRI) called for renewed attention by investors to the fragility of the global economy and the social risks it generates. The Investor Agenda, a transnational group of institutional investors and non-government organisations (NGOs) committed to action on climate change, is recommending a series of priorities to rebuild a sustainable post-COVID economy. The Investor Agenda argues that investors have the capacity to build 'greater resilience that will enhance the ability of our communities and economies to absorb both acute and systemic shocks' (The Investor Agenda, 2020). This proposition – the false prophecy that better management of environmental, social and governance (ESG) risks can build a better, fairer, more resilient capitalism – is the heart of what this book interrogates.

There is a steady flow of political projects and thought leaders demanding greater corporate accountability and urgent responses to pressing social and ecological crises. It was a key plank of Elizabeth Warren's failed presidential bid in the United States. Her Accountable Capitalism Act, sometimes described as a plan to 'save capitalism' (Yglesias, 2018), would have renovated corporate governance, requiring firms to bear moral responsibilities. Former chief executive and fellow at Harvard Business School Bill George has argued that '[c]apitalists must take the lead in reforming capitalism from its unrestrained vices into its responsible virtues' (George, 2019). Australia's federal Treasurer claimed that 2023 would 'be the year we build a better capitalism', one that had integrity, was evidence- and values-based and 'more capable of building resilience' through partnership with the private sector (Chalmers, 2023). The editorial board of the *Financial Times* has favourably endorsed calls from business leaders and CEOs for a shift from strategy focused on shareholder value towards 'inclusivity, sustainability and purpose' (FT Editorial Board, 2019). But the FT's editors also pointed out that this shift will only be meaningful if 'purpose' can be measured. Once relegated to the domain of marketing and public relations, corporate responsibility is being driven into questions of risk and measures of financial accountability.

In early 2020, the Bank of International Settlements (BIS), the bank of central bankers, published a book about financial stability in the era of climate change (Bolton et al., 2020). Written before the COVID-19 pandemic, when the front-of-mind global existential threat was climate change, the BIS riffed off Nassim Taleb's (2010) notion of a black swan event, conjecturing that a 'green swan' could be the source of the next systemic financial crisis. Climate risks, said the authors, involve 'interacting, nonlinear and fundamentally unpredictable environmental, social, economic and geopolitical dynamics' (Bolton et al., 2020: 1) creating unprecedented uncertainties for those charged with maintaining international financial stability. As the global economy is increasingly threatened by unpredictable economic, social and political risks, the BIS heralds two momentous breaks in finance. First is the proposition that backward-looking portfolio management is not appropriate to a world that cannot be predicted on the basis of the past. Making plans for the future increasingly depends on forward-looking scenario analysis rather than probability analysis from distributions of past events. The second break the BIS identifies is an imperative for central banks to take a more active role in advocating large-scale, coordinated climate action by states and the private sector. Given the complexity and severity of the green swan risk, the BIS claims that the central bank function of supporting financial system stability is likely to be unachievable without widespread action on emissions. These two shifts proposed by the BIS suggest a new orientation to the temporal dimensions of risk management; an understanding of financial risk that is more deeply intertwined with ecological and social issues; and a model of cooperation between public and private economic actors for long-run stability.

Business leaders are also joining this chorus of concern for sustainability and social impact. In May 2020, Business for Inclusive Growth (B4IG), a coalition of major multinational firms, issued a 'call to action' for 'an inclusive, green and resilient recovery' from the COVID-19 crisis (Rodriguez et al., 2020). Reflecting the BIS projections of a collaborative approach to building long-term economic stability, one of the founding members of B4IG claimed, 'The idea is to create international *solidarity amongst companies*, to scale up best practices and to have an inclusive recovery ... We believe that *tackling inequality is a matter of ethics but also a matter of business*' (Rodriguez et al., 2020, emphasis added).

Larry Fink, Chief Executive of the world's largest asset manager BlackRock, has become infamous due to his support for ESG investing. Fink declared in his January 2020 open letters to clients and investee companies, 'we are on the edge of a fundamental reshaping of finance ... a company cannot achieve long-term profits without embracing *purpose* and considering the needs of a broad range of *stakeholders*' (Fink, 2020, emphasis added). He insisted that BlackRock would put 'sustainability' at the heart of its investment strategy, specifying that '[s]ustainability in the investment context means understanding and incorporating environmental, social and governance (ESG) factors into investment analysis and decision-making' (BlackRock, 2020). Fink has since stopped using the term 'ESG', which he claims has become too divisive in the face of recent turmoil in the media and financial markets (Megaw et al., 2023), but his interventions continue to foreground resilience, sustainability and, above all, the commonality of interests between all 'stakeholders' (Fink, 2023, 2022).

What unites the positions of the BIS, BlackRock and B4IG is their insistence on the relationship between ecological and social issues and economic risk; the importance of the long term for financial stability and investment performance; and a cooperative, collective orientation to maintaining economic stability. These elements comprise what I characterise as the "responsible capital imaginary" that animates the public debate around corporate accountability. This imaginary drives the faith in the proposition that better management of ESG risks will produce a more resilient economy. Fink and other champions of stakeholder capitalism have come under fire in the early 2020s, especially from conservative politicians in the US, as the responsible capital imaginary has become more prevalent and ESG investing, in particular, has grown in size and influence.

As the integration of ESG risks into investment decision-making becomes more mainstream, this book investigates what those practices mean in reality. Going beyond a study of the limitations of responsible capitalism, this project aims to understand what responsible capitalism does, the changes it facilitates in capital accumulation, and what this implies for class relations. The proposition is that rather than building a "better" or "safer" capitalism, the practice of ESG integration drives ethics to the frontier of accumulation. Ethics become risks, absorbed into and transformed by financial calculus, subordinating this fundamental element of the human being (ethics) to capital accumulation.

What is ethical capital?

The book offers a series of interrelated propositions about ethics, risk and value. First, ethics are material, historically specific and grounded in social, economic and political institutions. The recently expanded concept of 'moral economy' (Palomera and Vetta, 2016; Sandberg, 2014; Sayer, 2007, 2015; Sippel, 2018) is used to explore the materiality of ethics and its application to the contemporary economy. Second, ethics are treated as risks, which are commodified in today's "speculative moral economy". Firms manage those ethical risks along a spread of possible ethical positions. Third, in this economy where risks are commodified and constitute a form of connectivity between economic actors, "abstract risk" is a frame for understanding contemporary value relations. Fourth, the process of identifying, measuring and managing ethical risks renders ethics legible for capital accumulation. Finally, by translating derivative positions on ethics into commodities and intangible corporate assets, speculating on ethics becomes an accumulation strategy.

This accumulation strategy produces ethical capital: a process through which challenges to capital, based on social and ecological concerns, are subsumed and transformed into opportunities for speculation and profit. This process is manifest in contemporary phenomena such as responsible investment and consumption, and corporate social responsibility. The concept of ethical capital, as I use it, makes no claim that the ethics expressed in the process will conform to the ethics of any particular person or group. Ethical capital generates intangible assets, including commodities such as brands and ESG scores. These assets are commodities in a dual sense: they impart use value to consumers who purchase branded goods and services, and they can be bought and sold by firms as a form of intellectual property. This is a point where production and circulation are melded (Martin, 2015: 5). Importantly, ethical capital is a commodity in the Marxian sense because it facilitates the alienation and subordination of ethics, a fundamental element of the human being. On this basis, I argue that it is also a potential site of contestation.

Ethical capital, then, is a frontier of accumulation. The responsible capital imaginary is a dominant capitalist realist (Fisher, 2009) frame through which social change is being envisaged and enacted. This is represented most clearly in movements and campaigns that focus on ethical consumption and investment activity through which consumers and investors are implored to vote with their dollars and to achieve social change through an aggregated expression of individual preferences. This book explores the mechanisms through which ethical capital is produced and the subordination of labour to the process.

The argument is organised into three parts. The first, 'Moral economies', uses the moral economy concept to understand how ethics are mobilised at different times and places. It also establishes the contours of a particular moral economy that pertains to the contemporary period: a speculative moral economy. The second, 'Risk and value', conceptualises value in the context of risk and finance. This enables a new approach to understanding why ethics are mobilised as they are and the function ethics play in accumulation, which is explored in the third part, 'Producing ethical capital'. This final part reveals the role that ethics, transformed into risk, play in the process of ethical capital: how ethics-as-risk support profit-making, how they facilitate the subordination of labour and life to capital accumulation, and what political possibilities this opens up. These dynamics are explained in relation to economic and legal theory relevant to intangible assets, the relationship between consumers and brands, the production of ESG information in the finance sector, and the emerging regulation of ESG information.

The overarching concern of this book is to identify how ethical concerns about ESG risks are shaping contemporary capital–labour relations and accumulation. This concern is addressed through a series of sub-questions which are addressed chapter by chapter. How have moral economies manifested at different times in capital's development? What is a contemporary form of the moral economy? What is a theory of the relation between value, ethics and risk that can elucidate the function of today's moral economy and, in particular, ESG integration? How do social and environmental accounting initiatives render ethics legible to capital? How, and in what forms, does ethical capital manifest? What opportunities are there for contesting ethical capital, the alienation of ethics and their subsumption into the process of accumulation? Grappling with these questions encourages an analysis of one instance of capital subordinating labour outside the wage relation, namely through finance and intangible assets. These questions also move beyond the observation that ethical capital is an inadequate vehicle for social change, and instead focus on what ethical capital does, and how to contest it.

Ethics

This book does not offer a comprehensive survey of the philosophical literature on ethics. Rather, it aims to understand how ethics are mobilised by, and through, capital. A persistent premise of this research is that, throughout history, ethics are consistently mobilised as a means to resolve social and political tensions. The particular ways in which this occurs reveal elements of the social relations underlying these dynamics. The book addresses the particular ways in which ethics are mobilised today, in the context of financialised capitalism. As observed above in relation to the claims that ground the responsible capital imaginary, ethics are ostensibly mobilised to resolve conflicts between economic actors and to address contradictions of capital accumulation. But in this particular moment, I argue that ethics move beyond a defensive orientation and become part of the capital–labour relation in a more comprehensive way. As part of capital's constant drive to expand through 'capturing' different aspects of our lives and being (Massumi, 2018), ethics become the subject of quantification and accumulation.

The argument here is grounded in a materialist understanding of ethics and morality. Recognising that there are debates on this point, the discussion does not distinguish between ethics and morality; it uses the terms interchangeably. What is important, though, is that ethics and morality are not understood as transhistorical or universal principles. Rather, expanding Engels's position in 1878 that morality is based in class interests (Engels, 1947), it is argued here that morality is dynamic across space and time, and influenced by subjectivities of race, class, gender, age and more. In opposition to both Marxian and orthodox economists who imagine the possibility of a scientific, ethics-free basis for economic analysis, the position here is that morality is material, political and inescapable.

On the basis that ethics grow out of the material circumstances in which people live and work, the book will explain why ethical debates manifest in certain ways in the contemporary moment. It will explain why the extant institutions of capital require ethics to operate as they do in this moment, why governance is taking place as it does in this moment, and what possibilities these realities hold for those people who would construct political and economic institutions differently. It will be argued that institutions of capital have begun to price ethics because these are increasingly relevant to the creation and accumulation of value. As a result, corporate governance is incorporating ethical questions into its analysis and operation. This is creating both opportunities for and barriers to social and political change which are not always understood through existing political economic frameworks. Methodologically, the book is eclectic. It draws together historical analysis, key informant interviews with ESG analysts and other finance professionals, a critical reading of social accounting standards, and jurisprudential analysis of intellectual property law, to understand how ethics are mobilised, commodified and rendered productive for capital. The following gives an outline of the book, narrated through its key concepts and ideas.

Moral economy

The concept of the 'moral economy' is employed to understand the function that ethics plays in the contemporary economy. This is an expanded version of the moral economy as used by E.P. Thompson (1971) to understand the morals and norms of pre-industrial England and how they clashed with the emergent capitalist economy. For Thompson, and those who have adopted his conceptualisation (Castree et al., 2013; Scott, 1976), the moral economy describes a particular set of ethical constraints on the production and distribution of goods and services in pre-industrial or peasant economies. By contrast, the expanded version argues that all economies are moral economies (Palomera and Vetta, 2016; Sandberg, 2014; Sayer, 2007, 2015; Sippel, 2018). This approach reveals 'the moral norms and sentiments that structure and influence economic practices, both formal and informal, and the way in which these are reinforced, compromised or overridden by economic pressures' (Sayer, 2007: 262). This articulation of the moral economy is akin to the approach of Marion Fourcade and Kieran Healy to understanding the morality of markets. That is, 'markets are explicitly moral projects, saturated with normativity' (Fourcade and Healy, 2007: 299) and that the role of economic sociology should be to open 'the black box of morality' (Fourcade and Healy, 2007: 305) that operates in particular contexts.

This conceptualisation has a strong relationship with Karl Polanyi's (1945) theories of economic and social embeddedness, and indeed, Polanyi is sometimes recognised as a moral economy theorist (Palomera and Vetta, 2016). However, the moral economy is used here because of its specific focus on morals or ethics, and how they interact with economic institutions, actors and practices. While all economies are culturally and socially instituted, the analysis developed in this book is focused on ethics, their legitimating function and other political functions they play in economic life. It is an attempt to overcome the schism between ethics and the 'engineering' approach to economics that Amartya Sen has recognised and contested (Sen, 1999) and to render explicit the morals underlying economic phenomena, and the work those morals do.

The first thing the book does, then, in Chapter 1, is to go back in time, to offer a brief history of capitalism through this lens of the expanded moral economy. Chapter 1 explores the constantly evolving relationship between ethics and economics, the contours of the moral economy in different moments, and the function that these moral economies have played at different times. This historical narrative grounds a materialist approach to ethics that this book will pursue, alongside an account of how conceptions and practices of business ethics have evolved in parallel with developments in the organisational and institutional form of capital. The chapter casts capitalism's development in four broad periods: liberalism, establishing the moral foundations for capitalism and (un)free labour; socialisation of capital (factories, trade unions and limited liability firms); the morality of monopoly (welfare capitalists and philanthrocapitalist robber barons); and restraint and stability (the state as administrator of the moral economy and the emergence of responsible corporations). Chapter 1 explores these transitions in the moral economy through and alongside the concept of speculation. Risk, and speculation, has always been at the heart of profit, growth and dynamism in capitalism. In today's financialised economy, with a prevalent derivative logic (Martin, 2015), risk plays an especially important function.

Risk

Speculation has been persistently unpopular, ever the scapegoat in times of crisis, and with a renewed degree of unpopularity since the financial crisis of 2007–8. Despite this, it is the foundation of capitalist enterprise. A positive yield on investment is legitimised by the fact that it involves risk. The "progressive" capacities of capitalism to generate increasing living standards are predicated on speculative investing in new technologies, processes and products. This is a framing that is hostile to John Maynard Keynes's distinction between frothy speculation and steady enterprise (Keynes, 1936: 159).

Risk is premised on an element of uncertainty, contra the distinctions between the two famously made by Frank Knight in 1921 (Knight, 2014) and Keynes (1921, 1936). Assessments of risk have become more sophisticated since the Enlightenment, with the emergence of probability theory, increasingly complex techniques, theories about risk diversification and assessment, and financial products designed explicitly to trade risk. The history of Wall Street reflects the struggle to find the most accurate way to identify, measure and manage the uncertainty of the future, and to maximise the risk/return trade-off (Bernstein, 1993). But if outcomes complied with formal models of risk, diversification would be its own solution, and risk would be merely about distributions of particular outcomes. This is a de-socialised and de-historicised notion of risk that presumes new events will comfortably be understood in terms of past distributions. At different points in recent history, ambitious financiers have presumed their ability to transcend this problem using sophisticated mathematical tools, sometimes with ruinous consequences.

In a rapidly changing world, it is becoming even more apparent that the models of risk and risk management are fallible. James Bridle (2018) explains in *New Dark Age* that much of the knowledge and predictive capacity that has been developed in the modern era, such as being able to forecast the weather, is being undermined by the uncertainties of the twenty-first-century climate. Louise Amoore (2013) argues, in line with the above BIS observation of forward-looking approaches to risk, that we live in an age of possibilistic rather than probabilistic risk. While probabilistic risk management looks backwards to determine the future based on the past, possibilistic risk looks ahead. In an era of over-abundant data, Amoore's possibilistic risk operates on anticipation of what could happen, however improbable. Pre-emptive action and algorithm-based reasoning are characteristic of this mode of risking.

Such uncertain uncertainty compels not so much a neutralisation of risk as, rather, mechanisms which use risk to make profits. The derivative is the risk management tool at the centre of the current moment. Since the 1970s, the emergence of derivative markets has drastically changed how risk is understood and managed. State institutions through which risks were collectivised have been reconfigured (Baker and Simon, 2004; Hacker, 2008; Rafferty and Yu, 2010). Beginning with foreign exchange and interest rate risks, the versatility of derivatives contracts and the facility provided by the Black–Scholes pricing model meant the rapid dispersion of the derivative as a tool not only to manage but to price and trade all manner of risks. Leigh Johnson explores catastrophe bonds as one instance of this process through which such 'ontologically disparate' phenomena as 'epidemics, seismicity, demographic aging, and meteorological extremes' (Johnson, 2013: 31) are rendered commensurable through financial risk. Johnson argues that this is dependent on the transformation of 'ideas of responsibility, liability, and acceptable sources of profit' (Johnson, 2013: 31). Dick Bryan and Michael Rafferty (2014, 2018) explore the dispersion of a derivative, financial logic into the 'banal' domains of life. They show how derivatives facilitate the securitisation of household payments, extracting financial stability from the imperative for social reproduction. They reframe contingent employment relations by conceptualising the zero-hours employment contract as a type of embedded options contract. Social benefit bonds outsource public policy to private investors who "bet" on the achievement of social objectives such as reducing recidivism. These developments imply that derivatives 'are now a way of conceptualizing and organizing social relations' (Bryan and Rafferty, 2014: 898). Randy Martin (2013) explains the utility of thinking through the logic of the social derivative. First, it reveals the ways in which connection and engagement operate in the context of apparent isolation and fragmentation. Second, the social derivative demonstrates that production happens inside circulation. Finally, it reveals how the management and trade of risks, as commodities, becomes profitable.

Speculation takes on a particular role in this conjuncture. Risk is commodified, an object of trade. In this process of commodification, 'the vast ensemble of socioeconomic relations that engender specific risks (re)appear as a singular or homogeneous object' (LiPuma, 2017: 60). Abstract risk emerges as the connecting thread between these concrete and specific risks, not because all the forms of risk are equivalent, but because they are traded, mediated and managed through the same processes. Risk becomes a form of social mediation, 'the principal means by which people and companies organize their interdependence' (LiPuma, 2017: 61).

Chapter 2 argues that in this context, the moral economy and speculation have merged. The contemporary speculative moral economy has two key, contradictory features. First, it is underlaid by the responsible capital imaginary that insists it is possible to simultaneously "do well" (make profits) and "do good" (be ethical). According to this imaginary, business not only delivers the unquestionable benefit of increased material wealth, but it treats social problems and ethical dilemmas as opportunities for profit. The underlying philosophy of this moral economy is that "good" business is more profitable. Contemporary business ethics asserts that profit-making and social justice are not merely compatible but mutually beneficial.

By contrast, though, this moral economy is operationalised through risk management. Ethical questions are treated as risks and are managed, like other risks, through financial mechanisms. The processes by which ethical risks are managed reflect a derivative logic, producing an ethics that is an expression of capitalist risk: contingent and profit-driven. This is the second key feature of the speculative moral economy: a derivative logic of ethics. The derivative is a historical form in which moral economy and speculation converge. Ethics become capital, but at the same time, capital accumulation produces a particular ethics. The speculative moral economy produces both a derivative form of market-compatible ethics and "ethical commodities": corporate assets that are built on ethical claims. Understanding how ethics are rendered as risks and commodified demands a reconsideration of value as the particular form of connectivity that the capitalist economy requires.

Risking value theory through finance and intangible assets

Many scholars have engaged with challenges to value theory in the late twentieth and early twenty-first centuries (Bryan and Rafferty, 2006b; Christophers, 2016a; Hardt and Negri, 2000, 2004; Harvie, 2005; Lazzarato, 2004; Martin, 2002; Massumi, 2018). Activities and phenomena which were once marginal have become prevalent, and even dominant, in the global economy. This book focuses on two of these phenomena: intangible assets and finance. Intangible assets were identified as a small part of a firm's inventory in the late 1800s. But today, intangible assets are often

Introduction 11

more valuable than the tangible. Connected to this, in the contemporary economy, knowledge, affects and human relationships are commodified and constitute major drivers of trade. Similarly, the role of finance has transformed since the 1970s. Though finance has played an important role in the global economy since its earliest days, the rise of derivatives has revolutionised how risk is understood and managed. Financial innovations in risk management have filtered through to other domains of life (Bryan and Rafferty, 2006b; Martin, 2002).

The increasing significance of intangible assets and the dispersion of financial innovation throughout socio-economic life both present challenges to a conventional Marxian understanding of capital accumulation and value. It is virtually impossible to meaningfully analyse capital accumulation by firms which are driven by intangible assets, like Facebook and Google, through socially necessary labour time (Fuchs, 2014, 2015). Similarly, attempts to understand the role of finance through a theory of value based on time spent in waged labour are condemned to debates about (un)productive labour and treating finance and its institutions as parasitic on the "real" economy (Lapavitsas, 2014; Soederberg, 2014). These debates often tend towards, strangely for Marxian scholars, a reification of both waged labour and industrial, tangible forms of economic production.

For some this might suggest that Marxian value theory is now defunct. On the contrary, and inspired by a tradition of unorthodox Marxian thought, I argue that a rethinking of Marxian value is necessary. This rethinking should retain the understanding of value as the primary form of connectivity (Alessandrini, 2016: 52) in capitalism, but should consider new measures of value, going beyond socially necessary labour time.

Value is the organising principle of the capitalist economy because it facilitates the commensuration of disparate commodities. Value reveals how we are connected within a whole that is an economy based on generalised commodity production and exchange. Like other critical Marxian value theorists (Alessandrini, 2016; Gawne, 2014; Mann, 2010; Postone, 1996), I argue that value has no singular substance; it is a social relationship of domination that produces an abstract form of social wealth, based on 'equivalence and substitutability' (Mann, 2010: 177) of commodities. Value theory approached in this way enables an analysis of what value does: the processes by which things are made fungible, and the tensions and contradictions these processes create and resolve. Diane Elson's (1979) value theory of labour, for example, considered the particulars of labour's subordination to capital, exploring how and why work and social relations are structured as they are at any given time. Samuel Knafo (2007) has similarly argued that value analysis shows how the imperatives of value transform labour processes for greater productivity.

As the economy transforms, the processes by which value is produced also change. Strict adherence to labour time as a source of value has required scholars to treat vast areas of economic activity as fictitious or parasitic on the "real" economy. By contrast, a more flexible approach that recognises the 'plasticity' of value (Konings, 2018: 7) is sensitive to the new ways that capital is renovating and reproducing itself. Such an analysis provides a more meaningful understanding of how value is produced, and a more interesting and fruitful political orientation. Sites of accumulation are potential sites of struggle.

Chapter 3 uses value theory to understand how ethics are produced through contemporary responsible investment practices and, in particular, the integration of ESG issues into investment decisions. The chapter offers an interpretation of value theory that is specific to understanding how ethics are translated into financial decision-making frameworks. This theory is then applied to empirical evidence about ESG integration in practice, to develop the argument that ESG integration produces a derivative logic of ethics.

The production of ethical capital

The commodification of ethics-as-risk manifests in intangible assets such as corporate brands and ESG scores. Ethics become a form of capital, as part of corporate identity and reputation. This process of commodifying ethics is dependent on two key mechanisms that are explored in Chapters 4 and 5. In Chapter 6, I consider how consolidation in the ESG information industry and recent attempts to regulate that industry are exposing the limits of the responsible capital imaginary.

First, ethics must be made legible to capital through processes of rationalisation and standardisation comparable to those of political arithmetic, metricisation and double entry accounting. Capital is developing its ability to account for ethics through many new forms of social accounting standards which allow businesses to attach numbers to their ethical claims. Chapter 4 employs a critical reading of the Integrated Reporting framework and the Sustainability Accounting Standards Board (SASB) standards, methodology and guidance documents. The analysis explores how key concepts like materiality, value, capital, accountability and risk are deployed in these frameworks, to understand the function this form of accounting or reporting plays in the speculative moral economy. The discussion in the chapter draws together several strands of accounting literature. Recognising the debates in accounting regarding the challenges presented by social and environmental accounting and intangible assets, SASB and the Integrated Reporting framework are chosen as the empirical focus for this chapter because they connect and aim

Introduction 13

to account for both intangible assets and sustainability. Guided by historical accounting research (Bryer, 2000a, 2000b, 2005; Carruthers and Espeland, 1991; Levy, 2014), and recalling the propositions developed in Chapters 1 and 2 of the book, this chapter develops an understanding of how ethics are rationalised and made ready for commodification.

The production of "ethical capital", and the capacity of firms and investors to leverage their speculations about which ethical claims will be the most profitable and which ethical risks are most profitably minimised, depends on information from labour. Chapter 5 examines how labour, and specifically labour-as-consumer, informs markets about ethical risks. This information becomes the basis on which capital takes speculative ethical positions that are valorised through intangible assets like brands. The chapter charts the developments in intellectual property law, particularly around the protection of trademarks and brands, which facilitate the production of ethical positions, images and ideas. Branding strategies and practices have transformed from a direct communication by firms to consumers about the origin and quality of goods into a co-creative dialogic process through which consumers and firms produce images, meanings and emotional responses. Today's brands are crucial to an 'economy of qualities' in which many producers trade on ideas and feelings rather than goods and services (McDonagh, 2015). Intellectual property law enables brand owners to control and monetise the wide array of meanings and images associated with a brand, facilitating the capture of an incredible range of the human experience, including ethical debates and positions. This chapter reveals how labour co-produces brands, including their ethical dimensions, and the ways in which digital technology is accelerating this process.

In this context, where image and affect are drivers of trade and consumption, ethics are often an important part of the package. While it is not claimed here that this means that businesses are in fact operating more "ethically", it is the case that businesses are leveraging different ethical positions. The same firm often offers a conventional range of goods alongside a sustainable or green range, for example. This is one of many ways that contemporary firms manage their exposure through contingency along an ethical spread. As new accounting practices emerge to measure intangible value, to codify ethical standards, and to quantify corporate performance on social and environmental issues, this must be understood as something more than mere window dressing. A conception of value that can elucidate these phenomena and explain why it matters is crucial. This book uses risk as a measure of value and a derivative logic of ethics to show that ethical capital activities go beyond marketing and render ethics productive.

Finally, Chapter 6 explores the recent consolidation and concentration of the ESG information segment of the financial sector, and the emerging regulation of this sector as the political contest over defining the limits of ESG heats up. While ESG advocates present the practice as one that is value-free and objective, opponents reject the imposition of "left-wing" principles through financial markets. As the economic significance of ESG investing grows, these debates become more pointed and have led to new rules and proposals from securities regulators defining ESG and setting disclosure requirements. These regulatory processes, often positioned as a mechanism to standardise and clarify ESG practices, are exposing the limits of the responsible capital imaginary and creating new platforms to contest the accumulation of ethical capital.

In short, the argument progresses through the subsequent chapters as follows. Chapter 1 develops a selective survey of different moral economies throughout capitalism's history, interwoven with a discussion of speculation and risk. This chapter establishes the materialist approach to ethics that the book adopts. Chapter 2 builds on that analysis to posit a speculative moral economy in operation in the current moment. The speculative moral economy is based on a responsible capital imaginary and expresses certain crucial contradictions in its treatment of ethics as risks. Chapter 3 delves into these contradictions in more detail through the frame of Marxian value theory. Here a value theory of labour, ethics and risk is used to elucidate the operations of contemporary responsible investment (in particular, ESG integration). This analysis shows that risks are shaped by assessments of both economic and socio-cultural values, and that the types of ethics and the types of risks addressed by ESG integration are mutually constitutive and mutually constraining. ESG integration expresses a derivative logic of ethics, a dynamic and political phenomenon. Chapter 4 demonstrates that emerging social accounting standards render the dynamic and political phenomenon of ethics legible to capital through rationalisation. Social accounting standards create both a technical and a rhetorical basis for ethical capital production and accumulation. Chapter 5 draws together a critical reading of intellectual property law and marketing practices to reveal how brands become a locus for ethical value through co-production by capital and labour-as-consumer. Finally, Chapter 6 explores recent developments in concentration and regulation of the ESG information industry, exposing some of the contradictions of ethical capital.

Part I

Moral economies

Chapter 1

A history of capital's moral economies and speculation

> Morality has always been class morality; it has either justified the domination and the interests of the ruling class, or ever since the oppressed class became powerful enough, it has represented its indignation against this domination and the future interests of the oppressed. (Engels, 1947 [1878])

Introduction

How do prevailing debates about morality express the economic and social conditions in which they arise? Inspired by Engels's declaration regarding the class-based nature of morality, this chapter sets out a materialist analysis of ethical debates and settlements throughout capital's history. The intention is to reveal the dialectical relationship between those ethical debates and their historical context. This opens the possibility, taken up in later chapters, to analyse current ethical debates as a product of current material conditions: the form that ethical debates and settlements take is historically specific.

The analysis in this chapter adopts two primary frames as heuristic devices to orient the discussion. The first is the notion of a moral economy. The concept is used here in a broader sense than the Thompsonian pre-industrial peasant moral economy. The classic example in Thompson's work is the 'crowds' of working people who forcibly took control of grain supplies at certain moments during the seventeenth and eighteenth centuries in England. These crowds distributed grain at what they considered to be a just price to prevent profiteering and to ensure that people who needed food could access it. The price of bread was a crucial point of conflict between rural and urban England as the capitalist economy emerged, and the moral economy of the pre-industrial era was a source of legitimation for the regulatory and redistributive work of the crowds (Thompson, 1971).

For Thompson, these events revealed the tensions between the declining peasant moral economy, encumbered by paternalistic restrictions on prices and standards for commodities, and the 'new political economy' that he described as 'disinfested of intrusive moral imperatives' (1971: 90). Though Thompson recognised that philosophers of the new political economy such as Adam Smith were not unconcerned about the public good, he argued that the new model was not a moral one because it concealed its inherent morality with the 'de-moralised scientism' of the laissez-faire doctrine. The core principle was that '[t]he natural operation of supply and demand in the free market would maximize the satisfaction of all parties and establish the common good' (Thompson, 1971: 90).

Recent interventions in sociology, geography and anthropology have re-enlivened the moral economy concept (Götz, 2015; Palomera and Vetta, 2016; Sandberg, 2014; Sayer, 2007, 2015; Sippel, 2018). This work has tended to expand Thompson's use of the term, with some arguing that all economies are moral economies. Recognising the risk of emptying the concept of analytical purchase, Jaime Palomera and Theodora Vetta (2016) highlight the importance of incorporating class and capital accumulation. This development of moral economy discourse is also reflected in recent economic sociology scholarship that theorises the morality of markets. Fourcade and Healy (2007), for example, argue that all markets are moral projects, and aim to understand the ways in which particular markets reflect certain values, set moral boundaries or facilitate explicit moralising. Framing this recent expansive approach, Andrew Sayer offers a useful definition of the moral economy as 'the moral norms and sentiments that structure and influence economic practices, both formal and informal, and the way in which these are reinforced, compromised or overridden by economic pressures' (Sayer, 2007: 262). Similarly, Joakim Sandberg presents the moral economy as a set of 'economic practices based on moral attitudes' (2014: 178), which might be a set of beliefs that are shared by a certain population, or a set of morals that are institutionalised through certain social practices or structures (Sandberg, 2014: 177).

Here, the moral economy concept is employed in a way that is inspired by both Thompson and the recent expansive approach. From Thompson, the moral economy is understood here as a vehicle for legitimating political and economic action, and as a product of class conflict and evolutionary economic processes. From the recent moral economy literature, the moral economy is used here as an analytic tool (not as a normative one) to understand how economic actors, institutions and processes are shaped by moral claims, debates and controversies. It is argued here that different manifestations of moral economy throughout history demonstrate how and why ethical debates are changing, and how ethical debates operate not only as manifestations of abstract beliefs, but as an expression of tensions that emerge from people's lived experience. Importantly, the moral economies described here are not intended as exclusive: different moral economies may operate at the same time. As an example, see a compelling analysis of riots in the United Kingdom as an instance of a moral economy that differs markedly to the depiction of a contemporary speculative moral economy in this book (Harvie and Milburn, 2013).

The second heuristic device that guides this chapter is speculation, a practice which is central both to the accumulation of capital and to a persistent moral critique of capitalism. Speculation is often the focus of tensions around the sources of wealth, legitimation of wealth-creating activity and the proper relation between humanity and god (see, for example, Konings, 2018; Tawney, 1926). It has commonly been understood that risk-taking and speculating on the success of a business venture is what drives the market economy forward. This type of activity came into conflict with certain teachings of the medieval church because of its pursuit of wealth (Tawney, 1926) and because of its presumptuous approach to the social organisation of time (Postone, 1996). The doctrine of St Thomas Aquinas, for example, insisted on the moral requirement to labour to meet one's needs, rather than accumulating wealth to enrich oneself or to provide for future sloth. The 'idolatry of wealth' and 'the attainment of material riches' as 'the supreme object of human endeavor and the final criterion of human success' was not consistent with dominant Christian systems of thought in the prehistory of capitalism (Tawney, 1926: 286). With respect to the organisation of time, medieval European society centred around variable, canonical hours. The demands of a capitalist economy built on the productivity of labour and the measurement of labour time required the imposition of an abstract and constant hourly regime that displaced the church's regulation of time (Postone, 1996; Thompson, 1967).

Modernity and the development of a capitalist economy put the basic principles of god's control of the future and the church's disdain for commerce into question. Struggles over how to negotiate the relationships between time, labour, god and commercial life have been interwoven with moral debates about appropriate, moderate, reasonable, ethical approaches to economic activity. Attacks on what is perceived to be rampant or irresponsible speculation pre-date capitalism and have long provided reason to restrict business activity on ostensibly moral grounds. By contrast, the practice of moderate speculation (usually in the realm of industrial production of tangible commodities) serves as a proxy for what is often considered to be responsible, virtuous business activity. Indeed, for Keynes (1936), this was the distinction between speculation and enterprise.

The forthcoming narrative reveals that what is considered to be responsible enterprise is dynamic. Forms of financial risk-taking that were banned in the early 1800s (limited liability incorporation) became the engine of the mid-1800s economy. Those same speculative engines became the subject of

20 *Moral economies*

moral condemnation as their unprecedented success in accumulating capital became clear by the beginning of the 1900s. When financial markets collapsed in 1929, the state took responsibility both for more closely regulating financial risk-taking and for administering a moral economy of restraint. Speculative activity is at the heart of the capitalist economy, but it is always subject to moral claims. The management of risk and uncertainty is an ever-present challenge for those negotiating and contesting moral economies throughout the history explored below.

Framing this discussion around these two heuristic devices of the moral economy and speculation establishes a narrative of capitalism's history in which ethics can be seen as dynamic, material and conflict-driven, rather than as objective and transhistorical. The analysis is driven by key moments in the development of the institutions of capital, class relations and their relationship to ethics. It is not intended to enter into the fine details of this debate. History is divided into four broad periods: liberalism, moral capital, and (un)free labour; the socialisation of capital (factories, unions and limited liability firms); the paternalistic economy of monopoly and welfare capitalism; restraint and stability (the welfare state as the administrator of the moral economy and the attendant rise of corporate responsibility as a bulwark against regulation).

For each period, a critical debate (or range of debates) represents some ethical dilemma(s) of the period. This reflects the ways in which ethics are shifting, and being reframed, as capitalism develops. A class-driven analysis illuminates why particular ethical issues rise to prominence at particular times, in particular places, and why and how they are resolved. Resolutions are always partial and create the conditions for new social conflicts and dilemmas to emerge. The partitions between the periods are permeable, with hints of the next appearing in the previous. The chapter asks: what do these moments in the history of economics and ethics reflect about the social, economic and political conditions in which they occur? How do those conditions shape what is considered to be ethical?

Liberalism, property and freedom

Formal legal freedoms are central to the competitive dynamic on which capitalism depends. The emergence of capitalism relied as much on social, cultural and political change as it did on shifts in economic organisation (see, for example, Federici, 2004; Hobsbawm and Wrigley, 1999; Thompson, 2002). Social structures and political institutions were reconfigured to accommodate capital accumulation. In particular, the money-mediated economy of capitalism relied on the tenets of classical liberalism. At the most fundamental level, this meant individual freedom for the worker and for the owner of capital, and protection for the privileges of private property.

There were persistent tensions between peasant struggles for political freedom and the historical moral economies of mutual responsibility (Dobb, 1976; Sweezy, 1976; Thompson, 2002). Pre-industrial economies were characterised by a lack of freedom of movement, for example, but also by a complex network of shared obligations, often mediated through a local parish (Blackburn, 2004; Tan, 2002). Despite many limitations, these forms of support and relief were important for the survival of the poor in the pre-capitalist period. The emergence of Enlightenment notions of selfhood and individuation was the basis for pursuing freedoms of movement, of labour, of contracts and of property ownership, which often contradicted pre-existing bonds, including bonded labour, as well as bonds for medieval forms of social security. Freedom for workers meant that people were at liberty to seek waged work outside of feudal structures, but separation from those structures meant that people were compelled to enter into the market for wages. This tension was captured in 1867 by Marx's (1990) notion of the capitalist worker's 'double freedom'.

This dynamic was central to the clash of Thompson's pre-industrial moral economy of the crowd and the emerging moral economy of capital. The pre-industrial moral economy included practices such as setting the price of goods at an accessible level during times of dearth and various other practices of making economic decisions according to criteria such as justice, political expedience or custom. The emerging moral economy of industrial capital, by contrast, was one of competitive market imperatives through which economic decisions were made according to criteria such as productivity, efficiency and cost control. The market itself became a source of virtue, as did wealth accumulation. Principles of prudence, thriftiness, time-discipline and diligence were imposed on the working classes, who were also required to respect the privileges of private property, including the right of property owners to capture the products of their labour.

Liberal philosophers such as John Locke (1993) and Adam Smith (1993, 2009), along with other leading moral and religious philosophers of the seventeenth and eighteenth centuries, constructed a theoretical basis for the emerging moral economy of capitalism. These foundations required private economic organisation based on exchange through markets by formally free individuals. The division of labour, which was integral to the blueprint that Smith set out for economic development, demanded a particular role for money, as a measure of value and as a means of exchange. The impersonal system of monetary exchange and accumulation had two corollaries. It required, first, that there be at least a perception that all participants in the market are, in some formal sense, equal; second, that their relations be framed legally and voluntarily, not by what Marx called extra-economic coercion, which had characterised the social and economic structures of feudalism. The money or exchange economy was then deeply embedded in impersonal legal norms. It was no longer possible to tolerate the human being as a commodity; equally, the (working-class) human being's labour power had to be commodified.

This enclosure and commodification of labour power was grounded on the political philosophy of liberalism and the economic philosophy of capital. Locke (1993) positioned capital as a moral project that increased the "common wealth" of all, with the aim of justifying two key elements of capitalist social relations. First, the theft (enclosure) of land both in England and abroad, and second, capturing the profit generated from putting that private property to work (the basic relation between capital and labour). The righteousness of accumulation, as characterised by liberal philosophers, stood in contrast to forms of investment or wealth that were framed as unproductive and idle.

This opposition between idleness and morally defensible toil was also a crucial feature of the religious defence of capital and the early critique of speculation. While the European church historically exalted poverty as a virtue (Federici, 2004: 53–54), a shift took place from treating the pursuit of wealth as taboo to faith institutions sanctioning industrious and profitable investment, albeit with the exception of breakaway orders, such as those of Luther and Calvin (Tawney, 1926; Weber, 2001). Speculation was juxtaposed to noble travail, which served as a justification for investment of capital in industry, as well as an imperative to the working class to accept the disciplines and strictures of the capitalist employment relationship (Tawney, 1926; Thompson, 2002).

The tension between the differential morality of purportedly productive and unproductive investment was reflected in early capitalist critiques of speculation in financial markets. The collapse of the South Sea Company in the early 1700s created controversy in part due to the fact that it had created a 'speculative frenzy' (Bathurst, 2013: 221). This controversy centred around the flurry of trade in the company's stock before it had even begun its intended business activity. The implication was that (immoral) speculation about the company's profitability had fuelled stock market sales and created instability. There is a gruesome irony in the notion that morality would have been better served if the South Sea Company had engaged in its intended business activity rather than being the subject of financial speculation, given that the company's intended activity was the trade in enslaved people.

Indeed, it was in this context of struggles around crumbling feudalistic and emerging market-driven political and economic structures that the institution of slavery became an unethical, as well as an uneconomical,

Capital's moral economies and speculation 23

proposition. Led by the resistance and abolition movements of enslaved people themselves (Harding, 2022; James, 1938), and economic drivers such as the declining profitability of slavery and the competition between slavery-dependent and other capitals, the imperative to establish formally free markets for labour power and other commodities created a political environment in which slavery could no longer be tolerated. A broad base of English society led by radicals, but also including legislators, the judiciary and a range of faith leaders, built a movement to prohibit first the trade and later slavery itself.

Often cited as the earliest instance of ethical investment (Eccles, 2011; Richardson and Cragg, 2010; Sparkes, 2001) is the self-imposed restriction on engagement in the slave trade by the Religious Society of Friends (Quakers) groups in the late 1700s. This decision came at a time of increasing political debate about slavery and its function in the economy of the British empire and the triangular trade. Throughout the second half of the 1700s, the movement to abolish slavery grew to encompass not only the self-imposed trade restrictions of the Quakers and other abolitionists, but also a boycott of slave-produced sugar by 300,000 British consumers, letter-writing campaigns, political lobbying, distribution of propaganda based on the testimony of people formerly enslaved, and several legal cases (the "freedom suits") in both England and Scotland which gradually expanded the rights of enslaved people.[1] Under pressure from this political debate and activity, the Westminster Parliament declared the slave trade illegal in 1807 and sought to use its naval power to enforce a prohibition. In 1833, further legislation abolished slavery in the British colonies of the Caribbean, the Cape Colony (contemporary South Africa) and Mauritius.

The embedding of the ethical debates around slavery within the philosophical frameworks of the early nineteenth century is reflected in the tensions between freedoms of labour and the privileges of property. The liberal principles that demanded freedom from forced labour were part of a suite of precepts that also required respect for property rights. As has been detailed in research by the Legacies of British Slave-ownership project, the 1833 legislation that abolished slavery in most British plantations also required the payment of compensation, not to enslaved people for the horrors they had suffered, but to their enslavers for the loss of property (Manjapra, 2018; Olusoga, 2018).

A constellation of political, social and economic dynamics created a space through which (a limited) political freedom for labour could become an ethical issue with broad support. This was a key plank of the moral economy of early capitalism and classical liberalism. By contrast, the unfreedoms that characterised the lives of working people in the market economy were neither visible nor contestable in the same way, nor subject to the same

24   *Moral economies*

ethical claims. The limitations of liberal freedoms for working people were explained by Engels in his description of factory working conditions in the 1800s: '[t]he slavery in which the bourgeoisie holds the proletariat chained is nowhere more conspicuous than in the factory system. Here ends all freedom in law and in fact' (Marx, 1990: 550). These conditions would become the subject of new ethical and political contests during the nineteenth century.

The socialisation of capital: factories, unions and limited liability firms

The 1800s brought capital's socialisation on several fronts. Factories, the heart of capital accumulation, had become a source of great social and political conflict. Though these concerns spurred a few ethical entrepreneurs, in many ways this was a period notable for the absence of an ethical imperative in business. While the abominable nature of factory working conditions was well understood and lamented by many amongst the middle and ruling as well as the working classes, it was understood as the corollary of capitalism's capacity to innovate in wealth creation. Eventually, regulation of factory work became a matter of both public order and reliable social reproduction to support accumulation. This drove changes in work organisation, and a rapid increase in technological development and productivity. Labour became increasingly valued for its skills and its capacity to combine with capital to create expanding value. In 1867, Marx (1990) depicted this as a shift from the 'formal subsumption' of labour (associated with increasing hours of work) to 'real subsumption' (labour's integration with machines, associated with increasing intensity of work). As labour became more comprehensively integrated into the circuits of capital accumulation, production became more socialised, more dependent on the collective of workers, and a particular collective with particular skills. At the same time, both labour and capital organised through trade unions and corporations, respectively, setting new terms for the moral economy of the late nineteenth and twentieth centuries.

Limiting working hours, intensifying exploitation

The real subsumption of labour was driven by the interconnected dynamics of political pressure and technological change. By the early 1800s, the moral economy of the factory became a primary subject of concern, particularly for social reformers like Chartist James Bronterre O'Brien, engineer Andrew Ure, and utopian socialist, industrialist and cooperative advocate Robert

Owen (Götz, 2015). Several ethical business projects developed around the issue of factory work but failed to gain significant traction. Owen applied new management principles to improve the conditions for workers at his factories in New Lanark, Scotland. While he was motivated by a paternalistic drive to 'remoralise the lower orders' (Thompson, 1971), Owen's work was nonetheless locally impactful and inspiring to workers' movements elsewhere in Britain.

As well as these management practices, Owen advocated factory reform, restrictions on child labour, and cooperative approaches to business ownership and management. The principle of cooperativism, whereby workers share in the ownership of their employer, was popular amongst Chartists, early trade unionists, and was supported by the leading economist of the nineteenth century, John Stuart Mill. Though worker-owned cooperatives did not become a significant feature of the economy, the Principles of the Rochdale Society of Equitable Pioneers were adopted in 1844 and were the basis of a widespread consumer cooperative movement.

These fringe projects of isolated factory reform and worker-owned cooperatives could not become dominant given the particular social and production relations at the time. As Marx's (1990) analysis demonstrated, for any individual capitalist to improve the working conditions of the people in their employ would see them lose competitiveness as against other producers. So, while the majority of the capitalist class firmly resisted change in factory conditions, a combination of great mobilisations of political power by working people along with intra-class conflict between capitalists did lead to reforms. A range of crises emerged in the 1830s and 1840s, many of which centred around the deplorable conditions of factory work (Hobsbawm and Wrigley, 1999). Struggles over the length and intensity of work were a central feature of industry and politics, 'the product of a protracted and more or less concealed civil war between the capitalist class and the working class' (Marx, 1990: 412–413).

Following decades of agitation, and some fairly ineffectual regulation of factory labour in the 1830s (Hobsbawm and Wrigley, 1999; Thompson, 2002), legislation limiting factory working hours to ten per day was introduced in 1847. The passage of the legislation was achieved, in part, on the basis of an alliance between workers' movements and free traders campaigning to repeal the Corn Laws (Satz, 1989). The deal could be construed as a success for labour, but one that also served the interests of accumulation, not only with respect to lifting the trade barriers in the Corn Laws, but also with respect to the preservation of the capacity of labour power to reproduce itself and the maintenance of social order.

Once limitations on the length of the working day became effective in practice, though, employers intensified factory work to increase labour productivity through the extraction of relative, rather than absolute, surplus value. This included strategies like increasing the speed of machines or giving workers more machines to supervise and operate. Factory inspectors recognised that while reduced working hours responded to some of the impacts of factory work, the intensification of labour which had accompanied the reduction in working hours became so damaging to worker health as to undermine these achievements (Marx, 1990: 542).

The intensification of production processes and the extraction of relative surplus value also shifted the dynamics of the employment relationship. Workers who had been, until this point, relatively expendable and easily replaceable became more skilled and more valuable. Real subsumption into capital accumulation meant that labour became a more integral part of capital, and capable of exerting collective power more effectively. The more comprehensively workers were subordinated to capital accumulation, the more socialised and interdependent the labour of the factory became, the greater their capacity to disrupt that accumulation. It was also in this period of the mid-1800s that trade unions were decriminalised. Although divisions between skilled and unskilled workers (not to mention divisions based on other grounds such as race and gender) limited the burgeoning trade union movement, labour began to socialise on its own terms, to recognise the power of that socialisation, and to build the collective institutions which would challenge the increasingly monopolistic power of capital into the turn of the twentieth century.

Limiting liability, socialising capital

The increasing productivity of factories associated with intensified work processes opened up potential for larger-scale, technologically driven capitalist enterprise, but it also required a reframing of the ethics of speculation. Larger-scale production was beyond the funding capacities of individual capitalists but required longer-term, more stable organisational structures than business partnerships would permit. It is no accident, then, that in Britain the repeal of the South Sea Bubble Act in 1825 and legislation expanding the availability of limited corporate liability (in 1844 and 1855) closely coincided with the Factory Acts. Limited liability incorporation provided a mechanism for collectivising and restricting the legal and financial risk of business failure while depersonalising the moral responsibility associated with such failures.

By the mid-nineteenth century, capital was exhibiting its extraordinary tendency to concentrate. And concentration required more finance, which favoured larger firms and undermined the interests of small manufacturers (Marx, 1990: 304–307). Laws relaxing conditions for incorporation and limited liability laid the foundations for massive concentrations of capital by the late 1800s. Though these company law reforms are often thought to have been an inevitable consequence of economic development (see, for example, Berle, 1954), there was considerable contingency and dispute (Djelic, 2013; Harris, 2020; Lipton, 2018, 2020; McQueen, 2009). Those contingencies reveal the expansion of limited liability as a highly contested process, shaped by material conditions as well as disputes over basic questions of moral economy and speculation.

The dispersal of capital through financial markets was based on the legal fiction of the corporation's separate personality, which enabled segregation between the owners of the firm and the firm itself, creating tensions regarding the moral responsibility for corporate conduct. Competing interests around whether the law should be reformed to expand limited liability included both debates about the moral economy of the firm and arguments about the "proper" role of speculation. Widespread limited liability enabled incorporation and large-scale business activity on a radically different basis than that which had operated before. Not only was the scale much greater, but the risk structure and the relations between investor-owners and managers were transformed. Investors were able to participate in more expansive economic activity with much lower financial exposure and much lower exposure to the ignominy associated with business failure. This was a crucial factor in debates about company law reform (Djelic, 2013; Lipton, 2018; McQueen, 2009).

At stake were moral arguments about how capitalists ought to behave and what their responsibilities should be, as well as how markets should properly operate and be regulated. Opponents of limited liability legislation included established capitalists who feared competition from new companies that could agglomerate the finances of many small investors, as well as those who argued that limited liability undermined moral responsibility for one's own economic activity. Generalised limited liability might lead to greater negligence, mismanagement and even fraud (Djelic, 2013). Opposition, both from conservatives and from social(ist) reformers and critics, also harkened back to tropes regarding the immorality of speculation, contending that people would 'gamble' in shares rather than engaging in 'patient labour' with 'moderate expectations' (McQueen, 2009: 104).

Support for a more relaxed approach to incorporation came from (amongst others) middle-class investors and small capitalists who were eager to exploit opportunities to pool their capital in less risky business structures (Djelic, 2013). The financial consequences of business failure weighed heavily on this group, with relatively smaller capital to risk. Limited liability was positioned as promoting competition and creating a new era of economic freedom, to enable 'working and practical men of small means … to compete with leviathans of wealth' (shareholders circular, 1864, cited by McQueen, 2009: 84). Through this social justice frame, limiting corporate liability was promoted within the workers' rights and cooperatives, Christian Socialist and Chartist movements, and as a mechanism for mobilising small capital for the benefit of the poorer classes. Mill, for example, saw incorporation as a vehicle for profit-sharing schemes for the benefit of workers and general social improvement (Djelic, 2013).

Perhaps the most decisive factor in the debate, however, was the very material threat of capital flight in Britain in the 1850s. Middling investors seeking safer ways to invest were taking up opportunities in the colonies, where economic and industrial capacity was growing rapidly. The British Board of Trade supported limited liability legislation as a way to give these investors safer business opportunities in Britain (Lipton, 2018; McQueen, 2009: 98–99).

Despite the claims that limited liability incorporation would promote competition, it quickly became a vehicle for further industrial consolidation and anti-competitive behaviour. The conditions were created for the establishment of monopoly power within asocial corporations, with no capacity for moral agency, feeding into new debates about the morality of capital and business.

Fathers of philanthropy: the paternalistic morality of monopoly capitalism

The turn of the twentieth century brought what Adolf Berle (1954) described as a capitalist revolution: a monopolistic economy, headed by limited liability corporations. The scale of these firms, or empires, fundamentally changed the nature of economic organisation and the context in which moral economy was understood. This was no longer the capitalism imagined by Smith and his contemporaries, albeit that capital's 'classical competitive' era was always something of a myth (Christophers, 2016b: 41). The captains of this economy quickly came under pressure not only from workers and trade unions, but also from small business owners, farmers and other reformers. The following century gave rise to a contest over how the moral economy would be administered. The private sector asserted its capacity to respond to this critique from the late 1800s through welfare capitalist projects. Many reformers were suspicious of capitalist philanthropy and argued instead for the state to act as the arbiter of public morals. At this time, with the rise of large firms, the locus of the global economic growth began to shift to the US, where the concentration of capital was more rapid and pronounced.

Capital's moral economies and speculation

By the early 1900s, the US economy was highly centralised, with a handful of industrialists controlling key industries like oil, railways and steel manufacture (see, for example, Zinn, 2016). Employment and economic output were dominated by less than 5 per cent of all firms (Carroll et al., 2012). At the head of these vast enterprises sat the celebrity industrialists sometimes referred to as "robber barons". Perhaps the first prominent industrialist was Jay Gould, a speculator and railway magnate who waxed lyrical about his omnipotence in the late 1800s. Unlike some of the later robber barons, Gould did not succumb to public outrage regarding his wealth and influence. He engaged in no significant philanthropic activity and was renowned for his ruthlessness (Mason, 2007).

As the monopoly economy became further entrenched and the influence of a couple of dozen men consolidated, public pressure accelerated. The trade union movement was building all over the world, including in the rapidly growing economy of the US. Syndicalists agitated for workers to form 'one big union' with the Industrial Workers of the World, who exerted considerable influence in key moments of labour organising in railways, mines and textiles factories (Mason, 2007; Zinn, 2016). The socialist threat was becoming more ominous, strengthened by myriad movements of Black, migrant and women workers, and driven by tragedies like the 1911 Triangle Shirtwaist factory fire in New York City, one of tens of thousands of industrial incidents in which workers lost their lives (Zinn, 2016: 327). The influence of syndicalism at this point demonstrated the popular understanding of capital's ubiquitousness and the necessity for a broad, well-organised and transnational opposition to capital. This opposition included the emergence of parties representing worker and trade union interests in the parliamentary arena, especially as working people gradually won the right to vote and as revolutionary Russia began to exert pressure on the capitalist state. The working class was establishing itself as 'a historical protagonist in its own right' (Negri, 1988: 5).

The increasingly violent clash between social movements and monopoly capital forged a critique of monopolists as 'irresponsible' or 'corrupt', divorced from the image of the properly constructed market economy of early capitalism – notwithstanding the horrific conditions for working people which prevailed in early factories. In the evocatively titled *Decay of Capitalist Civilisation*, Beatrice and Sidney Webb (1923) detailed their thesis about how monopolies and unscrupulous capitalists were warping market mechanisms. They advocated a strong role for the state in regulating labour and providing for social reproduction. Associated organisations like the Fabian Society and the Labour Party took up a gradual reform agenda based on social democracy, including policies such as reducing competition over wages; establishing minimum standards of education, sanitation and leisure; and providing extensive poor relief (Webb and Webb, 1909, 1911). Similarly in the US, the Progressive Party cohered a range of political interests largely centred on opposing corrupt business and politics. The party's platform included some labour reforms like the eight-hour day and minimum wages for women. It also advocated social insurance provided by the state and some regulation of both the corporate and political spheres.

Under this pressure, monopolistic firms began to self-regulate to moderate the social impacts of their activity, a process Keynes described as 'the tendency of big enterprise to socialise itself' (Keynes, 1926: 9). Whether to reduce their exposure to government regulation, to temper their reputations for greed and ruthlessness (Kristoffersen et al., 2005), or to fulfil personal and idiosyncratic god-complexes (McGoey, 2015), capitalists of the early 1900s constructed a paternalistic moral economy of philanthropy and welfare capitalism. Through this frame, captains of industry managed their own public images and negotiated social conflicts on their own terms, by pursuing welfare initiatives that complied with their own understandings of morality and justice.

The major industrialists became the first practitioners of philanthrocapitalism (McGoey, 2015; Ponte et al., 2009). They established foundations in the early 1900s that were unlike other charitable endeavours at the time, and which continue to dominate philanthropy a century later. Structured legally and financially to exist in perpetuity, the Carnegie, Rockefeller and other similar foundations had large endowments and open-ended objectives such as 'improving the human condition' (Barkan, 2013: 635). Although these philanthropic initiatives were often managed in a business-like manner and according to the dictates of efficiency, Taylorist principles and similar (McGoey, 2015), there was little connection between philanthropic work and the daily business operations of their founders. The Rockefeller Foundation's initiatives, for example, included donations to the American Red Cross, the establishment of scholarships for research in physics and chemistry, and investments in medical education. So, the philanthropy of the major industrialists did not extend to workers in their employ. On the contrary, the robber barons were noted for the deplorable conditions under which their employees worked, and for the use of violence against union organising.

While the morality of the monopolists was limited to charitable works at a distance from their own businesses, around the same time, various other pioneering ethical business practitioners adopted welfare initiatives that were more integrated into their own business operations. The US National Civic Foundation (NCF), established in 1900, brought together former politicians, business leaders and union leaders, ostensibly to promote social cohesion. The NCF advocated firm-sponsored programmes for social welfare, including housing, pensions, paid holidays and healthcare. By 1925, more than 300 companies had instituted pension plans, and by 1920, more than 100 had instituted employee stock ownership (Mizruchi, 2013: 30). Similar welfare capitalist projects included those of entrepreneurs such as Pullman, Heinz, Patterson, Eastman, Kellogg and Johnson. They pursued a range of business management practices to improve both living and working conditions for employees and local communities, but also to meet the direct needs of their own business operations. Initiatives included the provision of facilities such as gymnasiums, playing fields, libraries and dining halls. In some cases, employers provided much-needed decent housing, located close to workplaces. This both addressed a pressing social need and also ensured that workers had little excuse for tardiness at work (Brejning, 2012). Quality housing and amenities were justified on the basis that they would ensure healthier workers, more productivity and more profit. Reflecting the paternalistic nature of this moral economy, welfare capitalists typically disciplined employees through religious instruction, citizenship education and thrift clubs. Such initiatives promoted 'self-improvement' and 'social mobility' through abstinence, thrift, prudence and enterprise (Brejning, 2012) and were 'designed to turn the slothful, ignorant, or intemperate into strong middle-class citizens' (Carroll et al., 2012: 82).

Henry Ford took the integration of business and benevolence to a new level. Fordist management combined technological development and shifts in the organic composition of capital through assembly lines, tight control of work organisation, using Taylorist time-and-motion studies, along with relatively generous wages as a model for facilitating a mass market for consumption. Paternalistic authority over the labour force, according to Ford's moral expectations, was central to the employment relationship. The company's Sociological Department took Taylorism and the moral economy into life beyond the factory, monitoring workers to ensure they were sober, thrifty and otherwise of good character.

The moral economy driven by welfare capitalists gave way with the financial crash of 1929 and the ensuing economic crisis. Massive capital accumulation, high spirits in financial trading and associated stock market volatility gave rise to familiar debates about rampant and irresponsible speculation. Economic collapse meant the withdrawal of many welfare capitalist initiatives, not to mention high unemployment, leaving many working people without the basics of survival. The perceived excess and lack of moral continence of the 1920s financial markets, as well as the economic deprivation and political unrest of the 1930s, created the conditions for the New Deal, which would pitch the nation state against the monopolistic power of capital.

Restraint and stability: the state as administrator of the moral economy

The post-World War II social compact between the welfare state, organised labour and the industrial capitalist class promoted a moral economy of restraint, primarily for labour and financial markets. This moral economy was largely mediated through the state, in service of stability: social, economic, financial and geo-political. The foundations of the post-World War II moral economy were laid as revolutionary fervour took hold in the 1920s, followed by economic collapse. The 1929 financial crash and the ensuing Great Depression cemented the conditions for the US Government to undertake large-scale social programmes and regulatory reforms directed towards stability. Unemployment hit around 25 per cent and industrial production ground to a halt. Social unrest and political tensions represented by recent global events like the Russian Revolution (1917) and the British general strike (1926) formed much of the basis for the state's intervention in social provisioning and management of conflict (Holloway, 1996; Negri, 1988).

In the heady atmosphere of the 1920s, many markets had become saturated as productive capacity exceeded demand. Over-accumulation gave rise to debates about the future of economic organisation. Trade unions and other working-class institutions argued for decreased working hours, while the business community warned against the risks of working-class idleness and advocated maintaining work hours but increasing consumption (Beder, 2004; Cleaver, 2005). The business case was that an increase in material wealth should be traded off against a greater compulsion to work. Though Ford had opened a politics of consumerism in the early 1900s by offering relatively high wages to its workforce to support mass consumption (Beder, 2004; Zinn, 1966), this did not become a dominant feature of the economy until the boom conditions of the post-World War II period. Nonetheless, these debates about how to organise the employment relationship contributed to political pressure around economic organisation.

Keynes (1926) laid much of the rhetorical and philosophical basis for the welfare state in his challenges to the principle of laissez-faire. He showed that classical political economists had often supported pragmatic regulation of the market economy by states (for example, regarding restrictions on usury, legislation on factory working conditions and trade laws). By the 1930s, Keynes argued that state action was essential to save capitalist economies, indeed 'civilisation', from the threat of communism and revolution (Mann, 2017). Franklin Roosevelt responded to the pressure identified by Keynes, and earlier by the Webbs and other democratic socialists. The New Deal offered a series of social security legislation, including protections for labour unions, fair competition codes and public works projects (Zinn,

1966). More ambitious programmes followed to support farmers, to regulate corporations and securities trading, to provide unemployment insurance and age pensions, and to establish minimum working conditions.

F.D.R. stole the moralistic mantle from the welfare capitalists whose initiatives had been undermined by economic crisis. He asserted the government's responsibility both to ensure human well-being and to contest the growing power of business (Zinn, 1966: 49–50, 145). The problem, he argued, was "economic royalty" and "princes of property". In response, the state was mobilised to constrain the hyper-exploitation of (white, male) workers and intra-capitalist competition, and also to contain political unrest. Unlike his predecessor, Herbert Hoover, who welcomed the robber barons' philanthrocapitalist foundations to deliver social services, F.D.R. sought the taxation revenues that industrialists avoided paying by channelling funds into those foundations (Martin, 2015: 85).

An equally important, and related, element of stability in this moral economy was that of the financial markets. After the collapse of thousands of financial institutions, the US Government abandoned the gold standard, and established national financial controls and protections for bank deposits through the Federal Deposit Insurance Corporation (FDIC). The need for financial stability in the face of what was considered irresponsible speculation was one of the grounds for the government to overtly participate in regulating financial markets, and laid the foundations for the later Bretton Woods agreements, which would expand financial market regulation transnationally. Construction of this stability was a crucial element of the state's function, according to Keynes. He characterised 'speculation' as a practice of forecasting market sentiments, as opposed to 'enterprise', a practice of forecasting the yield of assets. In this way, Keynes divorced speculation from industrial production and relegated it to the realm of the casino, and cast it as a danger to the rest of the economy, stating, 'Speculators may do no harm as bubbles on a steady stream of enterprise. But the position is serious when enterprise becomes the bubble on a whirlpool of speculation' (Keynes, 1936: 159).

The consequence of this concern with speculation, as opposed to justifiable investment, was Keynes's stipulation that the state should regulate and participate in investment to maintain stability. Core to the critique that motivated the welfare state was the distinction between responsible and irresponsible capital, between reckless speculation and prudent investment. The state took up the task of regulating and adjudicating to restore stability and, with that, prudence.

During the post-World War II period, the nation state became the administrator of the moral economy of Anglo-American capitalism, at both the national and the international level. This moral economy was characterised by a social compact that combined welfare state measures and greater economic management by the state, with institutionalised wage bargaining, and the containment of social and workplace conflict through the Fordist compromise whose basis had been laid much earlier. The political, economic and cultural influence of World War II strengthened the position of the state to act as an arbiter of the moral economy in several ways. The war effort had demonstrated the state's economic planning and coordination capacities. Public participation and sacrifice for the war effort created a level of expectation regarding compensation and support for working people, which was sharpened by the emergence of communist states and an alternate economic imaginary.

Having established itself as the leading global military power, the US confirmed itself as the economic hegemon with the Bretton Woods agreements, which positioned the US dollar as the global currency. This new era of 'embedded liberalism' (Ruggie, 1982) was marked by government taking significantly more direct responsibility for welfare and economic management. In Britain, the Labour Party electoral victory of 1945 led to sweeping changes, including nationalisation of several industries (Crosland, 1959), introduction of the National Health Service, improved access to free education, and an expansion of social security through amendments to National Insurance legislation. In the US, post-World War II social security, such as pensions and health insurance, was largely channelled through the workplace. These work-based welfare developments extended the earlier Fordist initiative of compensating (white, male) workers well as a mechanism for alleviating conflict, at the same time as greasing the wheels of consumption for the benefit of accumulation. The decade after World War II in the US involved a combination of aggressive foreign policy to establish the 'permanent war economy' favoured by leading American industrialists, and Truman's Fair Deal social welfare policies (Zinn, 2016).

The responsible corporation as a response to state regulation

Almost as soon as the state began to assert itself as the arbiter of the moral economy, the business community responded with its own assertions of responsible conduct (Kaplan, 2015). The concentration of economic power into a few firms had created questions of legitimacy regarding the social impacts of business and the containment of corporate power (Bowen, 1953; Mason, 1959). Optimistic commentators argued that the modern corporation was a 'soulful' one (Kaysen, 1959) which would take account of a wide range of interests beyond just shareholder profits. A range of proposals were made to integrate stakeholder interests into corporate decision-making and to impose checks on corporate power (Bowen, 1953; Chamberlain,

1959; Chayes, 1959; Crosland, 1959; Mason, 1959; Rostow, 1959). By the late 1950s, Berle argued that corporations were developing a 'conscience' and were 'more reasonable, more perceptive, and (in plain English) more honest, than they were in 1929' (Berle, 1959: xiii).

Contesting much of the recent history of corporate social responsibility (CSR) which suggests responsible business is a more recent project, Rami Kaplan (2015) shows that business leaders were active promoters of corporate responsibility for social issues from the early to mid-twentieth century. Rather than a sober acceptance of moral responsibility, as Berle perceived, Kaplan argues CSR was a corporate strategy in response to government regulation of business. According to this view, the 1929 financial crisis was a catalyst for CSR because the crisis triggered the New Deal policies of the 1930s and tight government regulation of the economy during World War II. Concerned about these intrusions by the state, businesses used a number of strategies to promote their own capacity to act in the public interest. A rhetorical shift was driven by the Harvard Business School and *Harvard Business Review*, along with major corporations like Standard Oil New Jersey (later Exxon). This discourse derided the welfare state while pursuing stakeholder-focused public relations initiatives. By the time new social movements began in the 1960s to agitate for corporate responsibility on social issues, Kaplan says that '[c]orporations were not merely receptive; they invented the concept of [CSR] and had been promoting it for many years, precisely because they wanted to channel social supervision of themselves in that direction' (Kaplan, 2015: 149).

Faced with a more activist nation-state, the capitalist class reasserted itself as a moral actor. In the context of the welfare state, though, capital's assertion of social responsibility differed from the previous monopoly or welfare capitalist era. Self-styled responsible businesses of the welfare state era broadened their remit. Howard Bowen, a business ethics theorist of the time, claimed a wide range of 'social responsibilities' for business, asserting, 'The unrivaled freedom of economic decision-making for millions of private businessmen, which characterizes our free enterprise system, can be justified not if it is good merely for the owners and managers of enterprises, but only if it is good for our entire society' (Bowen, 1953: 5).

Bowen framed business social responsibilities as a consequence of the maturity of industry. Many major US firms had been operating for over half a century by this time, generating a sense of security in their status as going concerns and an enduring presence in civil society. John Galbraith (1967) made a similar argument that mature corporations are not subject to the same 'vagaries of the market' as newer firms. This stability, Bowen argued, afforded the leaders of giant corporations statesman-like qualities and obligations: 'their top managements can afford the luxury of philosophizing about their social role. Moreover, because of their large size, they can think in terms of the effects of their decisions upon the total economy and on society' (Bowen, 1953: 82). This claim reflects the "responsible" corporation's attempt to usurp the state as arbiter of the moral economy.

Uncontainable tensions

The post-World War II moral economy of restraint could be also be observed through the containment of social conflict through institutions (particularly trade unions) and the exercise of countervailing power (Galbraith, 1952). Large industrial firms were challenged by the institutions of labour, and this conflict was mediated through the apparatus of the state. Minimum wage and other labour legislation, along with the extension of various social security programmes, underlaid the post-World War II Fordist consensus through which white male workers, in particular, enjoyed access to relatively stable and standardised work, higher living standards than had prevailed in the past, and access to various forms of social insurance for basic needs like housing and healthcare.

The standardisation and stability of labour in the workplace and the stability of the household through the post-World War II social security apparatus were deeply imbricated with the New Deal financial stability arrangements (Cooper, 2015). Federal deposit insurance for banks was initially posited as a protection against runs on the banks and associated financial crises. This type of collective insurance, underwritten by the state, became a model for many of the credit, welfare and social insurance initiatives that comprised the Fordist social compact, covering matters like health, education and housing. The model was dependent upon risk calculations that were, in turn, dependent upon standard working time and wages and stable employment. According to Melinda Cooper, the New Deal financial stability arrangements, such as those established by the FDIC, were the 'foundation for a new class compromise between unionized labor and the state' (Cooper, 2015: 401). The close connection between workplace, household and financial stability created a new frame for the persistent critique of speculation, especially in financial markets. The moral economy of restraint demanded disciplined markets for both finance and labour.

The welfare state containment strategies were effective in limited contexts and for a short period of time, but eventually succumbed to both internal and external pressures. Internal contradictions arose from capital's incapacity to maintain the Fordist compromises on which labour's appeasement was based, due to the demands of competition and accumulation. External pressures came from those excluded from the social compact and the welfare state.

Capital's moral economies and speculation

Marginalised groups, including non-white workers and women, engaged in political action which forced an expansion of the compromises of the welfare state, but which also made the welfare state much more expensive.

Internal tensions arose from the incorporation of working people, particularly the Fordist subject and *his* family, into advanced industrial society, which created an opaque form of domination (Chamberlain, 1959; Marcuse, 1964). What appeared as freedom or transcendence often disguised containment. Central to this dialectic was consumption. The foundations of the 'consumer republic' (Cohen, 2003) had been laid by Ford in 1914 but were picked up more broadly as part of the post-World War II consensus through which labour conflict was contained with relatively generous wage bargains (Holloway, 1996). Leisure increasingly became a time for consumption, with a proliferation of goods, entertainment and recreational services, which ensured leisure was subordinated to, and dependent upon, work. Consumerism was capital's response to workers' struggles for greater freedom from work, reasserting capitalist class control (Cleaver, 2005) and maintaining the centrality of work (Beder, 2004). While the working classes had often been subject to moralistic dictates of thrift and prudence, consumerism required a shift in the moral economy that undermined those principles (Beder, 2004). Though it seems that there is a contradiction between thrifty Victorian workers and spendthrift mid-twentieth-century workers, the thread of restraint remains. Post-World War II workers were constrained both by the demands of work which was necessary to fuel their spending, and by the shifts in consumption culture which created insatiable needs and demanded ever more purchases.

By the late 1960s and early 1970s, the Fordist consensus was breaking down. Worker frustrations with limited avenues for expressing dissent manifested in sabotage, wildcat strikes and absenteeism. The widespread use of Taylorist techniques to manage work processes exposed capital to considerable risk due to worker capacity to disrupt production (Holloway, 1996). As economic crisis hit in the 1970s, the interests of the collective capitalist – specifically, the right to make profits – came to the fore. What Harry Cleaver describes as 'a wide variety of seemingly unrelated disorders in which a number of basic social institutions began to fall apart' led to a 'global cycle of struggles, a complex yet interlocked whole that shook the entire capitalist social order to its roots and pitched it headlong into a crisis of historic proportions' (Cleaver, 2001: 24–25). This eventually contributed to the breakdown of the Bretton Woods institutions and the stable financial basis of the post-World War II period, as well as the Fordist social compact itself.

In addition to discontent regarding economic issues such as inequality, Luc Boltanski and Eve Chiapello (2005) describe the 'artistic critique' of capitalism, which demanded a life less bounded by the strictures of waged work. Similarly, Angelo Quattrocchi and Tom Nairn (1998), analysing the events of May 1968, argue that young people rejected the 'secondary alienation' of the Fordist compromise between stable waged work and post-scarcity levels of consumption. Under these conditions, drivers of revolutionary politics were not so much (or not only) material but aesthetic, including demands for greater autonomy and a 'truly social control of society' (Quattrocchi and Nairn, 1998: 118). Post-World War II struggles for civil rights, women's liberation, environmental protection, and for greater freedom and choice were often framed in terms of collective freedom, although they have since been reinterpreted through an individualist frame.

The Fordist social compact and the welfare state represented a short-lived concessionary period for certain fractions of the working class, fuelled by economic boom conditions and by the exclusion of many marginalised groups. This social compact eventually gave way in the early 1970s with the collapse of Bretton Woods and associated financial controls, as well as political pressures from both within and outside the Fordist compromise. The ensuing deregulation of financial markets, reduction of protection for trade unions and dissolution of workplace rights, proliferation of precarious employment and other instances of social and economic precarity, and structural change in advanced economies have made way for yet another set of ethical debates and accommodations.

Conclusion

This chapter has presented a particular reading of some key institutional forms and moments of capital. That reading has combined a characterisation of the prevailing moral economy at each moment, and also the various ways in which speculation has been constrained and mobilised in service of both accumulation and the moral economy. From the earliest days of capitalism's development, the moral foundations of the market economy were laid by philosophers such as Smith and Locke, interacting with social movements of that period to produce liberal rights to property and freedom of movement. Capital was socialised in the mid-1800s through limited liability firms, large-scale factories and workers' unions. The mobilisation of capital in this period was fuelled by unleashing the speculative energies of the stock market. By the turn of the twentieth century, speculators and large industrialists were under fire after having amassed unfathomable fortunes, creating the basis for a new philanthrocapitalist moral economy. After the 1929 financial crash, this privately funded welfare gave way to the organisation of the moral economy by the state through the restraint of financial and labour markets.

By focusing on the dynamic manifestations of moral economy and the politics of speculation, this history reveals the grounded and contested nature of ethics. Dominant moral principles change according to material conditions and exertions of political power. At any given time, the dominant ethical concerns and propositions are specific to that moment in history, as are the settlements and compromises made between capital and labour.

The analysis in this chapter draws out and relies upon a few key variables in capitalist social relations that drive these shifts in moral economy. These variables include the institutional form of capital; production relations and the organisation of labour and other social movements; the role played by the state as an economic actor as well as a regulator; and the role of finance as a facilitator of economic activity, a target for moral condemnation and a site of struggle. The following chapter will explore how these variables have changed in the current period. The contemporary financialised corporation has moved beyond the containment of social contest over ethics, and rather has incorporated ethical claims into its process of value creation and accumulation. And as the post-World War II state controls on finance have been lifted, or reoriented, a new space has been opened for speculation.

Note

1 For example, the 1772 *Somersett's case* in England and the Scottish case of *Knight v Wedderburn* in 1788.

Chapter 2

A speculative moral economy

ESG Risk Ratings *empower investors* by providing them with the tools to assess *financially material* ESG risks that could *affect the long-term performance of their investments* at the security, fund, and portfolio levels. (Morningstar, 2023: 5, emphasis added)

Introduction

This extract from Morningstar's annual report to the US Securities and Exchange Commission (SEC) speaks to a core element of how the speculative moral economy works and the function it is designed to perform. That is, ESG integration enables investors to identify, assess and manage financial risks to their own portfolios, facilitating speculation about which of these risks is most important to minimise or hedge and which ESG opportunities should be pursued. This is an important aspect of the speculative moral economy represented by ESG investing and stakeholder capitalism. This moral economy is not grounded in a specific set of principles. Rather, it is based on the capacity of market actors, primarily firms and investors, to speculate on which moral principles translate into financial risks, the degree of financial impact those risks might generate and the actions that should be taken to manage those impacts. To the extent that there are principles underlying the speculative moral economy, they are the principles of choice and liberal individualism, mobilised through financial markets.

This chapter charts the shifts in corporate governance practices alongside the developments in financial risk management and statecraft which have created the circumstances in which ethics are treated as a source of economic risk and opportunity. Speculation is central to the ways in which social life is ordered in a financialised economy. Changes in statecraft with respect to management of political, economic and social risks have opened a space into which financial markets have stepped. Life course risks, such as those associated with education, retirement and healthcare, which were often collectively managed during the post-World War II period, have been privatised. Financial markets have been established for private pension savings, education debt instruments and private health insurance.

The growth of financial markets has been accompanied by an expanded role for financial derivatives in managing risk. This chapter details how the institutional forms of capital are changing in this period and the forces propelling capital to adopt positions on ethical issues. Drawing together theories of financialisation and corporate governance, the chapter puts these in conversation with public statements, reports and initiatives of transnational economic and political institutions like the World Economic Forum (WEF) and the United Nations (UN); prominent financiers and corporations; human rights, environmental and non-government organisations; and political leaders. This analysis reveals a collective responsible capital imaginary that asserts not only that capital can be ethical, but that ethical capital is more profitable and more efficient and can reduce systemic risk. In contrast to this imaginary, an analysis of the speculative moral economy in practice reveals important contradictions.

The example of ESG integration – the integration of environmental, social and governance issues into investment decisions – illustrates the contradictory machinations of a speculative moral economy. ESG integration purports to responsibilise capital, but in fact facilitates speculation on different ethical positions. It is the derivative position on ethical investing. Rather than establishing an ethical capitalism that is devoid of systemic risk, the speculative moral economy translates ethics into financial calculus, via risk, producing an ethics that is contingent and profit-driven. This chapter both shows that ESG integration is central to the speculative moral economy and also lays a basis for understanding how ethics, risk and value interact to produce ethical capital, as explored in later chapters.

Between the responsible corporation and a bundle of risks

The socially responsible corporation, as an element of the post-World War II moral economy discussed in Chapter 1, was always a contested proposition but came under particular attack in the crisis-ridden 1970s. Milton Friedman's famous essay in the *New York Times* declared that the only social responsibility of businesses is to make as much profit as possible, within the bounds of 'ethical custom' and 'law' (Friedman, 1970: 33). Friedman insisted that business managers should consider themselves agents of the firm's owners (shareholders), rather than submitting to any wider social accountability. A new theory of the firm emerged from the law and economics school associated with the University of Chicago and other pillars of neoliberal thought. According to this view, the firm is a 'nexus for contracting relationships' (Jensen and Meckling, 1976: 9). Michael Jensen and William Meckling specifically rejected thinking about firms 'as if they were persons with motivations or intentions' (1976: 10), and rather saw them as akin to markets, providing a forum for equilibrium processes to take place; open, neutral spaces in which actors pursue their own ends. This contractarian view is grounded in Ronald Coase's (1937) theory of property rights and agency, privileging the interests of shareholders as the owners of the firm's property.

Consistent with Friedman and the contractarian theory of the firm, shareholder value maximisation became the dominant perspective on corporate governance during the 1980s. With increasing influence of institutional investors, relaxation of strictures on financial markets, and the thirst for hostile corporate takeovers during the 1980s, shareholder value maximisation had significant material impacts on corporate governance (Aglietta, 2000; Froud et al., 2000; Lazonick and O'Sullivan, 2000). Rather than retaining corporate earnings for reinvestment in the long-term growth of the firm, managers more often chose to distribute earnings to shareholders and to downsize, reducing labour costs and increasing labour's precarity (Lazonick and O'Sullivan, 2000). The firm was increasingly treated as a 'bundle of investment projects' (Froud et al., 2000: 87) which could be broken down, repackaged and spun off, if particular financial metrics indicated that would improve performance in capital markets. Building on this idea, it is also possible to see the firm being reconceptualised as a bundle of risks. Corporate managers were beginning to parse business activities to exclude those with an undesirable risk–return profile. Here was the emergence of an approach to investing influenced by the rise of derivative markets and their capacity to unbundle 'bits' of capital to intensify competition through the commodification of risk (Bryan and Rafferty, 2006b).

Risk was the fissure through which the shareholder value maximisation approach to corporate governance gave way to questions of ethics. The contractarian view of the firm resisted calls for CSR or considerations of stakeholder interests which grew throughout this period. The movement for divestment from apartheid-era South Africa and its associated Sullivan Principles was accompanied by an increasing awareness of the business role in environmental degradation that led to the UN approach to sustainable development of the late 1980s. It was becoming more difficult for firms to refuse some recognition of their ecological and social impact. By the turn of the new century, even Jensen, a leading proponent of the contractarian view, was advocating 'enlightened shareholder value' (Jensen, 2002), which has since become a building block of the speculative moral economy.

A speculative moral economy

Jensen's treatment of the 'stakeholder' concept is crucial both to his reworking of the contractarian view of the firm and to establishing the foundations of a speculative moral economy. He recognised that firms should not 'ignore or mistreat any important constituency' (Jensen, 2002: 246). But he defined stakeholders slightly differently to advocates of a stakeholder approach to the firm (such as Freeman, 1984). He was not concerned with those *who will be impacted by* a firm, but with *those who can impact* the firm. So, the stakeholders Jensen was interested in are those who pose or who can create *risks* for firms. Risk was the frame through which ethics were squeezed into the model of the financialised firm: a bundle of risks. And crucially, it is financial risk to the firm, rather than other types of risks to the firm's stakeholders, which are being managed. This is an important distinction which is often elided in contemporary debates about corporate responsibility and business ethics, and which has been highlighted in critiques by Tariq Fancy (2021) and Adrienne Buller (2022).

Enlightened shareholder value is, then, a foundation stone for the speculative moral economy. It is the expression of a struggle between an insistence on markets as the optimum apparatus for achieving social welfare against the need to manage class conflict and political tensions around ecological, social and political challenges. The business impact on social and ecological issues is hard to deny. Demands for increased corporate accountability for ecological destruction, poverty and inequality, human and labour rights abuse, and other social impacts have accelerated since the 1990s. Climate change, in particular, has brought the destructive capacity of capitalism into sharp relief, prompting calls for drastic social and economic restructuring from a broad spectrum of actors and activists, including anti-capitalists and social democrats, techno-optimists and deep green theorists, and increasingly, schoolchildren. In his relatively radical 2015 encyclical, Pope Francis cited climate change, along with access to basic resources such as water, biodiversity loss, inequality and decreasing quality of life in his condemnation of 'a global problem with grave implications: environmental, social, economic, political and for the distribution of goods. It represents one of the principal challenges facing humanity in our day' (Pope Francis, 2015: 36). As the climate crisis escalates, with each new UN report revealing more devastating predictions, with each year generating new climate-driven disasters, the weight of this social and political pressure grows. Business and political leaders have developed and extended Jensen's rhetoric of enlightened corporate management to improbably posit the market as the place to manage these contradictions and political pressures, producing a responsible capital imaginary.

A plethora of multi-stakeholder initiatives, codes of conduct, ethical standards and more have emerged in an effort to harness corporate influence for good and to temper the worst impacts of business activity on the biosphere, on human rights and on social phenomena such as inequality. The ideological strength of the market was reinforced when this rhetoric accelerated in the wake of the financial crisis of 2007–8, arguably one of the most significant market failures in capitalism's history. Mark Carney, the former Bank of England Governor, recognising the depleted faith in the market economy, implored business leaders to develop an 'inclusive capitalism': 'We simply cannot take the capitalist system, which produces such plenty and so many solutions, for granted. Prosperity requires not just investment in economic capital, but investment in social capital. It is necessary to rebuild social capital to make markets work' (Carney, 2014). Around the same time, Christine Lagarde, former Chief of the International Monetary Fund, and now of the European Central Bank, similarly argued that '[b]y making capitalism more inclusive, we make capitalism more effective, and possibly more sustainable' (Lagarde, 2014).

Since the late 2010s, there has been yet another acceleration of this kind of corporate responsibility rhetoric through the frame of 'stakeholder capitalism'. Two journalists working for the *Financial Times* cast 2019 as 'the year that capitalism went cuddly' (Edgecliffe-Johnson and Mooney, 2019). The United States Business Roundtable (US BRT), which represents many of the US's largest firms, declared in late 2019 that 'the free-market system is the best means of generating good jobs, strong and sustainable economy, innovation, a healthy environment and economic opportunity for all' (US BRT, 2019a). Echoing twenty-first-century Jensen (2002), the US BRT also stated that corporations should be driven by 'purpose', long-term value and a concern for stakeholder interests (US BRT, 2019a). Similar statements have been made by the British Academy, which launched its 'Principles for purposeful business' in 2019, and the UK's Institute of Directors, which called in 2019 for firms to explore 'new ways to combine the profit motive with social responsibility', while the US Chamber of Commerce told its members that 'empathy' drives free markets (Edgecliffe-Johnson and Mooney, 2019). The WEF, a long-standing advocate for CSR, launched a revised manifesto in January 2020, claiming that when a company engages in 'shared and sustained value creation' it serves all of its stakeholders, not only shareholders (WEF, 2020). This updated document replaced the 1973 WEF founding manifesto, which stated, 'The purpose of professional management is to serve clients, shareholders, workers and employees, as well as societies, and to *harmonize the different interests of the stakeholders*' (WEF, 1973, emphasis added).

Implicit in the 1973 manifesto's requirement to harmonise different interests is recognition of a conflict of interests which corporate managers are called upon to negotiate. The 2020 manifesto, by contrast, claims that a company 'serves not only its shareholders, but all its stakeholders' when it engages in value creation (WEF, 2020). This shift in emphasis is crucial. It is a central feature of the contemporary moral economy and its underlying responsible capital imaginary. Dispensing with the notion of conflicting interests, it is assumed that all stakeholders are served when business is successful.

The work of the World Business Council for Sustainable Development (WBCSD) gives a window into the thinking that underlies this assertion of shared interests. The WBCSD aims to 'accelerate the transition to a sustainable world' (WBCSD, n.d.a) by building 'an economy based on *true value, true profits and true costs*' (WBCSD, n.d.c, emphasis added). Central to the WBCSD project is to 'redefin[e] value' by helping companies to 'measure and manage risk, gain competitive advantage and seize new opportunities by understanding environmental, social and governance (ESG) information' (WBCSD, n.d.b). The WBCSD's explicit reference to 'true' value, profits and costs highlights the role of externalities. Companies are implored not only to incorporate their direct economic costs, but to consider indirect social and ecological costs. Rather than being a drag on profits, incorporating externalities is reframed as a potential source of 'competitive advantage' and 'new opportunities' to be seized for the long-sighted investor or executive.

Ethical issues are a source of both risk and opportunity in this philosophy of enlightened business management. This moral economy contrasts with previous manifestations, as set out in Chapter 1. Victorian industrialists made no pretence to ethical conduct in the operation of their factories. The robber barons sought redemption for their massive wealth accumulation through charitable works but saw them as completely separate and independent activities. Welfare capitalists perceived ancillary benefits for workers to be a cost, but one which was justified by other benefits to the business. During the welfare state period, business profits were constrained in the service of ethics through institutionalised wage bargaining, the operations of countervailing power and trade-offs through the welfare state. Even classical liberals, who perhaps come closest to today's moral economy by arguing for the inherent moral good of wealth accumulation, increasing the common wealth and putting idle resources to work, fell short of treating ethical conundrums as business opportunities. For today's capitalists, business not only delivers the unquestionable benefit of increased material wealth, but it treats social and ecological problems as risks to be managed and as opportunities for profit. In the speculative moral economy, through prescient management of ESG risk and opportunity, speculation is a mechanism for ethical action.

46 *Moral economies*

Following and developing the line opened up by Jensen at the turn of the century, contemporary business ethics asserts that profit-making and social justice are not merely compatible but mutually beneficial. The assertion that capital, properly managed, can overcome its own social, political and ecological contradictions by reducing or eliminating ESG risks is the conceptual foundation of today's speculative moral economy. But this moral economy in action reveals crucial contradictions. While the rhetorical or conceptual claim is that responsible capital can eliminate ESG risks, what the speculative moral economy facilitates in practice is leveraging different ethical positions for profit. Given the particular role of finance with regard to risk management in the contemporary economy, this practice is most clearly seen through trends in finance, especially the strategy of integrating ESG issues into investment decision-making (ESG integration).

Finance and the contemporary moral economy

A social or ethical turn in finance has been observed both in scholarly literature (Dowling, 2017; Dowling and Harvie, 2014; Harvie and Ogman, 2019; Langley, 2018; Ouma, 2018) and in popular business management and political discourse, represented, for example, in the extensive coverage in the *Financial Times* of trends in 'Moral Money'. David Harvie and Robert Ogman (2019) and Emma Dowling (2017) frame the emergence of a social investment market as a response to a legitimacy crisis for capitalism. Stefan Ouma sees the 'moral evolution of modern finance' (2018: 71), as a process in which finance becomes a 'problem-solving machine' through which 'moral and social questions are reframed as economic ones' (2018: 81). But as Sarah Sippel has pointed out in her exploration of the financialised moral economy, 'financial logics and rationales ... do not emerge out of nothing. They both rely on, and actively participate in the production of, certain norms and values while being grounded within the broader sociohistorical context' (Sippel, 2018: 551). This compels a consideration of why finance has become a locus for ethical debate, for taking action on social dilemmas, and for asserting a moral stance.

Finance occupies a special place in the contemporary moral economy for two key reasons. First, the growth in size of institutional investors and, more recently, asset managers has created the conditions under which investors adopt a quasi-regulatory role in the global economy (Hawley and Williams, 1997, 2005, 2007). Second, the risk management revolution that has taken place since the 1970s has created a particular function for finance and its techniques beyond the stock market. Under these circumstances, the treatment of ethical issues as risks has become more plausible. This opened the possibility of an ethical spread which can be priced. Through an approach to corporate governance driven by leveraging different risk positions, ethics become cells in a spreadsheet, representing several different possibilities.

Investors as intra-class regulators?

The notion that investors can or should act as an intra-class regulating force is closely related to the development of private governance in the global economy (Ford and Nolan, 2020; Fransen and LeBaron, 2019; Herman, 2020) but also has a particular financial character, based in the 'fiduciary capitalism' thesis. According to this thesis, the particular interests and perspective of institutional investors mean that they should use their power to reduce systemic risk across the economy (Hawley and Williams, 1997, 2007).

Fiduciary capitalism, or 'financially intermediated society' (Bogle, 2009), is characterised by the ownership of corporate entities by institutional investors rather than individuals. Share ownership has concentrated throughout the twentieth and twenty-first centuries, with institutional investors like pension funds increasing their share of equities compared with other investor categories. Globally, institutional investors own more than 40 per cent of market capitalisation (De La Cruz et al., 2019). This makes them the largest single category of investors in stock markets and represents a significant shift from the mid-twentieth century. In the 1960s, individuals held 84 per cent of all publicly listed stocks in the US. By 2014, they held around 40 per cent (Çelik and Isaksson, 2014). In the UK, the shift to institutional ownership has been even more dramatic with the portion of shares held by individuals decreasing from 54 per cent to 11 per cent (Çelik and Isaksson, 2014).

Recent research on capital markets ownership by the Organisation for Economic Co-operation and Development (OECD) shows that the fiduciary capitalism thesis is strongest in the US, where institutions own over 70 per cent of all listed equities. Other economies in which institutional investors are particularly dominant include the UK, Canada, Japan and several other European states (De La Cruz et al., 2019: 12). However, as the majority of the money invested in public equity markets worldwide is held by investors from these economies, particularly the US, Japan, Korea and Europe (De La Cruz et al., 2019: 10), the influence of institutional investors is significant throughout the global economy.

In addition to the shift to institutional investors, stock ownership is highly concentrated at the level of the funds and their investee companies. The top ten global institutions control one third of all funds under management (Kennedy, 2019). As well, a small number of shareholders tend to own the majority of a corporation's stock. In the US, the UK, Canada and Japan, the three largest shareholders typically hold between 25 and 30 per cent of a given company's stock. The top twenty shareholders own, on average, 50 to 60 per cent of the company's stock (De La Cruz et al., 2019: 18).

Given these features of global equity markets, James Hawley and Andrew Williams have popularised the concept of the 'universal owner': a very large investment fund that depends on the performance of the economy as a whole; represents the entire market in its portfolio; and has long-term investment interests (Hawley and Williams, 2007). Universal owners are subject to particular pressures due to their long-term investment horizon and their exposure to 'systemic risk', which cannot be hedged by choosing outperforming stocks or diversifying a portfolio (Hawley and Williams, 2007; Quigley, 2019). Some emblematic examples of these kinds of systemic risks are those related to financial instability and climate change. In addition to the particular pressures to which universal owners are subject, Hawley and Williams (1997) argue that they have extraordinary power. This combination of external pressures and institutional power means these investors have a 'unique perspective and voice' (Hawley and Williams, 2005: 1995) which creates an incentive to adopt a quasi-regulatory function through investment strategies that manage ESG risk at the company level and at the economy level, where ESG risk is conflated with systemic risk (Hawley and Lukomnik, 2018; Kiernan, 2007).

This aspect of the corporate governance regime has been accelerated with the increasing growth in asset managers. Benjamin Braun (2021, 2022) has argued that the position of asset managers in the financial sector has established a new corporate governance regime. Throughout the 2010s, a handful of asset managers, led by BlackRock, Vanguard and State Street (the Big Three), have gained control over large pools of capital, often on behalf of institutional investors. BlackRock manages USD 8.5 trillion in investments, Vanguard USD 8 trillion and State Street USD 4 trillion. Combined, the Big Three manage the equivalent of over half of the market capitalisation of companies in the S&P 500 (Manjoo, 2022). Asset managers that are invested across the entire market are even more exposed to the corporate governance problem revealed by Hawley and Williams: they do not have the capacity to exercise control over investee companies via divestment. Further, as argued by Hawley and Williams, they are dependent on the health of the entire economy for their investment returns. This has created an environment in which both institutional investors and asset managers are encouraged to take on a quasi-regulatory role in relation to managing systemic risk.

Many institutional investors have self-identified as universal owners and have readily adopted this quasi-regulatory role. The Japanese Government Pension Investment Fund (GPIF), the world's largest asset owner, for example, describes itself as 'a classic universal owner'. The GPIF says this compels the fund to take a long-term view and to adopt strategies for reducing market instability (Eccles and Klimenko, 2019). Hiro Mizuno, GPIF's former Chief Investment Officer, has explained that 'as a universal owner, instead of trying to beat the market, our responsibility at GPIF is to make capital markets more sustainable' (UNEP FI, 2019: 25). In line with these statements, in 2018, the GPIF announced its intention to focus on enhancing 'beta' or reducing systemic risks (Hawley and Lukomnik, 2018). In March 2020, GPIF collaborated with USS Investment and the Californian Teachers' Retirement System (CalSTRS) on a statement affirming their commitment to long-term value creation, managing systemic and ESG risks, and working with companies and asset managers who share these views. This letter echoed many of the sentiments in an open letter to clients and investee companies from Larry Fink, BlackRock Chief Executive, in January 2020. Fink's letter made a series of commitments for BlackRock, the world's largest asset owner, to increase its ESG offerings and improve ESG risk management strategies, on the basis that doing so would produce a more 'resilient' portfolio (Fink, 2020). Prescient management of ESG risk has become a key part of the asset manager pitch to potential clients.

Transnational organisations like the OECD (2017) and the UNPRI also advocate investors taking a more active approach to managing their portfolios to reduce or eliminate ESG risk. The UNPRI and United Nations Environment Programme Finance Initiative (UNEP FI), in particular, have been engaged in nearly two decades' worth of advocacy and research, collaborating with legal and consultancy firms to develop jurisprudential arguments for a 'modern' approach to fiduciary duty (UNEP FI and Freshfields Bruckhaus Deringer, 2005, 2009; UNPRI et al., 2019, n.d.). Through this work, the UNPRI and UNEP FI have made an increasingly assertive case that taking financially material ESG issues into account in investment decision-making is consistent with investor fiduciary duties. Today, the UNPRI and UNEP FI take a particularly sharp line on the imperative for investors to take on a quasi-regulatory role with respect to ESG issues when they claim that '[i]nvestors that fail to incorporate environmental, social and governance (ESG) issues are failing their fiduciary duties and are increasingly likely to be subject to legal challenge' (UNPRI et al., 2019: 8).

To date, there is no evidence of any state or court taking such a hard line as this on the relationship between fiduciary duty and ESG issues, though some governments are taking action to facilitate investors taking ESG issues into account. In 2015, the US Department of Labor issued new guidance to trustees of pension funds regulated under the Employee Retirement Income Security Act (ERISA). Interpretive Bulletin 2015-01 stated that consideration of ESG factors in investment is consistent with fiduciary duties under ERISA as long as they are 'economically relevant'. In the bulletin and associated documents, the Department of Labor explained that this guidance was issued expressly to contradict existing restrictive readings of fiduciary duty. US President Biden reinforced this position in March 2023 by vetoing a potential change to the Department of Labor's interpretation of fiduciary duty. In the US in particular, this is becoming a vexed political issue with governments at the state level issuing contradictory instructions to pension and other investment funds with regard to the integration of ESG issues into investment decisions (Agnew et al., 2022; DeSantis, 2022; FT Editorial Board, 2023; Ropes & Gray, n.d.).

Pension fund regulations in South Africa, the European Union (EU) and the UK have been amended, recognising that fiduciaries are permitted to consider financially material ESG factors (OECD, 2017). The developments in the UK go slightly further, requiring pension funds to disclose how they are taking ESG risks into account for their investments. The Chinese Government also announced in January 2020 its raised expectations regarding ESG disclosure. Following action by the Chinese Securities Regulatory Commission in 2018, the stock exchanges of Shanghai and Shenzhen are expected to follow Hong Kong by requiring more ESG disclosures from listed firms (Lee and Moscardi, 2019; Temple-West and Liu, 2020). Meanwhile, US investors have requested guidance on ESG disclosure from the SEC, which has set up a Climate and ESG taskforce to establish and enforce standards (SEC, 2021). Recent expert legal opinion in Australia also indicates that investors' fiduciary duty extends to systemic risks represented by climate change, and that this position is accepted by superannuation (pension) funds in Australia (Hutley and Mack, 2021).

Aside from regulatory and policy initiatives, the expectations that powerful investors will act as monitors and moderators of corporate conduct has become a common rhetorical device for other political and business actors. In one of her final speeches as Chief of the International Monetary Fund, Christine Lagarde drew on inspiration from such diverse sources as Aristotle and Mary Poppins in a speech that argued that financiers have an ethical responsibility to drive a 'healthy economy' by using the 'magic of finance' to invest for the 'public good' (Lagarde, 2019). A former Australian Human Rights Commissioner declared during her tenure that pension fund trustees should assess investments 'through the prism of international human rights law' and use their economic power to encourage corporate adherence to human rights (Rose, 2016). Writing elsewhere, in partnership with accounting firm Ernst and Young, the Commissioner couched this proposal in the language of financial markets: 'human rights, just like any other aspect of business, *can increase the value of an organisation if managed appropriately, or decrease it, if neglected*' (Ernst and Young and AHRC, 2017: 1, emphasis added).

Taking a similarly pecuniary perspective and highlighting the long-term view, investment manager Patrick Odier wrote in the *Financial Times*:

> *most investors recognise that it pays to take into account the environmental, social and governance factors that affect companies.* From the accounting scandals at Enron and Parmalat, through the global banking crisis of 2007–09, the Macondo oil-well disaster, and recent vehicle emissions testing controversies, 'ESG' failures have had devastating financial consequences for businesses previously considered robust. *It is intuitive that the more sustainably a company is run, the more likely it is to be earning revenues tomorrow.* (Odier, 2017, emphasis added)

Despite the popularity of the universal owner thesis among some institutional investors and asset managers, the proposition that investors should act as quasi-regulators of corporate conduct regarding ESG issues is not the only, or even the dominant, view on corporate governance. Several scholars have highlighted the fact that institutional investors are not actually behaving like universal owners (Richardson, 2015; Richardson and Peihani, 2015), including one of the strongest advocates of the universal owner theory (Hawley, 2011). The business case for ESG is often less compelling than the case that it supports the legitimacy of the asset management industry (Clark and Dixon, 2023), and the adoption of a universal owner approach to investment faces 'institutional, social, and cognitive' barriers (Kiernan, 2007; Quigley, 2019: 5). Some of these barriers can be observed in Christophers' (2019) interviews with investment managers about their attitudes to climate risk. The degree to which ESG issues were integrated into investment decision-making varied between financial institutions. Most interesting, though, was the simple resistance of many investment professionals to assume any regulatory or socially oriented role. While some investment professionals felt that they were constrained by their fiduciary obligations to focus on financial returns, other fund managers thought only about returns because they believe 'often fervently, that this is the correct approach … whether legal guidelines happen to stipulate such single-mindedness or not' (Christophers, 2019: 762). As some fund managers said, '[i]t's not our responsibility to make oil and gas companies do anything … other than manage their risks responsibly—everything else is politicians' role' and '[w]e are not mandated to care about the planet' (Christophers, 2019: 762). As Christophers points out, these were normative statements about the proper role of finance.

While the integration of ESG issues into investment decisions is an uneven and emergent process, the reality of fiduciary capitalism in practice does not reflect the theory set out by Hawley, Williams and others. Fiduciary capitalism is not facilitating the management of systemic or ESG risks for a more resilient economy and society. But it is creating a space in which ethical issues are being measured, priced and traded for profit. The treatment of ESG issues as financial risks, and as undiversifiable systemic risk, is creating a space for a derivative logic of ethics to operate. This process has its grounding in the financial risk management revolution since the 1970s.

Risk management revolution

Risk management has taken on a particular character since the breakdown of the post-World War II political and economic order. 'Embedded liberalism' (Ruggie, 1982) depended on tightly managed labour and financial markets (Cooper, 2015), designed to manufacture stability through Keynesian governance practices. This did not mean the absence of risks but a specific approach to minimising and managing them through aggregate macroeconomic demand. The following considers how this transition in risk management has played out beyond the state, in households and, particularly, in corporate governance.

In the early 1970s, the containment strategies of the post-World War II boom period came undone. Social movements of the 1960s for racial and gender equality had increased the costs of the welfare state (Cooper, 2015). Transnational political tensions led the US to rescind its role as the global banker, undermining the Bretton Woods system for financial stability. Exogenous shocks like the oil price hikes drove inflation. As economic crisis hit, particularly in wealthy countries like the US and the UK, workers' frustrations were expressed in industrial action. Three decades of confidence in Keynesian economic management was dashed and a space created for those who had been advocating alternative economic policies since the 1940s.

Many states took up the principles of monetarism, privatisation of government services, reduction of social security benefits and attacks on labour organisations. This transition in statecraft, often called neoliberalisation, has variously been referred to as a class project to restore the power of capital (Harvey, 2005), a 'golden straitjacket' which all states must don to promote economic development (Friedman, 1999), and a vehicle to promote prosperity and freedom (Friedman and Friedman, 1980). To understand how these changes in statecraft have produced different risk relations, the most interesting theorisation of this period is that of Randy Martin (2014, 2015). Martin repurposes the commonly used concept of (dis)intermediation from financial practice and literature to understand the dynamics of financialisation and neoliberalisation. He explains that 'disintermediation … means that the field of economic activity becomes more porous, open to more and more actors working from ever more complex webs of rules and risks' (Martin, 2014: 199).

Contra common conceptions of deregulation and privatisation, disintermediation does not suggest that the state reduces its regulation of the economy or removes itself from the economy. Rather, the state makes space for other actors in both political and economic functions, and the distinction between these actors and their roles becomes more fluid. Regulation is not weakened or eradicated but altered, and often made more complex (Braithwaite and Drahos, 2000). What emerges from the forthcoming narrative is that in the context of disintermediation, multiple actors take on the role of managing risks that were previously collectivised, including ethical risks.

By dismantling the institutional and financial architecture that afforded stability to labour and financial markets, the state reconfigured its relationship to risk. One element of this change in risk management has been to disperse volatility and uncertainty by shifting risk from the state and the firm to the household and the individual (Bryan and Rafferty, 2018; Christophers, 2016a; Hacker, 2008; Rafferty and Yu, 2010). This is reflected in initiatives such as the privatisation of previously collectively funded and delivered health, education and other human services, and towards user-paid services and private insurance. At the same time, governments have opened economic and political space for private firms, through financial markets, with the sale of publicly owned utilities such as telecommunications, electricity, transport and water providers. The privatisation of retirement savings is of course central to this process, and a key factor in the emergence of the institutional investor and asset manager power discussed above (Braun, 2022).

Disintermediation (Martin, 2014: 199) means that many political and social risks are managed privately by individual actors and are increasingly subject to the dynamics of financial markets. Importantly, reflecting the practice of disintermediation as one that complicates regulation and invites more actors into the regulatory process, the state structures the way that risks are shared between public and private actors. Some theorists of risk have argued that this meant a transition from 'risk spreading' practices of collectivisation through the state to 'embracing risk' practices through which private firms and individuals are encouraged, or compelled, to engage more directly with risk (Baker and Simon, 2004). This plays out in many different risk structures, often dependent on the power relations between the parties. For example, Fleur Johns has examined infrastructure development contracts for several major projects in Australia to show the complexities of risk apportionment between the state, construction firms and financiers, and that the state often insures its contractors against various forms of economic and political risk (Johns, 2011). By contrast, Susanne Soederberg exposes the reluctance of US governments to indemnify individuals and households exposed to greater economic risks of unemployment and escalating healthcare and education costs, due to the phenomenon of disintermediation. This results in individuals' increasing reliance on financial markets, for example by accessing credit to meet basic subsistence needs (Soederberg, 2014).

54   *Moral economies*

From the perspective of capital, the breakdown of the inflation/employment trade-off meant the rise of volatility. This material condition gave rise to the development of derivative markets, as businesses sought to hedge (and speculate on) volatility. The invention of the Black–Scholes options pricing model at this time is significant, as it provided the formula not just to price options, but to create new derivative products and develop the capacity to define and dissect risks more precisely (LiPuma, 2017). A critical new market in the pricing, commodification and trading of risk exploded from the 1970s, forming the basis of enormous growth in trading on financial markets (Bryan and Rafferty, 2006a; Partnoy, 2000), which has been characterised by some as a derivatives revolution (Hu and Black, 2006, 2008). As derivatives markets spread into different economic domains, the Black–Scholes model provided a way to price and trade the risks that Julie Froud and her co-authors (2000) saw being outsourced through shifts in corporate organisation.

Derivatives enable economic actors to package, price and trade on the performance of attributes of an underlying asset. Modern derivative contracts are infinitely diverse and can be used to trade on any number of variables or attributes. The versatility of derivatives contributed to their rapid growth as a risk management mechanism. As a tool that prices and trades risk, the derivative has changed how risks are understood, assessed and managed. Through the derivative, the fortunes and survival of seemingly disconnected people, places and institutions can be connected by risk exposure and management. Perhaps the most well-known and catastrophic example of such connectivity is the financial crisis beginning in 2007–8 and the ensuing collapse of housing markets, livelihoods and financial institutions. That crisis revealed that the stability of the US economy, previously governed through arrangements like Bretton Woods and national fiscal policy, is now predicated, at least in part, on the regular payment of debts by households (Bryan and Rafferty, 2014).

The significance of the derivatives revolution extends far beyond the trading floor and the corporate boardroom, due to the role of derivatives in managing risk and the peculiar function of risk in today's economy (Bryan et al., 2015; Bryan and Rafferty, 2006a, 2014, 2018; Christophers, 2016a; Christophers et al., 2018; LiPuma, 2017). The intensive and extensive expansion of the derivative's function for managing risk means that a 'derivative logic' (Martin, 2014, 2015) permeates social and economic life. This logic represents an inextricable connection between finance, speculation and risk. A speculative ethos seeps from financial markets and into other areas of daily life, as is observed by scholars of everyday financialisation (see, for example, Allen and Pryke, 2013; Allon, 2010; Bryan et al., 2009; Bryan and Rafferty, 2014; Martin, 2002). These authors demonstrate the ways in which a financial or derivative logic becomes an integral part of workers' lives. From housing to health, education to retirement, finance is the avenue through which people increasingly access their basic subsistence. As collectively provisioned social services are depleted, working people rely on household debt and privatised savings (Bryan and Rafferty, 2018; LiPuma, 2017; Martin, 2015; Soederberg, 2014). Speculation becomes central to the experience of the neoliberal subject (Konings, 2018). Political, economic, social and personal decisions are made through the frame of speculation and positioning one's speculations in relation to the speculations of others. At the level of the individual or household, one must make a plethora of interconnected and weighty decisions about present and future economic security: do I really need health insurance? If so, at what level and which conditions do I need to cover? Which education scheme will be the best value for money? Do I need to save money for my children's education? Can I afford to buy a house? Can I afford not to? If so, where and when? Where are my pension savings? Should I take a balanced or aggressive investment strategy? How much do I need to retire? How long will I live?

This process of identifying, assessing and managing risks is central to the 'speculative lifeworld … in which each individual is condemned to decision making under uncertain levels of uncertainty, and thus to precarity and insecurity' (LiPuma, 2017: 235). In the terms of Randy Martin's (2014) 'social derivative' concept, individuals and households are increasingly compelled to think about themselves as a set of exposures (to risk) and to think about which risks to hold and which to sell off (through insurance). Through these processes of breaking the self down into exposures and separating those exposures from the self, the risks are abstracted, depersonalised and rendered commensurable.

It may not be immediately clear that there is a connection between individual and household risks, and corporate governance. What has my well-being in retirement got to do with whether a particular corporation uses forced labour? The answer lies in the emergence of abstract risk. Martin argued that the dissemination of a derivative logic means 'more finance everywhere, but also more socialization, more interdependence, more mutual debt' (Martin, 2015: 1997). Derivatives draw together different forms of risk (and social phenomena), subjecting them to a consistent process of management and leading to what some scholars of financialisation refer to as 'abstract risk' (Christophers, 2016a; LiPuma, 2017).

Abstract risk stands alongside Marx's (1990) concept of abstract labour. Through the commodification of labour power, concrete labours and their products come to reflect abstract labour. This is an essential feature of an economy based around the widespread division of concrete labours, mediated through exchange and money, because abstract labour facilitates the commensuration of these concrete labours. Bryan and Rafferty (2006b) situate the modern function of derivatives as a further development in this process of unbundling that began with the emergence of the capitalist mode of production. While capitalism necessitated the emergence of abstract labour to commensurate concrete labours, the derivative has broken down and unbundled capital itself. By breaking capital into 'bits' that can be recombined, traded and put into competition, derivatives create a different basis on which to understand value relations (Bryan and Rafferty, 2006b). Edward LiPuma (2017) has extended this analysis and argues that the commodification of risk through derivatives has led to the emergence of abstract risk. Processes of risk management through a derivative logic facilitate isolating attributes of particular individuals, events and organisations, and identifying risks to be priced and traded. This renders a vast range of different risks commensurable as qualitative and quantitative versions of each other, which are traded, mediated and managed through the same processes (LiPuma, 2017: 62). Risk becomes the 'principal means by which people and companies organize their interdependence' (LiPuma, 2017: 61). It is through this phenomenon of abstract risk that corporate governance issues and business ethics are bound up with individual and household risks. This relationship has become more pronounced with the recent innovation of sustainability-linked derivatives and other derivatives to manage various forms of ESG risk.

A speculative moral economy

While speculation is still a focus of blame in times of crisis (which was widely observable in the aftermath of the financial crisis of 2007–8) since Friedman championed it as a source of economic stability and liquidity in the early 1970s, a 'speculative ethos' (LiPuma, 2017), or a 'logic of specularity' (Konings, 2018), has become prevalent in social and economic life as a tool of risk management, and as a way of organising and understanding social relations. So, it is in the context of the risk management revolution, alongside the emergence of fiduciary capitalism, that a speculative moral economy emerges. It is useful here to recall the outline in Chapter 1 of the concept of the moral economy as a set of norms 'that structure and influence economic practices, both formal and informal, and the way in which these are reinforced, compromised or overridden by economic pressures' (Sayer, 2007: 262). This concept of the moral economy is a dynamic and historically contingent one that creates a framework for understanding the relationship between prevailing moral settlements or compromises and the lived antagonisms of capitalist social relations.

The nature of this speculative moral economy, then, is one in which ethical issues, including matters which have been collectively managed through the state, are reframed as financial risks. This is the process that Stefan Leins (2020) has described, based on an ethnographic analysis of ESG practitioners, as the 'post crisis ethical order', where ESG legitimates profit-making in finance while speculating on social conflict as a means to generate those profits. Labour rights, environmental regulation and consumer protection are just a few ethical issues that are subjected to this form of financial risk management. In this process, the ethical basis of the moral economy becomes speculative. Finance's method for managing ethical risks is, like its methods for managing other risks, grounded in estimations about which risks will be the most costly and which opportunities will be the most profitable. No longer just a subject of ethical critique in itself, the practice of speculation becomes a vehicle for managing ethical dilemmas.

This speculative moral economy has consequences both for the manifestation of ethics and for accumulation. First, in relation to ethics, the dissemination of a derivative logic produces an ethics that is contingent and profit-driven. Ethical issues are relevant to the extent that they have operational, legal or reputational consequences which have pecuniary implications. Second, in relation to accumulation, the speculative moral economy creates the possibility of "ethical commodities" or "ethical capital assets". It is not claimed here that these commodities are objectively more ethical than others, but rather that they are built on particular ethical positions. The most obvious examples are corporate brands that are built (in part) on ethical claims and other reputational elements (see Chapter 5 for more on brands) and ESG credit ratings (see Chapter 6 for more on these). The derivative logic of ethics facilitates speculation on different ethical claims. That is, firms and investors are able to price and leverage a spread between possible ethical positions. The clearest expression of this derivative logic of ethics is in the practice of ESG integration.

ESG integration and responsible investment

The integration of ESG issues into investment decision-making is now a widespread and relatively mainstream practice. The majority of institutional investors and asset managers use ESG ratings and analyses on a regular basis. Price Waterhouse Coopers research found that growth rates are much higher for ESG-mandated funds than for the rest of the asset management industry. Despite weak returns and political turmoil, ESG accounted for 65 per cent of inflows to European exchange traded funds (ETFs) in 2022

(Boyd, 2023). While figures vary, the evidence suggests that ESG investing is a growing part of the financial sector.

What is less clear is the relation between ESG investing and "responsible" capital. Though ESG and responsible investment are often conflated, the activities that comprise responsible investment are notoriously difficult to define (Eccles and Viviers, 2011; Langley, 2018; Sandberg et al., 2009). The nature of the underlying "responsibleness" or "ethicalness" is unclear. Contemporary responsible investment has its origins in divestment movements through which investors withdrew funds from enterprises that engaged in activity that offended ethical principles (Eccles and Viviers, 2011; Sampford and Ransome, 2011; Sparkes and Cowton, 2004). Divestment from the trade in enslaved people in the late eighteenth century by the Religious Society of Friends (Quakers) is a very early example, along with restrictions on trade in "sin stocks" such as pornography and gaming by faith-based trusts (Richardson and Cragg, 2010; Sampford and Ransome, 2011; Sparkes, 2001; Sparkes and Cowton, 2004). This kind of investment strategy was, and remains, a niche activity in which the profit motive is constrained by ethical standards.

The practice of responsible investment has emerged, claiming to marry the profit motive with corporate responsibility. The organisations that enact responsible investment include investment advisory and research firms that provide information and guidance to investors and funds regarding the performance of particular investment options in the form of social credit ratings and rankings. The contemporary responsible investment sector has emerged out of investment analysis based on ethical considerations in the early 1980s. Ethical Investment Research Information Service (EIRIS) was established in the UK in 1983 by a charitable organisation aiming to provide information to investors who wanted to screen their portfolios for certain ethical issues, such as investment in the nuclear industry. The other key precursor to today's responsible investment practices related to corporate governance. Institutional Shareholder Services (ISS) was founded in 1985 to inform and promote active ownership by institutional investors. ISS focused on corporate governance issues and provided a proxy advisory service for investors.

Since the 1990s, these two branches of practice have developed and merged. Business ethics have become a part of corporate risk management. Throughout the 1990s, several other services were established to provide information about the sustainability impacts of particular investment options. KLD was formed in 1989 in the US to provide social research on firms, and to inform positive and negative screening by investors. Other services were founded with similar objectives, including Jantzi Research in Toronto in 1992; GES International in 1992 and Ethix SRI Advisors in 1999, both in Sweden; and Oekom Research in 1993 in Germany, among others. These research organisations all developed their own methodologies for assessing corporate sustainability performance, or social and ecological impact. Towards the turn of the century, Jantzi Research, as well as larger and more conventional financial institutions, began to develop public rankings such as the Jantzi Social Index, the Dow Jones Sustainability Index (DJSI) and the FTSE4Good. The DJSI relied on research from Jantzi, while the FTSE relied on EIRIS to inform its rankings.

As the interest in responsible investment has spread since the early 2000s, a couple of shifts have taken place. First, there is a greater emphasis on the financial impacts of sustainability performance, as opposed to adherence to a strict set of ethical criteria for screening investments. The 'mainstreaming' of responsible investment, as advocated by the WEF and the UNPRI, for example, focuses specifically on financially material issues rather than ethics for ethics' sake. There has been a change in emphasis to integrating ESG issues into investment decisions, framing ethical issues as questions of risk and corporate governance, in line with Jensen's framing of enlightened shareholder value. The crucial question for ESG integration is how ESG risks impact on a firm's bottom line, *not* how a firm's business activity impacts on the realisation of ESG risks for others.

Second, as the market for responsible investment activity has grown, established financial institutions play an increasing role. In addition to the intervention of the Dow Jones and FTSE into the market for rankings, other investment research firms have begun to expand their ESG work. MSCI is a generalist investment research firm and publisher of stock market indices, which has established its ESG offerings through acquisitions during the twenty-first century. Similarly, traditional credit ratings firms like Moody's, Fitch and S&P have grown their ESG business, as have Bloomberg and several other financial institutions (see Chapter 6 for more recent developments and consolidations in the industry).

The reason for much of the opacity regarding the definition and purpose of responsible investment activity today arises from the tensions between profits and social responsibility. Early responsible investment activity, with its grounding in ethical investment, was focused largely on negative and positive investment screens. This meant ruling out investments in certain industries such as weapons manufacture and tobacco, or ruling out firms engaged in certain practices, such as the use of forced labour. By contrast, positive screens favoured investments in firms that have a strong record on social and ecological performance. As the field of responsible investment has matured, strategies have diversified with the emergence of social impact bonds and green bonds, a privately financed public policy tool under which financial returns are dependent on the achievement of prescribed social policy goals (Harvie and Ogman, 2019; Lee et al., 2020), and impact investing, where investment decisions are based not only on financial returns but also on the promise of some social or ecological impact.

The practice of ESG integrated investing emerges from the same trends as do other forms of responsible or sustainable investment, but differs from other approaches that fall under these umbrella terms. ESG integration means integrating financially material ESG risks into investment decision-making. As opposed to other forms of sustainable investment, it is not product, project or issue based. While other responsible investment strategies limit funding for particular types of projects (such as fossil fuel extraction) or target funding for achieving certain social or ecological objectives, ESG integration is a risk management process. It can be applied to any investee company, any type of economic enterprise or investment strategy. A guidance document jointly published by the UNPRI and the Chartered Financial Analysts (CFA) Institute says, 'ESG integration is defined as "the explicit and systematic inclusion of ESG factors in investment analysis and investment decisions". It is a holistic approach to investment analysis, where material factors—ESG factors and traditional financial factors—are identified and assessed to form an investment decision' (Orsagh et al., 2018). In addition to identifying and managing risks to accumulation, ESG integration also aims to identify and maximise ESG opportunities (Giese et al., 2018).

The practice of ESG integration depends on the identification, assessment and management of ESG risks and opportunities. Rather than excluding "bad" investments or promoting "good" ones, ESG integration takes an implicitly derivative approach to ethics. It prices ESG risks (ethical risks) and enables investors to take positions within that spread of possibilities. It facilitates the translation of ethical issues into drivers of competition. In this context, ethics become an accumulation strategy.

Despite the recent growth and convergence of the ESG industry, ESG ratings agencies use divergent methodologies, focus on different criteria and weight those criteria differently. They also have different approaches to the kinds of information they rely on and the extent to which they engage with or rely on information from the companies under investigation. The lack of standardisation in ESG ratings methodology is evidenced by low levels of correlation on ESG scores between current market-leading ESG rating agencies Sustainalytics and MSCI. The diversity of ratings between different agencies has led to widespread demands from investors and from the financial press for more consistent and comparable data and a standardisation of the foundations on which these decisions are made. This has been the basis for several projects like the establishment of the Sustainability Accounting Standards Board (SASB), the Taskforce on Climate-related Disclosures, the Global Initiative for Sustainability Ratings, and the International Integrated

Reporting Council (IIRC), as well as recent regulatory developments (see Chapters 4 and 6 for more on this).

ESG credit rating agencies like MSCI, Sustainalytics and their competitors are playing a market-making role that is comparable to that played by the Chicago Mercantile Exchange (CME) during the emergence of widespread financial derivatives in the 1970s. CME, a long-standing trader of agricultural futures, established markets for financial derivatives by codifying risks and designing tradable products for which there would be both asks and bids. CME played the dealer function in the establishment of financial derivatives markets, first in foreign exchange and later in a much wider range of futures. Although MSCI and other ESG credit rating agencies are not yet making markets in precisely the same way as CME, they are facilitating the stand-ardisation of pricing for ESG risk that establishes a basis for relative pricing or measuring the spread between different ethical positions. The emerging market for ESG-based and sustainability-linked derivatives is also a reflection of this trend (Varsani et al., 2021).

ESG risks and opportunities

At the core of the ESG industry are ESG risks. These comprise ESG issues that have a financially material impact on the performance of a particular stock or other investment product. ESG integration typically also includes an analysis of opportunities as well as risks to profits. A review of the various ESG reporting frameworks reveals the following broad typology of relevant risks. Under the environmental category, risks include those associated with climate change, natural resources, pollution and waste, and opportunities for developments of clean technology, green buildings and renewable energy. Under the social category are risks associated with human capital, including directly employed staff and workers in the supply chain, as well as product liability issues, controversial sourcing of materials, and opportunities in relation to promoting access to finance, healthcare and communications. In relation to governance are issues like board diversity, executive pay and accounting practices, as well as corporate behaviour opportunities such as tax transparency and anti-corruption measures.

The manifestation of ESG issues in financial risks and costs differs consider-ably depending on the nature of the issue and the context in which it arises. The risks canvassed for ESG integration can have *operational* implications such as environmental issues that limit access to natural resources; labour rights issues that lead to strikes and other disruptions to production; or human rights violations that lead to protest and social movement campaigns. ESG analysis also considers risks with *legal and regulatory* implications, which might include any wrongdoing that attracts fines for non-compliance;

damages payments that might be awarded by courts for any legal wrongs a firm has committed; or the costs associated with taking action to become compliant with laws and regulations. Finally, ESG issues might give rise to *reputational* risks. These could include loss of brand value; loss of market share; and diminished capacity to organise production through supply chains due to weaker market power. In many cases, ESG issues present multi-dimensional risks. For example, pollution of a local waterway could cause operational risks through limiting access to necessary resources for production, as well as attracting legal fines and reputational damage. The likely impact of these risks is dependent on contextual factors such as the extent to which the firm is exposed to reputation loss; the extent to which the issue has a public profile or whether unions and NGOs active on the issue are able to organise and gain media coverage; or whether there are effective enforcement mechanisms to apply fines.

Some ESG risks apply to entire industries or economies, while others may be localised and firm-specific. For example, water scarcity is likely to affect all firms operating in a particular region, to the extent that they depend on access to water. Industry-wide issues might include supply-chain exposures, such as human rights risk in fishing industries where forced labour is common; or workplace health and safety issues in construction or long-distance trucking. Firm-specific issues might arise where a particular company has a poor history on labour relations or corrupt practices.

A crucial limitation is that ESG integration only facilitates the consideration of financially material ESG factors. The core question for ESG analysis is to weigh the pecuniary implications of ESG risks. The head of ethics research at Australian Ethical funds management said in an interview with the *Australian Financial Review* (2019), 'irrespective of how concerning impacts on people, animals and the environment might be, the ESG fund can still invest if the risk return equation stacks up'. This is a reflection of the contingent basis of the speculative moral economy in which ESG integration becomes such a popular practice. The ethics underpinning ESG integration are profit-driven, contingent on the investment context, and volatile according to economic, political, social and ecological changes.

On this definition (and as is explored in Chapter 6, definitions of ESG integration vary wildly), ESG integration cannot be considered responsible or sustainable. ESG integration is conventional investing with a wider view of the types of risks which need to be considered in the investment analysis. The assertion that ESG integration is responsible investment depends on the questionable premise that it is possible to manage out the contradictions of capital. Specifically, if ESG integration is responsible investment, then environmental, social and political risks can be managed to the point where there is no contradiction between doing well (making profit) and doing good (promoting social justice and ecological well-being). There are parallels here with the assumptions that undergird disclosure as a vehicle for climate mitigation and adaptation (Christophers, 2017). The principal assumption is that properly informed markets will price climate risk to expedite an orderly transition to decarbonisation. Similarly, ESG integration is central to contemporary responsible investment because it implies that a benign, sustainable capitalism is possible.

Conclusion

The speculative moral economy is one in which ethical issues are negotiated through financial risk management practices. The financialised firm is a bundle of risks to be priced, managed and traded. Enlightened shareholder value maximisation has become a mantra in response to demands for more accountable and responsible firms, based on the myth that more responsible capital is more profitable. Institutional investors are a focal point for political pressure given changes in the structure of equity markets. Investors increasingly adopt (at least, rhetorically) a quasi-regulatory role in relation to managing for systemic or ESG risks.

An analysis of the speculative moral economy in practice reveals a divergence between the responsible capital imaginary – that more responsible capital is more profitable – and reality. The practice of ESG integration facilitates the identification, assessment and management of ESG risks. Rather than excluding "bad" investments or promoting "good" ones, ESG integration takes an implicitly derivative approach to ethics. It prices ESG risks (ethical risks) and enables investors to take a position within that spread of possibilities.

ESG integration represents a constrained and derivative ethical basis through which to negotiate our collective interdependence. The demands of financial materiality, the profit-making focus that guides ESG integration, imposes limits on the range of ethical positions that can be taken. Moreover, translating ethical issues into drivers of competition renders ethics an accumulation strategy. This is explored in more detail in Chapter 3 with respect to value theory and accumulation, Chapter 4 on accounting for the social, and Chapters 5 and 6 in relation to the production of ethical value through brands and ESG information products and services.

Part II

Risk and value

Chapter 3

Ethics, risk and value: the derivative logic in action

Unfortunately, protecting an investment portfolio from the disastrous effects of climate change is not the same thing as preventing those disastrous effects from occurring in the first place. It was a bit like reading that people who live near forest fires in California feel safer because one of their neighbours purchases wildfire insurance on their home. But wait — what does that do for you? And what about all the people that can't get insurance on their homes? And shouldn't we be trying to prevent the fires from burning down our neighborhoods in the first place? (Fancy, 2021)

Introduction

Tariq Fancy, former head of sustainable investing at BlackRock, has shaken up the responsible business scene with controversial interventions about the limitations of financial markets to manage ESG risks. Fancy (2021) points out that managing financial risks for investors is not equivalent to managing environmental and social risks, such as the risk of losing a house to a climate change-driven wildfire. The promise of the responsible capital imaginary explored in Chapter 2 – that there is no conflict between profits and ethics – is based on assuming an unlikely commonality of interests between investors and everyone else. In reality, profits can only be consistent with ethics if ethics are strictly defined. The ethics produced through ESG integration and the speculative moral economy are contingent, volatile and profit-driven.

This chapter offers a reinterpretation of value theory that elucidates how a derivative logic of ethics animates ESG integration. Value theory is uniquely positioned to support this analysis because it exposes the foundations of economic production and distribution, and provides an analytical vehicle for navigating the relation between economic and socio-cultural value. Importantly in the context of financialisation and the growth of ESG integration, value theory also provides a lens on the role of risk as a connecting thread and a means of commensuration.

Value analysis opens certain lines of inquiry, including: how is contemporary labour (and life) being subordinated to capital accumulation? How do value relations structure the interaction between capital and labour? In what ways are social or moral limits shaping capital–labour relations? In order to answer these questions, this chapter explores the relation between economic and socio-cultural conceptions of value, and it explores how value is measured. A core problem for ESG integration is negotiating the tension between economic value and non-economic values, and the translation of non-economic values through financial calculus. A central proposition of this chapter is that this translation process – a process of *measure* – is fundamental to capital's valorisation; and, crucially, that measures of economic value are shaped by questions of social and cultural value.

The empirical basis of this chapter is an analysis of responsible investment practice, based on both secondary materials and interpretations of a series of semi-structured interviews with key informants in the finance sector. These interviews were conducted with responsible investment practitioners in Europe, North America and Australia between September 2015 and July 2016. Interviews with key informants were chosen as the method for this analysis as the systems for valuation in ESG analysis were then, and still are, in their nascent stages of development. As is widely recognised by practitioners, scholars and mainstream financial press, there is little coherence in these systems of valuation and processes are evolving rapidly, so collating and analysing the views of key players was chosen as the best way to identify a critical perspective on the direction of the industry. This material is used to explore how practitioners translate ethics, or non-economic values, into a financial decision-making framework. The integration of ESG risks into investment decisions impacts on how value is measured and suggests some new ways to think about the relationships between ethics, risk and value.

Incorporating ethics into financial decision-making frameworks as risks, and determining methods for measuring those risks, generates a particular form of ethics. Chapter 2 introduced the concept of a derivative logic of ethics as one that is contingent and profit-driven. This chapter shows that logic in action, and how this form of ethics is produced. Linking this phenomenon to a Marxian value analysis reveals the role of abstract risk as a connecting thread of the contemporary economy, and how the speculative moral economy facilitates the alienation and commodification of ethics, which will be explored further in Chapters 5 and 6.

What is value?

The capitalist economy is built on conventions of measure, standardisation and commensurability. Double-entry accounting, political arithmetic, metric conversion and cartography were necessary foundations to render the world for capital accumulation. The contested social and political nature of this process means that the value(s) that underlie measures and standards cannot be seen in strictly economic terms. Economic assessments of value are informed by socio-cultural values, priorities and processes. The tension between economic assessments of value and socio-cultural ones has been an intellectual challenge for theories of value for centuries, and today it is a conundrum that confronts practitioners of ESG integration. This chapter employs value theory for three reasons. First, to understand how ethics (socio-cultural values) are incorporated into assessments of economic value through the practice of ESG integration. Second, to explain how this process of translating ethics into economic values produces a certain form of ethics. Third, understanding these processes through the lens of value demonstrates how ethics are commodified, expanding circuits of capital accumulation and deepening capital's subordination of labour.

The term 'value' is used in vastly different ways in the various social sciences and by different schools of economic thought. The approach here is to take a critical approach to both conventional Marxian value theory and autonomist value theory. Taking a lead also from feminist theory (Alessandrini, 2016, 2018; Fortunati, 2007; Jarrett, 2015), eco-socialism (Bigger and Robertson, 2017; Huber, 2017; Moore, 2015; Robertson, 2012), information economy scholarship (Arvidsson, 2005; Arvidsson and Peitersen, 2013; Foster, 2007, 2013; Hardt and Negri, 2000, 2004) and critical finance (Bryan et al., 2015; Bryan and Rafferty, 2014; Christophers, 2015, 2016a; Christophers et al., 2018; Johnson, 2013), the value theory developed here asserts a complex relation between economic value and socio-cultural value, troubles assumptions about fundamental value, and posits the practice of measure as key to understanding how contemporary value relations facilitate commensuration of the seemingly incommensurable.

In economic terms, value is that which renders commodities commensurable: it is the 'organising principle of capitalism' (Mann, 2010: 174; Marazzi, 2015). Economic thought often assumes a source of 'fundamental value'. For classical political economy and many Marxian approaches, fundamental value derives from the labour expended to produce commodities. The classical school focused on concrete labour time, while Marxian economics has broadly treated socially necessary abstract labour as the source of value. For the neoclassical school, price is the fundamental value because there is no distinction between value and price. The price reflects each individual market actor's subjective utility derived from the good or service being exchanged (Marshall, 2009). What unites these approaches is their attachment to the idea of an intrinsic value of the commodity. Fundamental value is understood as essential to capitalism because it is 'the analytical framework within which capital commensurates itself' (Bryan and Rafferty, 2013: 131).

It is an illusion which facilitates the circulation of goods and services that is crucial to a market-mediated economy of generalised commodity production.

The form of value changes as the institutional structures of capital, and its systems of production and exchange, develop and expand, drawing more people, places and things into the circuits of accumulation. Recognising these sorts of changes with respect to the role of finance, information and intangible assets in accumulation in the late twentieth and early twenty-first centuries, many scholars have drawn attention to the need to reimagine a value theory that takes account of these developments in the production of value (Bryan et al., 2015; Christophers, 2016a; Hardt and Negri, 2000, 2004; Jarrett, 2015; Knafo, 2007; Mann, 2010). Here value theory is reimagined by revealing the role of ethics in the production of use values and in the accumulation of the abstract social wealth represented by value. This conceptualisation of value moves beyond the concept of fundamental value. Contemporary financial practices and intangible production practices demonstrate that value relations facilitate commensurability *regardless of fundamental value*. Like other critical Marxian value theorists (Alessandrini, 2016, 2018; Gawne, 2014; Postone, 1996), I argue that value has no singular or independent substance. It is a social relationship; specifically, a relation of domination and mediation that produces an abstract form of social wealth. The core of value is 'a spatially and temporally generalising social relation of equivalence and substitutability' (Mann, 2010: 177). Through this relation, use values are produced and exchanged, facilitating the extraction of abstract wealth. The value form, then, is not a substance but 'a particular kind of connectivity' (Alessandrini, 2016: 52) that is realised through relations of equivalence and substitution.

Treating value as a substance is troublesome for a couple of reasons. Both result from a conflation of the economic meaning of value (that which facilitates commensuration) with a socio-cultural meaning of value (something that has worth). First, most closely associated with Marxian approaches to value, treating value as a substance creates a tendency towards the moralistic reification of labour (Mann, 2010). Relying on labour as a source or substance of capital's value creates an unnecessary reverence for transhistorical labour and, ultimately, waged work. It also results in a preference for supposedly productive over unproductive forms of activity (Harvie, 2005). Critical feminist scholars have explained how this problem translates into the domestic sphere. Celebrating tasks related to social reproduction as labours of love confuses the necessary distinction between the socio-cultural values attached to care work and the function of domestic labour 'as a key input into the reproduction of capitalist society and its attendant social misery and environmental destruction' (Munro, 2019: 454). Politically, the reification of labour seems at odds with the overriding objective of Marxian philosophy, which is directed at the destruction of capitalist value relations or, as Moishe Postone (1996) would have it, the destruction of the proletariat (as a subjectivity).

The second problem with a substantialist approach to value is that it may confuse use values and abstract value. This problem is exemplified in affective theories of value and, with particular relevance for this book, the work of Adam Arvidsson and Nicolai Peitersen (Arvidsson, 2011; Arvidsson and Peitersen, 2013). They argue, similarly to Michael Hardt and Antonio Negri (2000, 2004), that contemporary capital accumulation is based on labour that is done outside the workplace and the employment relation. According to this view, social life, relationships, goodwill, sharing and similar are sources of value. These social bonds, *philia*, are captured and capitalised through, for example, consumers' commitment to certain brands, or through users' contribution to the value of social media. Repurposing Marx's labour theory of value, Arvidsson and Peitersen (2013) argue that the valorisation of *philia* creates an *ethical surplus* which is the basis of contemporary capitalist value, and which can become the basis of a more socially and ecologically sustainable economy.

This argument demonstrates why it is important that a value theory does not rely on substance. While Arvidsson and Peitersen's observations about the productive nature of social bonds are important, and their theory is a useful way of thinking about post-capitalist value, this approach elides the fact that capitalist value relations are concerned with the imposition of social control and the domination of people by production (Cleaver, 2001; Postone, 1996). More broadly, the affect theory of value tends to blur the distinction between *use values* that affective social bonds provide and capital's *abstract value*. In the context of capital accumulation, affective social bonds are not produced in order to build relations between people or a sustainable economy. They are produced to generate an abstract form of social wealth which can be monetised and translated into profit. What is particular about labour under capitalism is not what it produces, whether commodities or affects, but rather the conditions under which it produces. What can be obscured by a substantialist reading of value theory is that the object of production under capitalism is not the use values – the commodities, the services or the relationships themselves – but the value, the abstract wealth, that is generated and accumulated, and the subordination of living labour to that process. As Harvie (2005) has argued, the distinction between value-producing (productive) labour and value-destroying (unproductive) labour is context – and struggle – dependent. Similarly, Donatella Alessandrini (2018) has shown that Marx's 'law of value' is not based in a substance (whether labour time, affect or something else) but is rather a social relation that actively constructs value measures. The utility of thinking in this way is that it enables a fruitful examination of how economic processes are organised; and reorganising the relations underlying production processes is crucial to challenging capitalist value accumulation.

Framings of value as a relation rather than a substance have been offered by various scholars as a way of understanding the particulars of how, and by whom, the wealth is produced, realised and accumulated. Elson's (1979) 'value theory of labour' reframed Marxian debates to assert that 'value is the form that labour takes under capitalism' (Harvie and Milburn, 2010: 631). Elson used this orientation to understand how labour is subordinated to capital accumulation, exploring why work and social relations are structured as they are at any given time (Elson, 1979). Knafo (2007) takes a similar approach, dispensing with the notion of value as a *product* of labour. For Knafo, the link between value and labour is the function that value plays in transforming labour processes, rather than the contribution made by the expenditure of physical labour to a quantification of value.

The argument here pushes the work of these critical value theorists further, inspired by literatures that have observed the expansion of labour's subordination to capital beyond the wage relation. I argue that Marxian value can be reworked to understand how developments in finance and the metrics it uses expand value relations to subordinate life and labour to capital in new ways. In particular, the following explores how processes of measuring and pricing ethics reshape the value relation.

The importance of measure

There is a risk in stretching the concept of Marxian value, as this book proposes, that it loses its specificity and analytical utility (Böhm and Land, 2012; Gawne, 2014). Critical Marxian value theorists have aimed to address this problem through a focus on how value is measured (Alessandrini, 2016, 2018; De Angelis, 2005; Dowling and Harvie, 2014; Gawne, 2014; Harvie and De Angelis, 2009). This is a challenge both to the autonomist position that capital's value has become immeasurable and to long-running debates regarding the incommensurability of certain objects.

While a central thread of Hardt and Negri's (2000, 2004) work is that value has become immeasurable, several other theorists respond that the question of measure is a point at which concrete connections can, and must, be made. De Angelis (2007), for example, demonstrates that how and what we measure, who decides how and what we measure, and the impacts of the measuring process are key issues for capital accumulation. Together with Harvie, De Angelis also explores the ways in which measure becomes 'a category of struggle', through an analysis of benchmarking, surveillance and workload models in the higher education sector (Harvie and De Angelis, 2009). These measurement tools, used to discipline labour, demonstrate some of the ways in which intangible knowledge-based labour is productive for capital, contesting the implication of Hardt and Negri's work that intangible production is immeasurable.

The importance of connecting autonomists' reimagined value theory to the concrete experiences of labour, including measure, is identified by Steffen Böhm and Chris Land (2012). Reading the 'new economy' theory espoused by Hardt, Negri and Arvidsson together with Labour Process Theory, Böhm and Land (2012) argue a reimagined value can be supported by a concrete analysis of the diversity of labours that the new economy includes. A crucial insight from Labour Process Theory is that 'labour is characterised by antagonism, control and resistance' (Böhm and Land, 2012: 233). The authors explore how the dynamics of antagonism, control and resistance manifest in relation to the labour ('value-creating activity') that consumers do in co-creating brands, giving a necessary specificity and tangibility to the immaterial labour thesis. Central to those antagonisms, control and resistance are practices of measuring value.

Dowling and Harvie's (2014) analysis of the UK Government's Big Society programme also reveals the important role of measures in understanding changes in the value form. A core element of this social investment initiative was the imperative for firms to demonstrate and measure their impact on 'social value'. The authors point out that 'the difficulties of measuring social value have not prevented attempts to do just that. This is because the need to measure is paramount in the imperative to control an activity, to harness it and render it profitable' (Dowling and Harvie, 2014: 880). These social investment ventures capture, control and valorise a vast range of unpaid and social reproductive activity, extending the realm of labour as 'value-creating activity', which can then be appropriated.

Struggles over measuring and managing labour reflect the importance of measure to capital accumulation, and to grounding an analysis of value as its forms change. In order to understand how value expands to subordinate different areas of labour and life to accumulation, a focus on how it is measured is crucial. The historical and social processes by which measures are established are the same processes which render commensurate the seemingly incommensurable. As Alessandrini (2018) has argued, building on the work of feminists in the 1970s, value has always been contingent, and that contingency is made concrete through the dynamic institution of value measurement.

Measures of value are socially and politically determined: commensurating the incommensurable

From neoclassical economics to anarchist anthropology, arguments persist that certain things are incommensurable. These arguments are made both on normative grounds, that it is incorrect to equate certain values, and on technical grounds, that it is not possible to equate certain values. Max Weber's assertion that it is technically impossible to measure substantive ends became part of Ludwig von Mises' defence for the neoclassical subjective utility function, which assumes that value is synonymous with price. Anthropologist David Graeber says certain things 'ought to be uncorrupted by the market, but at the same time, are unique and profoundly different from one another. Beauty, devotion, integrity—these things are *inherently incommensurable*. In other words, where there is no abstract medium to reduce value to a uniform, fluid form, one is left with concrete, particular crystallizations' (Graeber, 2005: 13, emphasis added).

The logic of incommensurability is employed to separate questions of economic from socio-cultural value, that is, to treat them as inhabiting separate and incompatible spheres or 'hostile worlds' (Zelizer, 2010). Margaret Radin (1996) argued a normative form of incommensurability when she railed against the law and economics school's assertion that social order is best organised through universal marketisation. Asserting the 'inappropriate commodification' of a range of matter from human organs to children, love, friendship and sex, Radin said these things are irreducible to price because there is no fundamental, quantifiable value which determines how one makes a choice between them (Radin, 1996: 12). While one might agree with Radin's normative claim, her observation elides the fact that value relations facilitate commensurability *regardless* of a fundamental source of value.

Viviana Zelizer (2010) has explored many iterations of what she calls the morals/markets dichotomy, including the emergence of markets for human organs, children, life insurance, compensation for care labour and ethical corporate conduct. For Zelizer, a strict division between morals and markets is politically limiting. For example, it may prevent advocacy for the payment of care labour on the basis that love and care are 'demeaned' by money (Zelizer, 2010: 292). Similarly, feminist economist Julie Nelson has argued that strict delimitation between morals and markets, between 'money and love', is 'a matter of ideology and rhetoric, rather than an economic or legal fact' (Nelson, 2011: 72). Questions of 'social meaning and relationality' are always at play in commercial activity and Nelson says that to suggest profit-making prohibits or excludes care and love creates too easy an escape for firms, which, she says, should be subject to moral principles. The problem, then, is how to bring questions of economic and non-economic value together.

Ethics, risk and value

Marx reconciled economic and non-economic value in discussing the value of what he considered to be the integral commodity in capitalism: labour power. In the chapter on struggles over the length of the working day in volume one of *Capital*, Marx sets out the ways in which the value of labour power is constrained by historically and socially determined limits:

> Besides these purely physical limitations, *the extension of the working day encounters moral obstacles*. The worker needs time in which to satisfy his intellectual and social requirements, and the extent and number of these requirements is conditioned by the general level of civilization. *The length of the working day therefore fluctuates within boundaries both physical and social. But these limitations are of a very elastic nature, and allow a tremendous amount of latitude.* (Marx, 1990: 341, emphasis added)

Marx's comments here demonstrate that the value of the commodity labour power is not a scientifically or objectively determined quantity. Labour power's value is determined through social contestation, in the context of shifting political and economic conditions. The moral constraints that labour sought to impose on its own exploitation were eventually instituted through labour law and enforced by trade unions. This is how the relationship between abstract value and socio-cultural value should be understood. It is not argued here that abstract value aims to capture what has worth in social, cultural or even economic terms, but rather that measures of economic value are shaped by questions of social and cultural value. The way that shaping process happens is through contest over how to commensurate the incommensurable.

Finding ways to commensurate diverse commodities is a crucial element of capital accumulation. This essential function of reducing qualities to numbers is what Alessandrini highlights when she describes the law of value 'as a powerful logic of commensuration that enables endless accumulation' (Alessandrini, 2016: 68). Indices, such as price, establish a measure of value regardless of the indeterminate qualities of commodities. Finance, in particular, is continually focused on reconciling incommensurability through the application of indices. This has particular application with respect to ethical capital because it avoids the problem of pricing ethics directly. Instead, ESG analysts can price the movement between different ethical positions through risk assessment. The conceptual dilemmas associated with commensurating the incommensurable that have vexed economists and social theorists for generations are core to the work of ESG analysts and responsible investment advisers. Indeed, these are two parallel processes of understanding value as a social relation of domination through commensuration, albeit with different politics and conversations. Recognising the dynamic social and political processes by which the socio-cultural qualities of use values and measures of value are instituted, one interview participant talked about the ways in which seemingly, or previously, non-financial issues are becoming financial issues through the changing political environment and changing perceptions of ESG risk. The distinction between financial and non-financial issues is described by one analyst as 'an old mindset, and out-dated way of framing things really. So [ESG risks] had been talked about as "non-financial" issues. Now the evidence is really strong that they are financial issues' (Australian Responsible Investment Advocate).

The translation of non-financial issues, or ethical debates, into financial metrics is central to the work of ESG analysts. A Senior ESG Consultant for a global investment advisory firm in North America said, 'Broader stakeholders [clients and the general public] are thinking about these issues [like climate change], but they're saying it in different terms. *It is two different languages*' (emphasis added).

The two different languages that the interviewee highlights here are the language of economic value and the language of non-economic, or socio-cultural, value. While the general public may not think about climate change, extreme weather events, involuntary mass migration, famine and mass extinction in financial terms, or through the lens of risk and opportunity, these are the terms that must be used to incorporate those issues into ESG analysis. When investment advisers consider the quality of an equity asset through the frame of climate or human rights risk, they are adding a layer of socially, spatially and historically determined ethical criteria. As a result, the use values being traded (both the corporate equities, as commodities in themselves, and the goods and services produced by those firms) incorporate these socio-cultural values. In addition, by assessing the worth of equities through the frame of ESG risk, investment analysts and advisers are adding a new measure for capital's value, which is also socially, spatially and historically determined. As the 'theory of the generalized reduction of social life to equivalence and exchangeability in the commodity form' (Christophers, 2016a: 4), value reveals how developments in finance, information and intangible assets facilitate the incorporation of ethics into use values and measurements of capital's value.

Risk as a measure of value

Key measures of value in capitalism to date have been money and labour. In the contemporary economy, where finance, the production of intangible assets and trade in information are so prevalent, different measures of value emerge. In particular, scholars of finance and financialisation have suggested that risk is an important factor to consider (Bryan et al., 2015; Christophers,

2015, 2016a; LiPuma, 2017). The following discussion uses an analysis of interviews with ESG integration practitioners to tease out how different forms of ESG risk (operational, legal and regulatory, and reputational) are produced in a dynamic, political relation between economic and socio-cultural value, and instituted through measure. Renovating Elson's (1979) value theory of labour as a way of understanding how value shapes labour's subordination to capital, we might think of the ways in which *ethics as risk* are expressed as value and therefore shape conditions for labour. This reveals the dynamic inter-relations between ethics, risk and value; how assessment, measurement and management of ESG risk shapes value relations and capital accumulation, and its domination of life and labour.

As discussed in Chapter 2, a risk management revolution has taken place since the 1970s with the emergence of the Black–Scholes formula for pricing derivatives. It is now possible to price and trade risks in infinite combinations. This facilitates the hyper-competitiveness of capital through breaking down assets into attributes and enabling those 'bits' to be blended and bound through time and space (Bryan and Rafferty, 2006b). Finance is central to this process, where risk is the 'stock in trade' and is commodified in financial instruments like bonds and insurance products (Christophers, 2016a). So pervasive is the trade in risk that it 'has become a connecting thread that links all things and places to one another, rendering them subject to the same normalizing financial logic' (Christophers, 2015: 4). LiPuma (2017) describes abstract risk as analogous to abstract labour in its capacity to connect economic actors. This can also be related to Alessandrini's (2016) construction of value as a form of 'connectivity' between economic actors and commodities. Thinking about value as a relation in the manner it is used by Elson, Knafo, Geoff Mann and others suggests that we may begin to think about risk as a measure of value (Bryan et al., 2015). This tradition of value theory inspires questions like: how does the identification, measurement, management and distribution of ESG risk shape the relation between capital and labour?

ESG integration is a prime example of risk being used as a measure of value and demonstrates the emergence of abstract risk as a form of connectivity. One interviewee described the role of ESG analysts as follows: 'It's our job to create ... a risk profile of what companies are exposed to, and then in turn, how well they are responding to that particular risk, in terms of their [inaudible] criteria, policies, reporting, performance and to put that into a system that enables clients to use it' (Second-in-Charge, boutique ESG research firm, Europe). ESG analysis, understood in this way, identifies and measures ESG risks for the purpose of enabling investors to adjust their assessment of the value of a firm according to a range of ethical possibilities. Chapter 2 set out a typology of the main operational, legal, credit and reputational risks encompassed by ESG analysis. ESG integration permits only the integration of financially material factors into its analysis. The financial costs attached to ESG risks are socially and politically determined. The cost of employing forced labour, for example, depends on the likelihood that the practice will be publicly exposed, the extent to which consumers or investors will act on that knowledge if it is exposed, and the legal and political penalties that may be imposed. The social and interdependent nature of these speculations is analogous to the Keynesian beauty contest for determining the value of investments. Keynes argued that the value of investments is not determined according to each investor's assessment of fundamental value, but rather that investors 'devote [their] intelligences to anticipating what average opinion expects the average opinion to be' (Keynes, 1936: 156). Contemporary investors speculate on which ESG (and other) risks will be the most costly and which opportunities will be the most lucrative, based on estimates of how other social actors and institutions will treat those ESG issues. This then determines which investments are made or not, and in this way 'our speculations are an active force in shaping the future' (Konings, 2018: 51).

Fossil fuels

ESG risks are constructed in a dynamic interaction of law, politics and social change. These are the boundaries that define the domain in which capital accumulation takes place. Particularly in the context of climate change, the exploitation of fossil fuels offers a prominent example of interconnected legal, operational and reputational ESG risks. Accumulation in the energy industry is structured by laws that regulate extraction and distribution, by policies that subsidise and support different forms of energy generation, and by social movements that create political and operational costs for companies profiting from fossil fuels. Assessments of climate risk in investment portfolios through the frame of ESG integration reflect these factors. In a briefing about its climate risk model, MSCI highlighted the anticipated financial impacts of California's Clean Energy Act 2015 and India's policy on electric vehicles, which both support profit opportunities in renewables technology. The firm also noted the realisation of operational risk for insurance companies, which received claims of USD 480 billion in 2019–20 linked to wildfires in Australia (MSCI, 2020). Setting out these risks and opportunities, MSCI's approach reflects the ways in which policy settings, physical risks and financial impacts interact through the frame of ESG risk to structure the organisation of capital, labour and nature.

The political and economic dynamism around ESG risk can also be observed in the fossil fuel divestment movement. Several research participants from

Europe, North America and Australia recognised the expansion of financial risk regarding fossil fuels. While research participants identified key factors comprising both physical and transition risk, the focus was often on those elements of risk that are shaped by the costs of political and legal factors, including the increased probability of stranded assets, the difficulty of obtaining and retaining social licence to operate and the increased costs associated with fossil fuel investment.

Many interviewees also highlighted the significant role of civil society in this process. The Research Manager for a responsible investment advisory firm in Australia referred to some economic actors and social movements who are 'driving the boundaries' of ESG risk through their political action. Recent examples in Australia, the world's largest coal exporter, include climate litigation which has focused on creating new legal risks in relation to the fossil fuel industry. A specialist climate risk law firm, Equity Generation Lawyers, has represented clients bringing various cases that aim to push these boundaries. One matter was brought by young Australian students arguing that the federal government has a duty, in particular to young people, to reduce greenhouse gas emissions. Another case involved a young superannuation (pension) fund member asserting that the fund was not properly discharging its fiduciary obligations to manage climate risk. Another case claims that the federal government in Australia has not properly disclosed climate risks to sovereign bond investors.

These observations suggest that the (perceptions of) transition risk associated with coal, oil and gas investments are increasing due to social movements and political pressure, in addition to the physical risks associated with accelerating ecological crises. While the low-carbon transition is weaker and slower than required, many financiers have tightened restrictions on lending to coal clients, spending on new fossil fuel projects has fallen significantly, and capital expenditure on renewables amounted to USD 1.4 trillion in 2022, accounting for almost three-quarters of growth in energy investment (International Energy Agency, 2022: 97). For the moment, this is creating a schism between those firms and financiers exiting fossil fuels and those continuing to exploit the profit opportunities.

Myriad contradictions are generated in this process. For example, Theodor Cojoianu and his co-authors (2021) have found perverse consequences associated with limits on new fossil fuel projects arising from the divestment movement, which drove decreasing fossil extraction in domestic markets but increased extraction elsewhere. Meanwhile, the firms retaining their positions in coal, such as Glencore, claim they are doing so in order to promote 'responsible stewardship' of the assets and to ensure prudent management of the ESG risks (Thomas, 2023). This spurious argument has been undermined by Glencore's recent indications that it intends to spin off its coal assets into a separate legal entity, in part due to the negative impact of coal on the firm's valuation (Hook, 2023).

While the ESG risks associated with fossil fuel investment may be changing, this does not exclude the possibility or probability of investment. It potentially creates more opportunities for investors to leverage their positions in relation to fossil fuels and related risks. While increased ESG risk does not exclude investment in fossil fuels, the developments discussed above reflect how the social, political and legal environment creates costs and risks for business activity through restricting access to certain resources and imposing limits on how conditions of production can be exploited. Political actors have scope to increase the costs of certain avenues of capital accumulation and open up others (such as renewable energy). The history explored in Chapter 1 details some of these dynamics regarding labour's exploitation. Access to natural resources for capital is filtered through politically determined limits. Contemporary struggles over the limits of surplus value are circumscribed by conflicts over how value (risk) is measured and calculated. By creating an atmosphere in which fossil fuel investment attracts different political and social (reputational and regulatory), as well as environmental and operational costs, NGOs and activists are shaping the calculation of risk. These dynamics have a material relationship to how both labour and the biosphere are being organised for accumulation.

Data security

Data security offers another example of the interconnections between operational, regulatory and reputational ESG risk. Research participants in the ESG sector identified this as an emerging issue in 2015–16, noting, in particular, the regulatory risk associated with privacy. Since then, data security breaches have become commonplace and financial consequences are escalating. In 2018, the exposure of Facebook's relationship with Cambridge Analytica revealed that 87 million user profiles were misused. This contravened privacy regulations in many of the jurisdictions where Facebook operates so the company was subjected to fines and regulatory inquiries, and privacy legislation was tightened in several jurisdictions. In the UK, the maximum fine for data misuse was increased from GBP 500,000 to GBP 17 million (NPR, 2019). In addition to stricter regulation, Facebook experienced a significant drop in user engagement, with some estimates around 20 per cent. The firm also saw its share price fall significantly over time, including a drop of almost 20 per cent in one day amounting to a USD 120 billion loss in market capitalisation, the largest single-day loss for a US public company (Sanders, 2019). Since then, decisions by regulators show that financial penalties for misuse of data are increasing. In 2021,

Amazon was fined USD 877 million in Luxembourg and WhatsApp faced USD 255 million fines in Ireland. In 2022, ride-hailing app Didi received a US 1.2 billion fine from Chinese authorities. Around the same time, several European regulators doled out fines for breach of the EU's General Data Protection Regulation. Also in 2022, Instagram and Meta faced hefty fines from the Irish regulator, while Google Ireland was fined by the French authorities. The financial losses, reputational consequences and regulatory tightening associated with privacy regulations create a dynamic terrain on which ESG analysts assess and measure the risks associated with business models driven by data collection and surveillance.

Global supply chains

The phenomenon of interconnected value and ESG risk structuring production and circulation can also be observed in relation to governing supply chains. One interviewee explained how their firm had changed supply chain management reviews following the collapse of the Rana Plaza textile factory in Bangladesh:

> After the Bangladesh fire in the garment factory, we did an engagement as part of a UNPRI taskforce, with other investors, to identify what are retailers doing to insure their supply chain … where they are violating human rights, labour rights, safety rights for the workers. You ask any company, it can quickly translate into reputational risk. You look at what happened with Nike in the 1980s and 1990s, in terms of the sourcing of their shoes, or GAP, the same thing. So, many protocols have been set up for these supply chain checks for these companies. The most recent Bangladesh fire brought that issue back. (Head of Corporate Governance, North American pension fund)

The Rana Plaza tragedy made visible the connections between investors and producers in geographically distant locations, and the 'violent underbelly' of transnational capital (Siddiqi, 2015: 171). The incident spurred firms controlling retail textile brands, and their investors, to take collective action with respect to labour rights in supply chains. This led to the establishment of two multi-stakeholder initiatives and several labour law amendments (Reinecke and Donaghey, 2015; Siddiqi, 2015). There are serious limitations to what these initiatives have achieved (Chowdhury, 2017) and, arguably, to what these initiatives can achieve (LeBaron et al., 2022). But with reference to the dynamics of ethics, risk and value in ESG integration, Rana Plaza revealed how abstract risk connects investors in wealthy countries and workers in Bangladesh. Crucially, this example also brings into sharp relief the great divergence between the way that risk is lived for investors and for workers. As Fancy (2021) has emphasised, managing financial losses for firms is not the same as preventing the losses from happening in the first place. These are some of the limits of a derivative logic of ethics in struggles for justice.

After the collapse of the Rana Plaza textile factory, among many other tragedies for workers labouring under appalling conditions, there has been a renewed focus on the prevalence of modern slavery throughout the global economy. Several jurisdictions have enacted legislation imposing requirements for firms over a certain size (for example, in the UK, above GBP 36 million annual revenue; in Australia, above AUD 100 million) to demonstrate how they have assessed and managed risks of modern slavery in their supply chains. These requirements create a framework through which activists, trade unions, lawyers and other civil society organisations may materialise ESG risks for firms. To date, much of the work around modern slavery has relied too heavily on social auditing of supply chains, which has limited effectiveness in delivering meaningful change (Ford and Nolan, 2020; LeBaron et al., 2017). Jolyon Ford and Justine Nolan argue, similar to many critics of the Bangladesh Accord and related processes (see, for example, Bair et al., 2020), that the most effective mechanisms for addressing modern slavery are those which facilitate robust participation by workers themselves and which provide for investigation and enforcement. They give the examples of the Cleaning Accountability Framework (CAF) in Australia and the Fair Food Program in the US. The Fair Food Program, developed with the Coalition of Immokalee Workers, empowers the Coalition to suspend purchases from suppliers who are not compliant, while CAF, which is partly led by the Australian trade union for the cleaning industry, gives workers paid-time meetings to engage collectively with the accountability process and ensures issues raised by workers are investigated and remediated.

Tax transparency

The risk environment for firms and investors regarding corporate tax accountability has shifted dramatically since the early 2010s, and in particular since the OECD and G20 commenced the Base Erosion and Profit-Shifting (BEPS) initiative in 2013. Recognising extensive possibilities for firms to arrange their transnational corporate structures to minimise corporate income tax payments, the BEPS initiative undertook research and policy development to eliminate these.

Key changes in the ESG risk calculation relate to both the increased risk of regulatory penalties and tax bills and investors' assessments of social and political risk. At the regulatory level, several notorious tax avoiders have been subject to significant tax assessments and fines. Amazon reported to its investors cumulative tax settlements of USD 1.5 billion between 2010 and 2020. As at 31 December 2022, the company reported to its shareholders that it had USD 4 billion in tax contingencies, up from USD 3.2 billion the year before and USD 2.8 billion in 2020. This means that Amazon recognises a reasonable risk that it may need to pay these amounts if its tax practices are successfully challenged. Microsoft's tax practices have also been subject to scrutiny. It reported to shareholders in 2022 that it paid a tax settlement of USD 1.7 billion in relation to liabilities between 2004 and 2013.

Recognising these financial liabilities and the changing regulatory environment, investors are demonstrating greater interest in corporate tax accountability. In 2022, shareholder activists were successful in bringing a resolution on tax transparency to the Amazon annual general meeting. This resolution reflected significant shifts in both regulator and investor approaches to tax. First, the regulator – the US SEC – accepted the resolution despite Amazon's objections that tax planning is a matter for managers and not suitable for investor oversight. Previously, the SEC had upheld these kinds of objections, but it recognised in 2022 that tax transparency was a significant social policy objective. Investors also showed a significant shift in their perception of tax risk. In 2014, a shareholder resolution calling on Google to pay its 'fair share' of taxes obtained less than 1 per cent support. The 2022 Amazon proposal calling for transparency about Amazon's income and tax payments around the world obtained more than 20 per cent support.

The BEPS initiative and the various regulatory developments associated with it, including the requirements for a global minimum tax and changes to how profits are allocated internationally for taxation purposes, and the requirement in some jurisdictions for greater tax transparency, are also contributing to a reconfiguration of tax as an ESG risk.

The role of social movements and NGOs

The identification and assessment of operational, legal and reputational ESG risks often relies on information from and action by NGOs, trade unions and social movements (Feher, 2018). Almost all ESG practitioner interviewees recognised their influence and the importance of their relationships with NGOs. A Research Director for an ESG research firm in Europe described their relationship with NGOs as being important for providing information to support the process of measuring ESG risk and assessing the value of equities:

> NGOs are a very important partner for us, especially when it comes to rating companies ... So, on almost all drivers, we have the question of whether the company is involved in controversies. The information for this we base on press sources, we have a specialized press review, but also on information from NGOs, Greenpeace, Amnesty, Human Rights Watch, trade unions. We

have a partnership with UNI and with IndustriALL. So, we consult them in a lot of cases to ask their feedback, or they proactively send us information on the companies. So, this information is for us of vital importance to balance the information we get from the company. Because most of our analysis is desktop research, internet research, based on the company's reports and other documents, but it is of course company reporting, so for us stakeholder information is very important.

The Research Manager for a responsible investment advisory firm in Australia highlighted the importance of NGOs identifying emerging ESG risks:

We do keep very close track of and speak regularly to NGOs, and particularly around issues that are starting to come onto our radar. Another example is the detention industry. We were right on the leading edge of that with some of the big institutional investors here because we have been tracking that issue very closely for quite a long time. And we spoke also to the NGO working on that. We saw that issue, and incorporated it into our engagement work, well before others in the market identified it.

The above interviewee was referring to a campaign for divestment from the immigration detention industry in Australia. While the interview participant described this as a process of being alerted to risk by the NGO, another interpretation is that the NGO, and the movement associated with it, created the ESG risk. This points to a further important function of social movements in the context of ESG, that is, in materialising previously immaterial risks. Another interviewee, discussing the same campaign for divestment from the immigration detention industry, said:

The question is how the ESG factors can translate into financial risk. Transfield is a really great case study because it absolutely translated into financial risk or loss. If you look at the Ferrovial bid of $2/share 2 years ago, down to $1.50 at the end of 2015, and the board recommending to take it, because our earnings are now 'uncertain', in their words, because of the PNG court case. This is the best case study I've ever seen for ESG and why it matters and why investors must try to get their heads around these seemingly non-financial risks or non-traditional investment risks. (Australian Responsible Investment Advocate)

In addition to the role that NGOs and social movements play in shaping ESG risk and providing information to ESG analysts, in some cases civil society has the capacity to render material a risk that may otherwise be financially immaterial. The campaign against Transfield (later Broadspectrum), the company that operated off-shore immigration detention centres for the Australian Government, is an example of how political action and social movements can concretise what would otherwise be financially immaterial ESG risk. A number of social movement organisations, unions and worker activist groups targeted the companies that operated detention camps, and related contractors, calling for divestment by shareholders as well as a boycott by financiers, clients and public institutions. Several interview participants perceived this campaign as a successful effort to turn an immaterial ethical issue into a financially material ESG risk. Human rights risk in Transfield's operations was rendered a financial liability through creating a political atmosphere in which it was difficult for the company to continue to make profits whilst it participated in those abuses of human rights. The impact of these efforts was reflected in the acquisition of the firm (by Spanish firm Ferrovial) at a reduced price, as discussed in the above quote. The broader impact of this campaign in structuring the risk environment for firms in the detention industry was revealed later. The political environment had become too fraught for most firms to seek contracts to run offshore detention centres. This forced the Australian Government to engage nefarious and inexperienced contractors, which became a political liability of a different sort (Knaus and Davidson, 2019).

In a different context, another interviewee, the Director of an ESG research firm in Europe, described the influence of NGOs on materialising ESG risks:

> NGOs are an extremely important, perhaps essential, part of the process. They bring information into the public space and create debate about particular issues, which generates a motivation for companies to change. Some examples include BP (with a terrible historic record on governance, especially safety; Gulf of Mexico spill); Shell (greatly influenced by Greenpeace campaign re Brent Sparr oil); the sale of weapons to questionable political regimes. NGOs threaten the 'social license to operate' by naming and shaming companies, they create a sense of urgency around particular issues.

What these examples of ESG integration in practice, investor–civil society relations, and social movement activity reveal is that socio-cultural values (ethics) are being incorporated, imperfectly and incompletely, into assessments of the economic value of corporate equities. This process of incorporation, through the frame of ESG risk, reveals the role of risk as a measure of value. We can begin to read the contemporary moment as one in which ESG risks to accumulation structure capital–labour relations, shaping the subordination of labour and life to capital. What ESG integration facilitates is the pricing of social and ecological issues through the frame of operational, legal and reputational risks that are legible to finance. While high levels of ESG risk will not necessarily mean that investors withdraw funds, these risks nevertheless influence the investment process and have

86 *Risk and value*

consequences for how labour's and nature's subordination to accumulation is organised.

The derivative logic of ethics in action: a different kind of 'social'

ESG integration produces a particular form of ethics. Despite the dynamism of ESG risk and the capacity that social movements and political institutions may have to shape it, the kind of socio-cultural value that can be expressed through capitalist finance is necessarily limited. A derivative logic offers a unique frame to expose this form of ethics and what the production of this ethics means for finance and for renewed understandings of value.

Paul Langley argues that social finance brings 'a logic of "financialization" into social policy-making and social welfare' to 'address collective social problems' (Langley, 2018: 2, 8). Langley defines 'social finance' to include impact investment and social impact bonds, which are more limited in scope than ESG integration. They provide financing for particular initiatives with very specific goals. Despite this distinction, there is relevance in Langley's analysis for understanding ESG integration. He uses the Deleuzean concept of 'the fold' to demonstrate how social finance markets are interrelated, shaping one another and generating a different kind of 'social', one that is grounded in liberal notions of ethics and entrepreneurialism. The liberal notion of ethics permits individuals to choose their preferred construction of ethics from the multiplicity of 'values' that social finance markets create. A vast array of new calculative devices is developed to assess social impact, enabling people to choose their preferred way to measure value. Everyone's ethics are recognised and there is no moral imperative (Langley, 2018: 12).

Langley's critique of this liberal notion of ethics broadly applies to ESG integration. It is true that there is no common ethics that binds ESG investors, and that an entrepreneurial spirit guides the ESG integration process: investors seek to maximise their opportunities to profit and minimise their downside risks. Interview participants frequently referred to both the normative and technical challenges associated with quantifying socio-cultural values. ESG analysts often avoid the problem of imposing a universal measure of ethics by mobilising a version of Langley's liberal notion of ethics. They suggest that individuals are free to adopt their own version of ethics in investment:

> [Our] version of ESG is not putting a worldview either. We just happen to have the best data set available so that no matter what worldview you have, you'll have all the tools and data *available to you to make the best investment decisions, given your point of view*. (ESG Consultant, global investment advisory firm, North America, emphasis added)

The Second-in-Charge at a boutique ESG research firm in Europe also explained that their approach gives clients (primarily institutional investors) the capacity to decide what 'ethical' means: 'We wouldn't necessarily hold ourselves up as having a normative role that means we should be defining what is ethical and what is not. In part because our diverse client base would not necessarily appreciate that we tell them what is and is not ethical.'

Similarly, an Australian Responsible Investment Advocate said, 'The question is how the ESG factors can translate into financial risk ... ESG is all about trying to put some kind of framework around how you identify and measure and monitor these non-financial, extra-financial risks, and *everyone is necessarily going to have a different approach to that*' (emphasis added).

This liberal framing conceals some of the financialised dimensions that a derivative analogy reveals. ESG integration permits a particularly financial reading of "the social". That is, the derivative logic of ethics that pervades ESG integration is not aimed at achieving particular social goals, like Langley's examples of social finance, but rather at leveraging the ethical spread on ESG risks. The point is not to identify what is good or bad, but to price exposure to one ethical reality or another – or positions along an index – and the movement and relationship between these positions. ESG integration is the derivative position on ethical investing because it facilitates measuring and managing investment returns between different ethical possibilities.

Understanding the ethics that underpin ESG integration as a derivative form alleviates much of the confusion about the nature of ESG and its relationship to sustainability or responsible investment. Recent political turmoil in the US, in particular, reflects this confusion, with advocates of ESG integration presenting themselves as objective profit-maximisers and ESG opponents arguing that the practice is a foil for left-wing politics on Wall Street. As explained in Chapter 2, ESG integration emerges out of the movement for responsible investing but concerns itself only with financially material ESG issues. The underlying assumption, then, if ESG integration is to be seen as 'responsible' or 'sustainable', is that all relevant ESG issues will have a financial impact.

In practice, decisions about the breadth of ESG integration are made by investment firms and analysts. There is great variation from one investment firm or analyst to another as to who decides, and on what basis they decide, which ESG factors are relevant. The weight to attribute to those factors, the evidence to use in assessing them, and so on are imbued with perceptions and speculations about the ethical standards expected by investor clients and/or the wider community. There is considerable variation between investment funds and analysts in assessments of firms' performance on ESG criteria, which is partly due to the absence of a well-defined baseline for analysis.

But it is also a function of the derivative logic of ethics at play. ESG integration is not directed at realising a particular worldview. Rather, it is a process that enables investors to assess and manage ESG risks across a portfolio. Consider the issue of forced labour. ESG integration is not interested in pricing freedom for workers, but rather the legal, reputational and operational risks of using forced labour for firms. This facilitates the assessment of risks along a spread of possible ethical realities, allowing investors to decide how to structure their exposure to those risks. It is unsurprising, given this derivative reading of ESG integration, that commentators observe this practice has an absent, or unstable, ethical foundation.

In 2022, the CFA Institute, which offers education for finance professionals, issued some guidance material that reinforces the derivative nature of the ethics underlying ESG integration. The CFA Institute instructs analysts to use ESG data, including financial, regulatory and market data, to 'identify investment risks and opportunities that they believe are likely to affect a company's fair value or share price' (CFA Institute, 2022: 2). The CFA Institute also stipulates that only financially material information is relevant to ESG integration.

Materiality is determined by analysts and investors according to the types of factors also identified by SASB (see Chapter 4), and the CFA Institute refers specifically to SASB's standards for materiality of ESG issues. Relevant factors will also include geography and legal jurisdiction; industry or sector; company-specific factors like corporate organisation; and investment time-line. Using a scenario analysis approach, ESG analysts consider a new development at a particular firm and consider the base-case (non-ESG financial analysis) as against the ESG upside (assuming that the new development improves revenue) and an ESG downside (assuming the new development materialises ESG risks).

The CFA Institute offers some examples of ESG integration in practice. For example, a chemicals manufacturer may seek to increase its revenue in response to consumer demand for sustainable products. Shifting from the use of petrochemicals to a renewable resource for its product base is estimated to increase sales by 30 bps (0.3 per cent). Combined with cost savings, this is estimated to increase net income by 100 bps over five years. In another example, the price/earnings ratio is used to adjust for an unaccounted risk exposure. In this case, it is assumed that new environmental regulations will be enforced stringently and that company X has a high environmental risk. As a result, the company is over-priced and the price/earnings ratio is discounted to reflect that.

One of the ways that the ESG sector (including the CFA Institute, as mentioned above) aims to address its ethical groundlessness is through recourse to ostensibly universal standards such as UN human rights codes or similar benchmarks for environmental or governance performance. There are on-going efforts afoot to establish consistent and comparable standards for corporate sustainability reporting and disclosure, for example through the recent merger of the SASB, the Integrated Reporting Foundation, the Carbon Disclosure Standards Board and the International Financial Reporting Standards (IFRS) Foundation. In this way, ESG analysts aim to put questions of ethical judgement to the side by applying standards that are supposedly beyond contest, above politics.

A Research Director for an ESG research firm in Europe noted the role of external standards in measuring ESG risk factors:

> [W]e don't take a particular ethical approach where we assess this because we think it's bad, but we find an international convention that says 'you should lower CO_2 emissions' or you should respect certain human rights, so that we can always make reference to this international law, a reference point. The OECD Guidelines, the United Nations conventions, the John Ruggie framework for human rights.

The tension between ostensibly objective positions against moralistic ones reveals one of the expressions of ESG integration as a derivative logic. ESG integration requires the translation of complex debates about morality, value and politics into ESG criteria, which can be assessed as compliant or not and given a rating according to financial risk exposure. There are unavoidable questions of values (both economically and sociologically conceived) at many points through the process of ESG risk assessment and management. Capitalist finance does not permit a fulsome engagement with ethics, priorities and values in relation to these issues. Rather, investment decision-making that is focused on the risk/return trade-off is concerned with managing ESG issues in order to maximise returns on particular equities and across an investment portfolio. Ethical issues become matters of financial risk (and its corollary, opportunity). And these risks will be largely dependent on the nature of the firm, the industry (or industries) it competes in, whether or not it is public-facing and similar. As one research participant said, 'there is no, and there never will be a, set definition of what constitutes ESG factors because for every company, industry, country it is going to be different' (Australian Responsible Investment Advocate).

This means that questions about whether businesses use child labour become questions about whether those businesses are public-facing and vulnerable to brand and reputational damage that could be associated with revelations of child labour in the supply chain. Debates about the importance of climate change mitigation will be dependent on the kinds of resources a firm needs to run its business, its geographic location and its revenue sources. Compliance with labour rights law is more important for firms which face strong trade unions and/or effective enforcement mechanisms. There is not a binary decision made about which investment is ethically good or bad, but a risk management decision about how to structure financial exposure. This is the derivative form of ethics that ESG integration produces: not ethics per se but an exposure to different ethical positions or possibilities.

The ultimate limit point of the derivative form of ethics is revealed in discussions about the constraint of financial materiality. ESG practitioners must identify a moment of financial materiality or the ethical issue falls away: 'There's all this perverse thinking about something that is an ethical or a moral issue, an ESG risk, that has reputational impacts; the question for most investors is, where is that going to impact on returns for the company? So, we're constantly trying to find those linkages back' (Australian Responsible Investment Advocate).

The profit-bound nature of the derivative logic of ethics is reflected in Matthew Lampert's (2016) critique of CSR. He argues that business ethics fails at precisely the moment where it is most needed, that is, the point at which "ethical" conduct is not more profitable than "unethical" conduct. Unless a particular ESG risk, or public interest issue, can be translated into a financial cost to a firm, then it will not be actionable through responsible investment mechanisms. To be successful in addressing harmful corporate conduct, arguments about ESG risks must fit into what one interview participant called an 'investment logic' (Senior Analyst 1, ESG ratings agency 2, Europe).

Participants were often quite explicit about the compulsion to find a link between an ethical or ESG issue and a financial impact. A Senior ESG Consultant at a global investment advisory firm in North America recognised that it is not always possible to identify such a connection: 'If you have child labour, for example, and you have grave concerns about it, … it's awful to say, is that always going to matter for a company? And then the question is, where is the line?'

Another respondent made similar comments regarding the differing dynamics of materiality between industry sectors:

> I'm working mostly with the primary sector. Mining and forestry, etcetera. It's products sold to other companies, *out of the public's view*. So, if you say, this company is killing orangutans, *they just look at costs and the legal risks that production stops*, and personally they may sympathise, but *it doesn't affect their business decisions*. (Senior Analyst 2, ESG ratings agency 1, Europe, emphasis added)

As the italicised phrases highlight, the pertinent issues are whether and to what extent the company is exposed to risk and the degree of financial consequences anticipated. In cases of low exposure and low financial impact, the ethical issues dissipate.

The approach analysts describe, of parsing different elements of a firm's activity and exposure to develop a sense of its ESG risk profile, reflects the function of a derivative. ESG analysis disassembles and re-bundles 'bits' (Bryan and Rafferty, 2006b) of portfolios according to a reductive set of ethical questions that are then funnelled through the ESG risk management framework. This enables investors or funds to mix and match their exposure across their portfolio according to their perceptions of the ethical constraints and ESG risks. For primary sector firms, which are less exposed to reputational risks, the legal risks and costs that attach to the destruction of the environment and harming wildlife may not be sufficient to constrain their business decisions. The stipulation that ESG risks must be financially material imposes a clear limitation on the issues that can be drawn into the analysis. One Senior ESG Consultant, working for a global investment advisory firm in North America, described their approach to ESG integration:

> [T]he belief is that these issues [ESG risks] have a material impact on the bottom line ... We work industry by industry to determine what might be the most materially impactful risk or opportunity in that industry, within an industry and then looking at the individual company level to compare them against their peers and see who is mitigating these risks best or who is taking advantage of these opportunities.

This approach reveals the close connections between the operations of the firm, how it makes profits, and the analysis of ESG risks and opportunities. Taking the example of an agricultural firm, an ESG analyst might consider the extent to which that firm had incorporated water use and chemical exposure in the farming process, and whether it was taking advantage of opportunities to build its share of the organic market segment. Through these analyses, ESG researchers interrogate and intervene on matters directly relevant to health and safety issues for workers exposed to agricultural chemicals; how nature is subordinated to agricultural production through water exploitation; and the terms on which worker-consumers are drawn into contributing more to capital accumulation circuits through paying a premium for organic food. By filtering ESG issues through a risk management frame, incommensurable ethical matters can be commensurated, priced and traded against one another. Assessment of the financial risks and potential windfalls associated with how companies respond to these issues is part of how contemporary finance is measuring capital's value, how environmental, social and political risks shape the measurement of that value, and how production relations are organised.

Conclusion

A common trope in the responsible investment domain is that there need be no choice between (ethical or socio-cultural) values and (economic) value, between principles and profit. This rhetoric is built on the responsible capital imaginary's premise that businesses can still be profitable, and can be even more profitable, if they manage their externalised social and environmental risks.

A value-driven analysis of ESG integration in practice demonstrates the flaws in this proposition. Value analysis reveals the underlying dynamics of connection and commensuration through production and distribution in a capitalist economy. Reimagining value for the contemporary economy demands a search for measures of value beyond labour time. In this chapter, abstract risk is proposed as a measure of value, given the ways that financial practices and instruments connect disparate economic actors through producing and trading in risk.

The above examination of ESG integration, through the frame of risk, reinforces and reveals two important points. First, it reinforces the fact that measures of economic value are shaped by social and political conditions. This has always been the case, as Marx showed in relation to the socially and politically determined nature of labour time's value. In the contemporary context, the practice of ESG integration reveals how measures of socially and politically determined ESG risk structure the exploitation of labour and nature. Second, ESG integration produces a particular ethics. The derivative logic of ethics that operates through ESG integration, subject to the dictates of financial materiality, opens up the possibility of risking a range of ethical futures.

Contrary to the claims embedded in the responsible capital imaginary, ESG integration does not facilitate internalising and managing externalised social and environmental risks. It is structured around a derivative logic of ethics that aims to leverage the spread between different levels of exposure to ethical risk. Where there is no financial cost associated with an externality, it bears no relevance to ESG analysis. To the extent that ESG integration renders firms and investments more profitable, it is because it facilitates more comprehensive management of *financially material* risks. The relation to ethics or social responsibility is necessarily vague, market-compatible and contingent.

Despite the very serious limitations of ESG integration as a political project, a value-driven analysis of its practices does reveal that seemingly disparate actors, events and objects are connected by abstract ESG risk. The dispersion of abstract risk, in the context of the conditions discussed in Chapter 2 (disintermediation of political and economic institutions, the

Ethics, risk and value 93

risk management revolution, and fiduciary capitalism), creates the conditions for organising our collective interdependence in new ways. Importantly, though, those connections are constrained by a narrow frame of financial materiality.

Through the process of ESG integration, many people seem to have the opportunity to express their ethics through investment. But, the limits of the ethical positions that can be taken are set. These are limited not only by the structures and institutions that define, assess and analyse ESG risks, but by the derivative logic itself. There is a range of investment possibilities, which comprise a range of ESG risk exposures. What ESG integration facilitates is not an "ethicalisation" of the financial sector, but the possibility of pricing the spread between different ethical options and profiting from predictions about the costs and opportunities associated with these different options.

Chapter 4

Accounting for ethics: SASB and Integrated Reporting

> We communicate reality: that is the myth; that is what people believe. It is even what most of us believe. And, in a sense, we do communicate reality. There is something there: bricks and people and so on. And the organization can, say, be 'doing well', or 'doing badly', in whatever sense you take that to mean. And it is our job to convey it. But what is 'the full picture'? There is no full picture. We make the picture. That is what gives us our power: people think and act on the basis of that picture! (Hines, 1988)

Introduction

Ruth Hines's provocation to accounting theory in the 1980s highlighted the constructive function of accounting practices which is at the heart of this chapter. By making (some) ethical issues legible to capital, emerging ESG accounting frameworks establish a foundation upon which a constrained form of ethics is mobilised via financial markets. A critical reading of these social and environmental accounting standards reveals how they open a frontier of accumulation. Establishing a foundation for identifying, measuring and managing ethical risks, these new accounting practices create a basis on which intangible corporate assets can incorporate an ethical dimension (as detailed in Chapters 5 and 6).

Accounting is a bellwether for capital, heralding major developments in accumulation because of the particular and crucial role of accounting in measuring profitability. Conventions about what is measured and how it is measured are driven by material conditions and, in turn, structure those material conditions. This chapter employs analogies to the role of double entry accounting in the early development of capitalism, including both the technical and rhetorical functions that accounting innovations have played in social and economic life, to analyse the development of accounting for ESG.

Two key challenges to contemporary accounting – intangible value and managing social and environmental concerns – are central to the developments in value relations documented in this book. The political pressures associated with managing social and environmental impacts of economic activity have been a core driver of the establishment of a speculative moral economy. The increasing significance of intangible value provides a vehicle for the accumulation of a new form of ethical capital. The accounting initiatives analysed in this chapter draw together social and environmental accounting (SEA) and accounting for intangible value. In doing so, they standardise and rationalise the ethical issues that arise in SEA, making those issues legible to capital, and creating the basis for ethics as an accumulation strategy.

Several accounting initiatives have taken up the twin challenges of accounting for intangible value and SEA. This chapter focuses on two of these in detail: Integrated Reporting and the Sustainability Accounting Standards Board (SASB). While there are many initiatives that aim to engage with these accounting dilemmas (such as the Global Reporting Initiative (GRI), the Carbon Disclosure Project, the Task Force on Climate-Related Financial Disclosures (TCFD)), Integrated Reporting and SASB have been chosen for several reasons. First, they most coherently connect intangible value and ESG issues, therefore speaking to the central concerns of this book. The changes in accounting represented by initiatives like Integrated Reporting and SASB are closely connected to transformations in value relations. Second, they both focus on the provision of information for investors and therefore for ESG integration, as opposed to other initiatives like the GRI, which have a broader range of stakeholders. Finally, both SASB and the Integrated Reporting project have garnered significant support amongst their stakeholder groups, notably accounting firms and advocates of responsible investment. SASB is closely related to the influential Bloomberg company, and its methods are being incorporated into Bloomberg's ESG analysis. Integrated Reporting is an initiative of the world's largest accounting firms, professional associations of accountants, major asset owners and managers, transnational organisations and other reporting organisations, including the GRI. Reflecting the accelerated demand for standardisation of ESG information, the IFRS Foundation, which oversees standards for financial reporting globally, announced in November 2021 that it would incorporate SASB, Integrated Reporting and several other organisations into the new International Sustainability Standards Board (ISSB).

This chapter employs a content analysis of the Integrated Reporting framework and associated guidance documents, and the SASB standards, methodology and guidance. In addition, it analyses some corporate reports that adopt Integrated Reporting and/or SASB standards, and related documents. The analysis reveals how key concepts like materiality, value, capital, accountability and risk are deployed in these frameworks, to understand the function this form of accounting plays in the speculative moral economy.

Putting this analysis in conversation with a reading of several accounting literatures demonstrates how new accounting practices are laying the basis for mapping, quantifying and coding social, environmental and political issues to be incorporated into capital's valuation regime.

Historicising accounting and the 'social'

What is counted by firms and investors (such as assets, profits, costs), and the means by which these are measured and managed, is shaped by socio-economic conditions. In turn, as accounting develops new metrics and practices, these have material consequences economically, socially and politically (Bryer, 2005; Burchell et al., 1991; Hopwood, 1976; Levy, 2014). This relationship between accounting and the social is illustrated in the historic role of double entry accounting. Double entry enabled the separation of capital accounts from profit and loss statements, which, in practical terms, facilitated the accumulation of capital (Chiapello, 2007; Levy, 2014). It introduced order, clarity and a rational approach to linking business and investment decisions to numbers in accounts. Abstractions enabled commensuration of diverse objects, with qualities reduced to quantities and uncertainty absorbed by the accounting framework. In technical terms, the adoption of double entry techniques fuelled the development of rationality, facilitating commensuration through the monetary unit and decision-making driven by profit, accumulation and competition.

In addition to these *technical* developments in accounting which facilitated the pursuit of profit, double entry legitimated the pursuit of profit. Bruce Carruthers and Wendy Espeland argue that it also performs an important *rhetorical* function. The rhetorical functions played by double entry were interwoven with, and arguably more transformative than, the technical innovations. Company accounts were drafted to make a compelling argument regarding business performance. Early accountants used 'pious invocations' such as 'In the name of God' in the preambles of their books to confer legitimacy, while the form of the balance sheet implies equality and equilibrium (Carruthers and Espeland, 1991: 37–38). Accounting rationalises, in the sense of both justifying and eliminating irrelevancies.

Accounting categories operate as ideology and change according to their social and historical context, with impacts beyond the corporate report (Bryer, 2005, 2015). One example of this is found in a legal case from the deindustrialising US rust belt in the 1970s. A labour union contested the closure of two Youngstown steel mills on the basis that they were still profitable, contrary to the claims of the company. The court acknowledged that the assessment of profitability turned on the accounting categories used.

Accounting for ethics   97

Deciding that the company was entitled to decide how profitability is determined, the court accepted the firm's chosen metric: the 'rate of return on capital invested', dismissing the union's claim and, with it, labour's interpretation of profitability (Levy, 2014).

Taking a cue from this historical orientation, this chapter hypothesises about the implications of contemporary developments in accounting for economic and social change. It reveals how Integrated Reporting and SASB's accounting standards are shaping socio-economic relations and vice versa. It asks: how do Integrated Reporting and SASB's accounting standards legitimate changes in social and economic relations? What is the rhetorical function being played by these accounting innovations? Do these initiatives impose new techniques for measuring accounting categories like value, capital, profit, costs and risk? How do these new techniques for measuring construct a new reality, in the manner predicted by Hines?

Accounting for ethics at the nexus of intangible value and SEA

Accounting has been grappling with both intangible assets and social and environmental challenges for several decades. From around the 1970s, they were contemporaneous but seemingly independent problems for accounting. Intangible assets are defined in International Accounting Standard (IAS) 38 as 'an identifiable non-monetary asset without physical substance'. They can include such diverse qualities as staff skills and knowledge, client base, corporate reputation, research and development capacity, and leadership. The conceptual and practical innovations required to account for intangible assets have required fundamental rethinking about the nature of assets, profits and value. In accounting for intangibles, the ephemeral needs to be 'framed and named and governed' (Eekelen, 2015: 452).

Early attempts at SEA included the triple bottom line approach and reporting standards such as the GRI, Accounting for Sustainability (A4S) and SA8000. These were complemented by voluntary corporate responsibility initiatives such as the UN Global Compact and by investing indices such as the Dow Jones Sustainability Index and the FTSE4Good. Accounting scholars and practitioners have engaged with these developments through an extensive literature on SEA since the 1970s.

While accountants observed a relation between the indicators used in intellectual capital reporting and SEA, there was a recognition that these reports were produced for different reasons, and for different audiences. Intellectual capital reporting aimed to make visible intangible assets that were not being captured by existing accounting methods. SEA aimed to defend firms against claims of social and environmental harms, and to re-establish corporate legitimacy in the face of political challenges. From the mid-2000s, though, corporate governance scholars (Gardberg and Fombrun, 2006) and accounting scholars (McPhail, 2009; Pedrini, 2007) began to think these two dilemmas, of intangible value and accountability for social and environmental impacts, together.

The proposition that responsible capital is more profitable – a core tenet of the responsible capital imaginary that is driving ESG integration – is at the centre of melding of accounting for intangible value and SEA. This convergence was expressed in shifts in corporate governance practice from the early 2000s, around the same time that the concept of ESG integration and responsible investment were promulgated by the UN and others. The establishment of Innovest's Intangible Value Assessment tool in 2004 is a pertinent example. Innovest used measures of social and environmental performance to account for intangible value that was otherwise not being measured (Eccles et al., 2019). The underlying premise was that the most profitable and resilient companies would be those that most effectively manage all of their 'capitals', including traditional financial and industrial capital, as well as intangibles like human resources, stakeholder relationships (reputation) and intellectual property.

Continuing this lineage, SASB and the Integrated Reporting framework are grounded in the premise that there is no fundamental conflict between ethics and the economic performance of firms. These initiatives assume that social and environmental challenges arise from a lack of adequate information about the externalised costs of business activity, and that properly informed investors will discipline the firms that they invest in to promote sustainability. As the Chair of the International Organization of Securities Commissions (IOSCO), a founding member of the International Integrated Reporting Council (IIRC), has asserted, '[a]cting ethically isn't more important than making a profit but the key to making a profit in the first place … It isn't that behaving well is more important than making a profit. It's that *it's necessary to behave well in order to make a profit. Good corporate governance is good business*' (Flower, 2015: 13, emphasis added).

The following draws out some key elements in the accounting literature about intangible assets and SEA, as a prelude to exploring how the accounting innovations of Integrated Reporting and SASB translate ethics into risk and capital.

Accounting for intangibles

While intangible assets are not new – they were acknowledged by economists and business managers more than 100 years ago, particularly in the form of "goodwill" – at the macro scale these assets were marginal and could be treated as an exception until the late twentieth century. Today, the scale of intangible assets is much greater and these assets are a source of competitive advantage for many firms. The OECD found in 2013 that intangible assets account for the majority of business investment in its member countries (OECD, 2013). The UK's Office for National Statistics (ONS) found that up to 2020, intangible investment in the UK private sector was on a par with investment in tangibles, but that intangible investment is growing more quickly (ONS, 2022). Brand Finance Institute's annual *Global Intangible Finance Tracker* report has consistently shown that intangible assets make up around half of the value of enterprises around the world since the early 2000s, albeit with variations in intangible intensity between nations and economic sectors (Brand Finance Institute, 2023a). Other estimates suggest that intangible assets make up 80 per cent of the value of major firms, such as those that comprise the S&P 500 (Palan, 2012), although this value tends not to be fully reflected in corporate accounts (Daum, 2002; Hand and Lev, 2003; Lev and Gu, 2016).

For present purposes, the most interesting and relevant intangible assets are those with a relationship to ethical claims. The rise of intangible assets has been consistently associated with corporate social and environmental performance, as the size of a firm's intangible asset base is in part attributed to its reputation and relational capital and the resources that it deploys to manage non-financial assets (like natural resources and employees). Primarily, the relevant intangible assets are brands, reputation and public image, which can be understood as a part of the 'relational' capital in Mark Wexler's (2002) taxonomy, and which have an impact on other intangible assets like consumer confidence. Already by the early 2000s, some credit rating agencies like Moody's, S&P and Fitch had begun to integrate brand value into their calculations of corporate worth through the category of 'relational capital' (Del Bello, 2008). Moody's considered issues like level and consistency of brand equity spending and other brand-building activities. Fitch took both a historical and a prospective view of company risk and financial risk. In considering relational capital, Fitch queried the strength of a company's brand, including potential impact of brand damage, sales loss, and the company's relationships with unions and NGOs (Del Bello, 2008).

Intangible assets present both conceptual and practical dilemmas for accounting, including the definition of an asset (Axtle-Ortiz, 2013; St-Pierre and Audet, 2011); establishing reliable measures where there is not a ready market for assets (Dahmash et al., 2009; Hoegh-Krohn and Knivflsa, 2000); how to treat internally generated assets (Nakamura, 2003); avoiding the circular logic of stock market valuation for company assets (Bond and Cummins, 2003; Perry, 2009); whether intangible assets should be capitalised or expensed; and how to deal with changes in value over time (Dahmash

100   *Risk and value*

et al., 2009; El-Tawy and Tollington, 2013; Lev, 2018; Lhaopadchan, 2010; Wen and Moehrle, 2016). Accounting has aimed to address these challenges through several measures, including incorporation into traditional financial accounts, the production of specific intellectual capital accounts and incorporation into corporate sustainability accounts or integrated accounts (de Villiers and Sharma, 2017). In traditional financial accounting, IFRS 3 (Business Combinations) and IAS 38 (Intangible Assets) both provide standards for intangibles accounting, although the circumstances in which intangibles can be recognised in financial accounts are very constrained.

SASB and the IIRC take a different approach to accounting for intangibles from that prescribed in traditional financial accounts. The Integrated Reporting framework aims to overcome the practical dilemmas of traditional financial accounting in providing information about intangible assets, by enabling firms to communicate with investors about how they manage various forms of financial and non-financial capital. The framework is very open and gives firms great discretion in determining how their non-financial capitals are defined and measured. SASB also enables firms to account for intangible value, to the extent that such value is associated with sustainability issues that SASB has prescribed to be material for the relevant industry. SASB's standards are relevant to all three types of intangible asset (human, relational and structural), but SASB reporting is not framed around the assets themselves. Rather, reporting is framed around the firm's management of risks and opportunities that will either grow or deplete those assets. Again, this allows the SASB framework to skirt many of the practical and conceptual issues in accounting for intangibles through traditional financial statements.

Social and environmental accounting

SEA emerged in the late twentieth century and has rapidly burgeoned as a field of practice and study. Early critiques of SEA questioned the proposition that firms become more profitable when they account for their social and environmental impacts. Jan Bebbington and her co-authors (Bebbington et al., 1999; Gray and Bebbington, 2000) argued that this was at odds with the fact that the pursuit of profits causes many of the problems that SEA aims to address. Concerned about the managerial agenda underlying SEA, these authors argued that to the extent that SEA remains centred on profit and the interests of business, it fails the environment. This conclusion contradicts a fundamental tenet of the moral economy that drives ESG integration: that profit and sustainability need not be in conflict.

Although some authors remain optimistic about the prospects for SEA (Thornton, 2013), much of the critical commentary since that time seems to confirm Bebbington and her co-authors' reservations (Andrew and Cortese,

2013; Cho and Patten, 2013; Chung and Cho, 2018; Deegan, 2013, 2017; Gray, 2013; Spence et al., 2013). Common criticisms among SEA sceptics arise from the tensions between financial accounting and sustainability. Authors argue that accounting is environmental only to the extent that the environment is commercial (Spence et al., 2013); financial accounting is not fit for purpose to account for social and environmental issues or to deliver meaningful change in these areas (Cho and Patten, 2013; Deegan, 2013; Gray, 2013); the focus is too squarely on business interests and profit, rather than ecological integrity (Gray, 2013); there is little correspondence between accounting concepts of debit and dcredit and complex social and environmental issues (Deegan, 2013); it is unclear who is the relevant responsible or reporting entity; the interests of investors and creditors are centred (Deegan, 2013); there is inconsistency in definitions for non-financial reporting, as well as in how and where the information is reported (Stolowy and Paugam, 2018); and financial accounting creates too narrow a frame for social and environmental accountability (Deegan, 2013, 2017; Gray, 2013).

Charles Cho and Dennis Patten (2013) point out that these contradictions in SEA lead to outcomes of environmental accounting that are sometimes quite perverse, such as in the case of disclosure bias. In these cases, the worst environmental performers disclose the most and seem to be rewarded for doing so. The problem is confirmed in comments by a responsible investment practitioner, Patrick Odier, who admits that his firm rates a company lower if it does not disclose its emissions:

> [W]e rate Cargill lower than Glencore on climate change mitigation: Glencore's activities are deemed highly-polluting and it has seen several environmental controversies, but it has made the effort to disclose its CO_2 emissions very precisely; whereas we had to proxy Cargill's emissions because its data is unreliable. (Odier, 2017)

Despite the inadequacies of SEA in meaningfully accounting for social and environmental impacts, the practice is growing rapidly. Sustainability accounting is being mainstreamed into global standards for corporate reporting through the incorporation of SASB, Integrated Reporting and other similar organisations into the IFRS Foundation. It is necessary to query, though, as Gray and Laughlin do (2012: 246, fn. 7), whether sustainability has become mainstream or if 'sustainability' has been redefined in accordance with what is already mainstream.

Grounded in stakeholder and legitimacy theories of corporate governance, SEA reduces ethics to pragmatism (Lehman, 1999; Mata et al., 2018). Liberal philosophical foundations of a 'social contract' between firms and stakeholders creates an instrumental approach to SEA through which firms are motivated to maintain their 'social license' to operate (Mata et al., 2018;

Stolowy and Paugam, 2018). There is an impetus for reporting firms to obfuscate, covering up corporate misconduct and reporting only favourable information (Cho and Giordano-Spring, 2015). In their analysis of A and A+ rated GRI reports from extractive firms, Olivier Boiral and Jean-François Henri (2017) highlight a lack of rigour in disclosures; lack of standardisation between reports; deliberate greenwashing; the corporate capture of information access and reporting; and the chaotic nature of sustainability topics, which is not suitable for rendering numerically. Writing elsewhere, Boiral (2013) argues that corporate reports are simulacra: disconnected from reality, reporting controlled and manipulated information, and using and creating misleading images.

In the existing SEA framework, social and environmental concerns are assets and liabilities. Craig Deegan (2013, 2017) points out that capital markets have little interest in environmental or social issues per se, but consider 'the environment' and 'society' to be key variables and markers of 'new value' against which to assess share prices, corporate profits and accounting measures. Firms engage with SEA so as to maximise their opportunities to profit and minimise their exposures (Boiral, 2013; Boiral and Henri, 2017). Recalling a core legitimating principle of the speculative moral economy, the business case for green accounting is premised on the false hope that profit and sustainability are consistent objectives (Lehman and Kuruppu, 2017). While the appearance of SEA is of a practice devoted to the process of accounting for social and environmental externalities, the underlying reality is rather a process of rendering social and environmental issues (ethics) for accumulation.

Many critical scholars observe that accounting and nature are fundamentally inconsistent and that attempts to reconcile them strip nature of its complexity and specificity. But, as Patrick Bigger and Morgan Robertson have pointed out, 'incompatibility between values is not an endpoint' (Bigger and Robertson, 2017: 69). Rendering seemingly incommensurable things measurable by the same criteria and deciding what to measure and how to measure it are political acts (MacKenzie, 2009). To assert incompatibility, or the absurdity of the valuation regime, is to retreat from the necessary politics of value and valuation (Bigger and Robertson, 2017). Bertrand Malsch's (2013) analysis of CSR and auditing reports demonstrates that retreating from the politics of value merely conceals the politics that are at play. When CSR audits treat social and environmental accountability issues as 'apolitical objects of risk', an instrumental form of morality is mobilised. The ethics are flexible and market-compatible, meaning that any ethical issues that conflict with profit become irrelevant (Lampert, 2016). Through this process, the accounting industry becomes an unwitting 'political mediator' (Malsch, 2013: 165).

The critical SEA literature, as outlined above, mostly addresses the disjuncture between the stated purpose of SEA (to achieve social and ecological sustainability) and the methods used to achieve it. The argument here extends beyond the limitations and failures of accounting for ethics by revealing what these accounting initiatives *do achieve*. While they may fail to comprehensively account for ethical issues, the accounting initiatives detailed here serve another purpose: to render ethics as a commodity. Though the full complexity of the ethical issues at hand cannot be addressed, as implied by the critics above, the rationalisation and standardisation of ethical issues through the SASB and Integrated Reporting frameworks makes ethics legible to capital and renders ethics for commodification. This is the function of these accounting frameworks at the frontier of accumulation.

Stefanie Hiss (2013) has made a similar argument with respect to the commodification of sustainability via financial valuation. Hiss (2013) argues that sustainability is being financialised in a three-stage process of (1) framing sustainability indicators by deciding what is to be calculated, such as water usage or greenhouse gas emissions; (2) constructing key performance indicators (KPIs) and deciding the measures to be used to quantify sustainability issues, from the qualitative to the numerical; and (3) financial marketisation through sustainability ratings and stock indices, adjusted for sustainability risk. Hiss (2013) posits these KPIs as the link between sustainability and financial markets, rendering sustainability issues translatable for investment purposes. This enables companies to claim that they are "sustainable", and in the process of financialisation, sustainability becomes a commodity in itself. A similar process can be observed in relation to SASB and Integrated Reporting, as detailed below, and further in Chapters 5 and 6.

Integrated Reporting

Integrated Reporting is a proposed transformation in corporate reporting norms to address the challenges of intangibles and sustainability. One of the accounting firm participants in the IIRC, Deloitte, says that '[the Integrated Report] is not a "complementary report" but a structural evolution in corporate reporting' (Deloitte, 2018: 9).

The Integrated Reporting initiative is based on the business case for sustainability and, as such, a creature of the responsible capital imaginary which asserts that there is no conflict between doing well (profit) and doing good (sustainability). The IIRC brings together its theories about the connections between intangibles, sustainability and market discipline when it claims that '[t]he cycle of integrated thinking and reporting, resulting in efficient and productive capital allocation, will act as a force for financial stability and sustainability' (IIRC, 2013: 2). Implicit in this assertion is that sustainability is undermined by deficiencies in capital allocation, which in turn are based on failures to integrate thinking and reporting. The integration here refers to the IIRC's 'six capitals' (financial; manufactured; natural; human; intellectual; and social and relationship), which include both financial and non-financial capitals, and tangible and intangible assets. The deficiencies in capital allocation on which IIRC relied for its solution to the question of sustainability are grounded in the assumption that when markets are properly informed about the full range of economic activity, they will reallocate capital to more sustainable economic activity.

This position is reinforced by investor advocates of Integrated Reporting and the 'fiduciary capitalism' (Hawley and Williams, 1997) view of institutional investors as agents of sustainability. An open letter by a group of self-described progressive investors claimed that Integrated Reporting would drive a shift to long-term thinking in capital markets which 'will facilitate more sustainable development and stable businesses in the longer term and the growth of more transparent and robust capital markets which will benefit us all' (IIRC, 2018).

These investors, like other advocates of Integrated Reporting (Adams, 2015; de Villiers and Sharma, 2017; Gleeson-White, 2014), also associate the increasing economic significance of intangible assets with questions of sustainability. Frequently referring to the volume of intangible capital in the global economy, Integrated Reporting draws intangible assets into its framework through its non-financial capitals. The six capitals identified by the IIRC are those things it considers to be relevant to value creation and which are at the heart of its proposed transformation of corporate reporting. In preparing Integrated Reports, companies are required to provide information about how their activities have impacted on the growth or depletion of each of these six capitals.

An Integrated Report should be prepared in accordance with the framework published by the IIRC. The framework adopts a principles-based approach, meaning it does not specify particular items or standards for disclosure, but provides a list of 'guiding principles' and suggested 'content elements' for Integrated Reports (see IIRC, 2013: 5). The guiding principles include a *future-orientation* that considers the organisation's ability to create value in the short, medium and long terms; *connectivity of information* that reflects the interdependency between the six capitals; and how the organisation relates to *stakeholders*, including how and to what extent the organisation understands, takes into account and responds to their needs and interests. An Integrated Report should disclose *material* information, that is, matters that substantively affect the organisation's ability to create value over the short, medium and long terms. Finally, Integrated Reports should be *concise*, *reliable and complete*, and *consistent and comparable*. The contents of an Integrated Report should include an overview of the firm's operations and business model, the risks and opportunities to which it is exposed, governance structure, past performance, outlook, and the 'basis for presentation' through which the firm justifies its methodology for preparing the Integrated Report and its inclusions and exclusions (IIRC, 2013: 5).

Crucially, the IIRC states that the 'primary purpose' of an Integrated Report is to inform 'providers of financial capital' (IIRC, 2013: 6) or investors. At the same time, IIRC claims that 'all stakeholders' of a firm will benefit from an Integrated Report (IIRC, 2013: 6). This claim is not substantiated explicitly but appears grounded in the assumption of a confluence of interests between stakeholders and the proposition that there is no contradiction between profit and the social and ecological impacts of business activity. Another stated aim is to 'enhance accountability and stewardship' (IIRC, 2013: 2) of all of the six capitals. Again, the connection between Integrated Reporting and better stewardship is assumed, and reflective of the ideological premises of the Integrated Reporting initiative and the moral economy in which it is embedded.

New capitals

The six capitals are essential to the Integrated Reporting framework, and the IIRC has a particular concept of capital: 'The capitals are *stocks of value* that are increased, decreased or transformed through the activities and outputs of the organization' (IIRC, 2013: 4).

Firms preparing Integrated Reports are required to provide details of the 'stock of value' for each of the six capitals that the IIRC defines (financial; manufactured; human; social and relationship; natural; and intellectual). In addition to the traditional financial statements which provide details of financial and manufactured capital, companies provide details of their non-financial capitals through information such as number of employees, ethnic and gender diversity among staff, the value of their brand, customer and/ or employee engagement figures, staff training expenditure, energy and water use, and greenhouse gas emissions.

Recalling historical developments in capitalist accounting, the rationalisation of assets, specifically tangible goods and money, was a central element of facilitating profit-driven decisions to propel 'the logic of enterprise' (Schumpeter, 1943: 123). The six capital metrics can be seen through both a legitimacy and a technical lens (Carruthers and Espeland, 1991). With respect to legitimacy, firms aim to present themselves as responsible stewards of the various stocks of value they maintain. In technical terms, Integrated Reporting metrics form the basis for building a firm's reputation and relational

Value creation

Integrated Reporting performs an ideological function by broadening the concept of value from strictly monetary to include ecological, human, social, cultural and other non-financial values. Integrated Reporting documentation frequently refers to increasing the capacity of firms to create 'real' value in an effort to capture these non-financial qualities (IIRC, 2015). KPMG, a member of the IIRC, sees the Integrated Reporting project as part of a series of projects which aim to 'develop metrics which will provide a more complete view of value creation' (Draaijer, 2014), incorporating systemic risks such as those associated with ecological deterioration, social conflicts and political turmoil. This points to a technical as well as a rhetorical function for Integrated Reporting in transforming corporate valuation measures according to risk. KPMG's 'true value' methodology, for example, reduces earnings expectations for firms according to its perceptions of ESG risk (Draaijer, 2014). In practical terms, the critical accounting literature reveals that the voluntary nature of Integrated Reporting means that firms are unlikely to fully disclose risks (Boiral, 2013). But the reorientation towards adjusting corporate valuation according to ESG risks, and investor interest in this information, is notable and indicative of the financialisation and commodification of ethics.

The Integrated Reporting framework also performs an ideological function by connecting its concept of value to stakeholder theory. The IIRC states that value is created through *relations with stakeholders* and the *external environment*, and that it is dependent on the capitals relevant to those stakeholders (IIRC, 2013: 10). Integrated Reporting is premised on the idea that '[t]he ability of an organization to create value for itself is linked to the value it creates for others' (IIRC, 2013: 10). At a surface level, this is consistent with the position here that value is created through relations between firms and others. Marxian value, as it is deployed in this book, aims to understand the relations of production and how life and labour are subordinated to the accumulation of capital. But the IIRC's framing of capitals as *interdependent* stocks of wealth in the value creation process ignores the crucial element of subordination and the conflicts of interest between the firm and the stakeholders whose interests are represented in its six capitals. The IIRC positions investors as the primary audience for Integrated Reports and implicitly assumes the primacy of returns to financial capital (Gleeson-White, 2014). By eliding conflicting interests and the centrality of profit, while presenting value creation as a cohesive, pro-social process, Integrated

Reporting performs an ideological function to buttress the speculative moral economy and its claims that capital can be ethical and sustainable.

Rationalisation

The IIRC framework reflects some of the critiques in the SEA literature regarding the challenges of translating ESG issues into metrics for corporate reporting (Hines, 1988, 1991; Lehman, 1999). The IIRC suggests that firms use a mixture of quantitative and qualitative reporting measures for the six capitals (IIRC, 2013: 8) and highlights the importance of the connectivity of the qualitative and quantitative (IIRC, 2013: 8, 16–17). Firms producing Integrated Reports tend to use a combination of numerical and narrative forms to report on their use, depletion and creation of the six capitals.

One interpretation of the use of combined qualitative and quantitative criteria is that the critical SEA literature accurately identifies the challenge, or even the impossibility, of rationalising the complexities of social and ecological values (Hines, 1988, 1991; Lehman, 1999; Radin, 1996). Another interpretation is that there is resistance to finding comprehensive measures for the social and ecological impact of business activity. Developing and applying quantitative measures inherently involves a level of abstraction and reduction that is dependent on ideology (Bryer, 2015). While some phenomena lend themselves more readily to this type of rationalisation, it is a process that can be applied to any phenomenon. The work of Viviana Zelizer, for example, demonstrates how quickly social conventions have changed with respect to valuing human life, through the development of a market for life insurance. Conversely, Zelizer shows that such conventions can also work in reverse, positioning certain people or things outside of monetary relations, through her examination of changing social and economic conventions regarding children, childhood and child labour (Zelizer, 2010). Through this work, Zelizer explicitly rejects the positions of Hines, Lehman and Radin that some things can never be marketised and that markets and morals inhabit 'hostile worlds' (Zelizer, 2010). Similarly, Bigger and Robertson argue that rather than simply asserting incompatibility, it is necessary to question how those incompatibilities are 'socially constituted through different measures and often reconciled in more or less violent or absurd ways' (Bigger and Robertson, 2017: 69). When incompatible socio-cultural values are 'made the same' (MacKenzie, 2009), there is a politics in interrogating the means by which this commensuration is effected.

Value theory scholars might adopt one of many positions on rationalisation of socio-cultural values, from Zelizer's instrumentalist approach to analysing markets and marketisation to the view that some forms of commodification are 'inappropriate' and not all social dilemmas and decisions can be framed in terms of costs, benefits and interests. But one should question why the leaders of the IIRC, comprising some of the world's largest accounting firms and most qualified accounting standard-setting organisations, are shying away from the business of rationalisation. The use of a combination of qualitative and quantitative information in Integrated Reports means that these reports will never be comparable in the same way as traditional financial accounts. Capitalist accounting requires the translation of values into money, as the universal equivalent, in order to facilitate managerial decisions about how to organise production, and investor decisions about how to allocate finance. The failure of the IIRC to complete this rationalisation process undermines the objectives of the IIRC to provide investors with information that is more consistent, complete, reliable and comparable.

The Sustainability Accounting Standards Board

The Sustainability Accounting Standards Board (SASB), funded by Bloomberg, the Rockefeller Foundation, Deloitte, Ernst and Young, PricewaterhouseCoopers and the Ford Foundation, among others, has developed standards for measuring and reporting on ESG metrics. SASB was established with a mandate to develop accounting standards for sustainability information, directed at investors, in a form comparable to the US Securities Exchange Commission's requirements for financial reporting. To that end, SASB's standards are designed similarly to those of the Financial Accounting Standards Board (FASB) and are positioned as a development or evolution of those standards. This project of evolving traditional financial accounting standards appears to be advancing with the incorporation of SASB into the IFRS Foundation in 2022. The IFRS issued its inaugural ISSB Standards in June 2023, for use in reporting from 2024. These standards have been endorsed by IOSCO, which is advocating the widespread implementation of ISSB Standards.

The work of SASB, which underpins the ISSB Standards and has been extensively adopted by financial market participants, is driven by two issues that are important here. First is the increasing economic significance of intangible assets. Bringing together accounting for intangibles and SEA, SASB's work focuses on reporting financially material information about what it calls 'sustainability topics', for the purpose of measuring the intangible value associated with ESG risks and opportunities. SASB explicitly argues that intangible value is composed of, among other things, sustainability performance (SASB, 2019: 10) and that good ESG performance increases the intangible value of firms (SASB, 2016a, 2018). Material ESG risks might include financial or legal exposure due to human rights abuse, failure to

Accounting for ethics 109

meet environmental standards, and reduced access to necessary resources due to environmental pressures. Material ESG opportunities might include the possibility to capitalise on a growing market for organic food consumption, markets for fair trade clothes, or renewable energy generation.

This leads to the second issue of interest here related to SASB's work. If firms' intangible value is increased by better ESG performance, then rationally self-interested investors can be expected to effect market discipline on those firms to demand better ESG performance. Consistent with an efficient markets hypothesis, SASB's work is premised on the conviction that the only limitation to this operation of market discipline and the power of investors as an intra-class regulatory force (see discussion of this concept in Chapter 2) is full disclosure of information about ESG risks and opportunities. SASB and its advocates recognise that ESG data and ratings are inconsistent, giving the examples of the divergence between ratings from ESG industry leaders MSCI and Sustainalytics (Anderson, 2019; SASB, 2018; Wigglesworth, 2018). Disclosure and documentation of ESG risks and opportunities, facilitating 'enhanced data quality' (SASB, 2016a), are presented as the basis of improving sustainability and ESG performance. Common themes are transparency in assessing ESG performance, accuracy, consistency and objectivity (SASB, 2018: 5–6). As one credit analyst says in an SASB white paper, 'everyone knows exactly what a BAA [rated] bond means no matter where they are. We want to bring that to the ESG discussion' (SASB, 2018: 14).

SASB emerges in a context where investors have an appetite for information about sustainability because of the proposition that it drives profits and is a factor of competition. SASB is one of several initiatives aiming to build, from this rapidly growing interest, an industry around the production of ESG information.

Materiality

Materiality, located at the top of SASB's conceptual framework, is central to how the organisation operates and its theory of change. SASB has developed a 'Materiality Map' that ranks the priorities of sustainability topics for each of the seventy-seven industries for which it has developed accounting standards (Table 4.1).

Materiality is the basis of the reporting under SASB standards, and the key driver of its work. This concept brings to the fore the importance of profit maximisation and the centrality of the investor perspective. Given its materiality focus, the issues that SASB highlights should already be reported in a company's 10K report, as required by the US SEC. Indeed, SASB recognises that much of the information relevant to its standards is already reported but says the quality and comparability of the information can be

110   *Risk and value*

Table 4.1 Sustainability topics in SASB's Materiality Map

Dimension	General Issue Category
Environment	GHG Emissions
	Air Quality
	Energy Management
	Water & Wastewater Management
	Waste & Hazardous Materials Management
	Ecological Impacts
Social Capital	Human Rights & Community Relations
	Customer Privacy
	Data Security
	Access & Affordability
	Product Quality & Safety
	Customer Welfare
	Selling Practices & Product Labelling
Human Capital	Labour Practices
	Employee Health & Safety
	Employee Engagement, Diversity & Inclusion
Business Model & Innovation	Product Design & Lifecycle Management
	Business Model Resilience
	Supply Chain Management
	Materials Sourcing & Efficiency
	Physical Impacts of Climate Change
Leadership & Governance	Business Ethics
	Competitive Behaviour
	Management of the Legal & Regulatory Environment
	Critical Incident Risk Management
	Systemic Risk Management

Source: SASB, https://materiality.sasb.org/ (accessed 14 February 2020)

improved. This reflects a faith in the power of fully informed markets and a functionalist theory of SEA, based on the idea that sustainability is a technical issue rather than a political one. The impact of this is that those developing the sustainability indicators decide the contours of the issues at hand. They determine what sustainability comprises and how to measure it. Consistent with Malsch's (2013) critique, this renders sustainability issues 'apolitical objects of risk' and means that sustainability will be redefined for market compatibility.

The requisite market compatibility was achieved through SASB's consultation process. In order to determine materiality for each of its industry standards, SASB coordinated a lengthy process of research and consultation for drafting its Materiality Map. The first few months involved using data-driven algorithms to mine publicly available documents such as financial news, SEC filings, corporate sustainability reports and legal cases to identify critical issues in each industry, where there was a concentration of attention on certain topics. This process highlighted ESG issues that are prominent in public debate and that also generate social, political, economic or legal risk. The resulting list was used as a proxy for issues that investors might be interested in.

Once this baseline of issues was identified, SASB dug deeper to assess market compatibility. The researchers looked for evidence that particular companies had experienced material financial impacts associated with any of the identified sustainability topics, for example if the company had lost market share because of a brand or reputational issue, or it had been fined, or it reported in its financial statements either increased revenue due to taking advantage of an ESG opportunity or losses suffered due to ESG risk. This second cut of research produced a list of subtopics per industry where there was both some evidence of investor or public interest in the issue and evidence of financial impacts. If there was either great public interest but no financial impact or significant financial impact but little interest, the topic was deemed not to be financially material. With these topics, SASB convened industry working groups comprised of companies in the industry, investors analysing the industry, and other 'subject matter experts' such as accountants, academics, lawyers and non-profits. The industry working groups voted on SASB's initial findings and provided guidance about the financially material ESG issues companies face in their industries (SASB, n.d.).

The result of this process is that the SASB standards provide a tightly constrained and industry-specific set of issues for companies to report on. For example, in some industries such as airline services and automobile manufacturing, SASB has concluded that employee collective representation is a material sustainability topic. In others such as retail, hospitality and education, it is not. The position of the International Labour Organization (ILO) is that freedom of association is a fundamental human right. Although every industry employs labour, the question from the perspective of SASB standards is how costly labour disputes may be and the relative power of trade unions, not respect for basic human rights. The dissection of sustainability topics and reporting frameworks according to financial materiality creates a very particular, market-driven form of sustainability. Ethical or sustainability issues that do not have a significant financial impact on the relevant industry or firm are excluded from consideration. This speaks to Lampert's (2016) intervention regarding the limitations of the corporation as a moral agent: that business ethics fail at precisely the point where they are most important, when they conflict with profit. This is how ethics must be constrained if the responsible capital imaginary at the heart of the speculative moral economy is to be realised. Profit is compatible with ethics only if ethics are moulded to fit the market. Market-compatible ethics are a particular form of ethics that privilege certain principles and exclude others. The process of producing this form of ethics creates a basis for its commodification, and the production of "ethical capital".

Rationalisation

There is great variation in the sustainability information provided in corporate reporting, and SASB identifies quality and comparability as the areas that it can improve. SASB claims that corporate reports often provide 'boilerplate' information that is vague, of little use and not specific to the relevant industry (SASB, 2016b). For this reason, SASB aims to produce information that can facilitate comparison, particularly between competitors. This standardisation facilitates commensuration of different firms' sustainability positions or different ESG risk profiles, within an industry, competing in the same financial markets for access to capital.

While the SASB framework provides for standardisation of information, rationalisation via the monetary unit is incomplete. Like the Integrated Reporting framework which provides for a combination of numerical and narrative data, SASB standards require a mix. Some information must be quantitative, such as quantity of greenhouse gas emissions; total water withdrawn or consumed; food safety violation rate; rates of non-conformance to suppliers' labour code of conduct; employee turnover rates; amount of materials used in production that are certified for environmental or social sustainability; and ethnic and gender diversity among employees. Other information required under the standards is discursive or qualitative, such as commentary on managing risks regarding data security or use of chemicals in production; strategies for managing labour and environmental risk in the supply chain; processes for identifying and managing emerging dietary preferences; or policies and practices regarding behavioural advertising and customer privacy.

Is this rationalisation process incomplete because the ESG industry is in its nascent stages? While this might be the case in the ESG industry, there may be other reasons that organisations like SASB, the IIRC, and the various accounting firms and professionals associated with these projects are holding back from the development of a more complete rationalisation and standardisation of sustainability information. As Carruthers and Espeland (1991) made clear, accounting plays not only a technical but also a rhetorical or symbolic function. The limits that SASB and the IIRC put on rationalisation and standardisation of ESG risks prevents a more comprehensive reckoning of the ecological and social costs of business which would be inconsistent with the dominant capitalist-centric, managerialist approach to SEA. But these limits do not prevent the rendering of ESG (ethical) risks for commodification. It is precisely these limits, in fact, which create the market-compatible ethics that can become the basis of producing "ethical capital".

Investors as change agents

The SASB conceptual framework focuses on the role of investors, requiring that information provided under SASB standards be "decision-useful", have the capacity to impact on value creation, be verifiable and be of interest to investors. These aspects of SASB's framework highlight the rhetorical function that the standards play in supporting the speculative moral economy. As explored in Chapter 2, the speculative moral economy elevates predictions about risk assessment as a driving force behind responsible decision-making in investment. That is, ethical issues that can be shown to present financial risks become "decision-useful" information because they have the capacity to impact on (financial) value creation. The SASB framework is built around the primacy of investor interests and the assumption that the only ESG issues that should be actioned are those with material (financial) implications. This supports several underlying premises of the speculative moral economy. First, that it is legitimate for investors to decide ethical questions. Second, that questions of financial risk should drive ethical debate. And finally, that fully informed financial markets will find a sustainable or ethical equilibrium.

Disclosure bias

Some of the concerns raised in the SEA literature regarding disclosure (Boiral, 2013; Cho and Patten, 2013) are borne out in the SASB standards and the case study documents issued by some SASB supporters. For example, Cho and Patten (2013) highlight the risk of disclosure bias in sustainability reporting whereby firms that are large enough, well-resourced enough or savvy enough to disclose ESG data obtain benefits even if they perform relatively poorly on environmental and social issues. A hint of this kind of bias is revealed in Bloomberg's case study on its experience in implementing SASB standards, which shows that '[a]s a result of publishing the SASB metrics, Bloomberg realized an enhanced reputation as measured through the earned media associated with their SASB-consistent reporting, Twitter chat, and social media campaign' (SASB, 2016a: 3).

This is possibly indicative of the function of corporate reporting in commodifying sustainability (Hiss, 2013), which does not depend on any meaningful change in social or ecological impact of business activity. That is, sustainability can be commodified and transformed into an intangible asset, a component of a firm's brand and other elements of relational capital, through disclosure and reporting, regardless of the social or ecological impact of the firm's actual operations.

One response to the problem of selective self-reporting is offered by a data analytics firm, TruValue Labs (TVL). Recognising that firms have a tendency to report only positive information about their ESG performance, TVL relies on third-party data and large, unstructured data sets, and has created an analytic process based on the SASB standards and Materiality Map. TVL aims to produce relevant (financially material), comparable, reliable, objective and timely data to inform investor decision-making. Scanning tens of thousands of sources to develop a score for over 8,000 companies, TVL generates various scores. One is an event-based 'Pulse' score that captures moments in time based on ESG risks and opportunities. Another is the 'Insight' score, a weighted average of Pulse. Finally, the ESG 'Momentum' score tracks the change in the Insight score over the course of one year.

Stephen Malinak and his co-authors (2018) have conducted preliminary research into the effectiveness of the TVL metrics for predicting stock performance. Using TVL Insight and Momentum scores against firms in the Russell 1000 universe and S&P 500, they found the TVL metrics can enhance traditional financial analysis. Outperformance was particularly pronounced for firms with median ESG scores on both TVL Insight and Momentum, suggesting high performers had already been recognised by the market. According to TVL, its SASB Insight and SASB Momentum metrics reveal and 'quantify many factors missed by traditional quantitative analyses' (TruValue Labs, 2017) and this is what it attributes to the capacity of its analysis to deliver high-performing investment strategies. This conclusion is unsurprising given the focus of SASB's standards on *financially material* issues. If it is the case that firms are exposed to ESG risks with the capacity to generate unexpected costs or to undermine returns, it is logical that the resulting financial analysis may be more effective.

What is less clear, though, is how this relates to the concept of responsible investing and what kind of "responsibility" or "ethics" is implied in the process. TVL says, 'Augmenting "business as usual" with additive behavioral data *isn't just responsible investing*. It's smart investing. It's ESG2.0' (TruValue Labs, n.d.: 9).

While it may be 'smart investing' from the perspective of shareholders, this is not meaningfully 'responsible investing'. Issues of corporate responsibility do not cut off at the limit of financial materiality. This is, yet again, a reinforcement of the particular ideology that sustainability accounting

Accounting for ethics

– and the responsible capital imaginary more generally – is embedding: the proposition that ethical issues must fit within a market logic, must have a financial impact, to be relevant. This is the only basis on which profit and sustainability can be seen as consistent with one another.

Conclusion

Analysing Integrated Reporting and SASB's standards through the critiques developed in the accounting literature, and through the frame of the responsible capital imaginary, reveals the technical and the rhetorical function of these two initiatives. In addition to performing a powerful rhetorical function, justifying capital accumulation through increasingly pressing ecological and social crises via the speculative moral economy, these new forms of accounting create a foundation for "ethical capital" accumulation, that is, capital that is based on certain ethical claims (as opposed to capital that is objectively ethical). One example of this kind of ethical capital is corporate reputations and brands that are built around ethical claims regarding business practices (see Chapter 5). Another form taken by ethical capital is the ESG data products and services generated by investment advisors, many of which are based on ESG accounting metrics (see Chapter 6).

The accounting initiatives analysed in this chapter create a foundation for standardising and mapping ESG information, making it legible for capital. This process is comparable to historical mapping and metricisation efforts, like those of William Petty and the political arithmetic movement, which has also been compared to intangible accounting (Mårtensson, 2009). It can also be understood as part of the rationalisation exercises that Jason Moore defines as 'abstract social nature': 'the family of processes through which states and capitalists map, identify, quantify, measure, and code human and extra-human natures in service to capital accumulation' (Moore, 2015: 194). SASB standards, in particular, are mapping, identifying, quantifying, measuring and coding social, environmental and political issues that may form the basis of ethical claims, and then "ethical capital" assets. SASB does this by determining the relevant (material) ethical issues pressing on a particular industry, through analysing news media, NGO reports and other elements of public discourse. These streams of information are generated by public debate, by expressions of ethical or political concern that create legitimacy risks for capital (see also Chapter 5). The work of SASB and Integrated Reporting performs a rhetorical function in legitimating capital accumulation against claims that business is a driving force behind many social and ecological challenges, and a technical one by creating a basis on which ethics can become a vehicle for accumulation.

The failure of the SASB standards and Integrated Reporting framework to develop fully quantitative measures is indicative of the limitations of SEA to quantify the social. Some argue that there are inherent constraints on quantifying the social (Hines, 1991; Lehman, 1999), but this ignores the fact that accounting has always imposed quantitative measures on social phenomena and facilitated the commensuration of things that seem inherently incommensurable (Bigger and Robertson, 2017; Robertson, 2012). So why does SEA pull back from the task of developing fully quantitative measures for social and ecological issues? Why do organisations like SASB and the IIRC, backed by influential global leaders in the accounting profession, permit the inclusion of qualitative and discursive information in these accounts which prevents them from performing the function that traditional financial accounts would perform? It is argued here that there are two reasons. First, a full reckoning of social and environmental costs would devastate the rate of profit. Second, a full reckoning is unnecessary. Accounting for ethics can perform the technical and rhetorical functions of rendering ethics for commodification on a constrained definition of ethics. Market-compatible ethics can suffice (indeed, a market-compatible approach is crucial) for this purpose of enabling firms to present as ethical and to generate ethical capital.

While the frameworks of SASB and Integrated Reporting reveal this limit-point for quantification of ESG issues – the point at which ESG issues conflict with and undermine profitability – the incompleteness of their accounting does not undermine their effectiveness in building a base for ethical capital. The ethics underlying these assets need not be meaningful or robust for the assets to perform their symbolic and economic function. Recalling Boiral's (2013) argument that corporate reports are simulacra, that they are disconnected from reality, based on manipulated information and misleading images, it is still possible for this form of reporting to serve its function in the production of ethical capital assets if the reports are misleading simulacra and if the information on which these reports are based is incomplete. Accounting for ethics, as established by SASB and Integrated Reporting, allows firms to engage in the responsible capital imaginary, where profit and sustainability are consistent, while obscuring the underlying conflict between them.

Part III

Producing ethical capital

Chapter 5

Brands and the (re)production of ethics

[Justin Rosenstein] When you think about how some of these companies work, it starts to make sense. There are all these services on the Internet that we think of as free, but they're not free. They're paid for by advertisers. Why do advertisers pay those companies? They pay in exchange for showing their ads to us. We're the product. Our attention is the product being sold to advertisers.

[Jaron Lanier] That's a little too simplistic. It's the gradual, slight, imperceptible change in your own behavior and perception that is the product. And that is the product. It's the only possible product. There's nothing else on the table that could possibly be called the product. That's the only thing there for them to make money from. Changing what you do, how you think, who you are. (*The Social Dilemma*, 2020, transcript)

Introduction

The marketplace being discussed above by Justin Rosenstein and Jaron Lanier in *The Social Dilemma* (2020) is what Shoshana Zuboff describes, in the same film, as

> a marketplace that trades exclusively in human futures. Just like there are markets that trade in pork belly futures or oil futures. We now have markets that trade in human futures at scale, and those markets have produced the trillions of dollars that have made the Internet companies the richest companies in the history of humanity.

The previous chapters have argued that ethics is an accumulation strategy in the speculative moral economy. In this chapter, that proposition is applied to a particular phenomenon: corporate branding, related assertions of responsible corporate conduct, and the manner in which labour, in its subjectivity as consumer, is subordinated to this process. As intangible and productive assets, brands mediate the relations between firms and their various stakeholders, including customers, suppliers and investors. In the contemporary economy, where trade often depends as much on image, ideas and affect as it does price, brands are an important strategic and competitive asset. They are commodities in themselves, with use value and exchange value, that deliver various forms of economic benefit, including increasing the value of the goods and services traded by their owners, facilitating communication between brand owners and other economic actors, and increasing the value of the brand-owning firm.

This chapter reveals how ethics become capital through the operation of brands, elucidating the productive relations between capital, labour, ethics and risk. Labour is subsumed into capital in novel ways through data mining, interactive communications and other efforts by firms to determine how to build affective connections with consumers, based on ethical claims. Pricing and trading on the spread between different ethical positions and realities becomes productive through the derivative logic of the financialised firm. In Chapter 2, the financialised firm was described as a bundle of risks which can be parsed, split off and traded in various ways. Social and ecological challenges, or ESG issues, become ethical risks to be managed for the financialised firm in a speculative moral economy. Having established how the finance sector (Chapter 3) and social accounting frameworks (Chapter 4) shape the derivative logic of ethical capital, this chapter demonstrates how ethics are alienated from labour and incorporated into capital through brands. In order to do this, the chapter brings together literatures from intellectual property jurisprudence, marketing and cultural economy. Through an analysis of brand valuation standards, techniques and processes, alongside intellectual property case law, the chapter argues that ethics become productive through the capital–labour relation and through branding practices that facilitate trading on ethical risks. This productivity is dependent on information about labour-as-consumer that provides a basis for pricing and trading ethical risks.

Finally, the chapter demonstrates the utility of approaching the phenomenon of ethical capital through the lens of Marxian value. New developments in information and communications technology (ICT), such as those discussed above in *The Social Dilemma* (2020), are intensifying firms' capacities to learn about consumers' preferences, ideas and priorities, transforming the labour processes underlying ethical capital production, expanding the scope for mass individualisation of ethical capital's propositions and for generation of ethical value. A value-driven analysis reveals the dynamism of these processes and the social relations underlying them, as ethics become a form of capital.

Brands as multifaceted commodities, co-produced by capital and labour

It has long been understood that brands are a ubiquitous, insidious feature of the contemporary economy. Reflecting on the twenty years since Naomi

Brands and the (re)production of ethics   121

Klein's anti-branding blockbuster *No Logo* was published, Dan Hancox describes

> the total branding of every aspect of our lives and culture … It is strikingly rare, in 2019, to encounter an unbranded, unsponsored cultural experience. Every festival, programme, public-awareness campaign and event has a series of 'partners', a cluster of familiar icons at the bottom of the poster. Every charity is led by its marketing team. Every TV programme is 'brought to you by …' (Hancox, 2019)

A creature of intellectual property, the brand has developed with and through the law such that brands, trademarks and commercial goodwill have become virtually indistinguishable (Seddon, 2015). Marketing scholar and practitioner Stefan Schwarzkopf describes brands as 'trademarks that have been loaded with social and cultural meaning' (Schwarzkopf, 2010: 165). The International Trade Mark Association similarly says that a brand is 'a trademark … [that] has acquired significance over and above its functional use by a company to distinguish its goods or services from those of other traders' (Davis and Maniatis, 2010: 120).

It is clear, though, that brands extend beyond those components that are legally registrable as a trademark to encompass the image, the relationships, the personality and the evocations that a brand creates (Mercer, 2010: 18; Seddon, 2015). Wider definitions speak to the role of brands as intangible use values and their function in creating a relationship between a firm and its stakeholders. One brand valuation agency describes them as 'the sum of all expressions by which an entity (person, organization, company, business unit, city, nation, etc.) intends to be recognized' (Interbrand, n.d.b). Intellectual property scholar Neil Wilkof suggests a similarly broad definition, that a brand 'comprises all publicly identifiable knowledge associated with a particular product, service, or company' (Wilkof, 2018: 341), as do Leslie de Chernatony and Francesca Dall'Olmo Riley, for whom a brand may be 'a legal instrument, a differentiating device, a company, an identity system, an image in consumers' minds, a personality, a relationship, adding value, and an evolving entity' (cited by Davis and Maniatis, 2010: 121).

Importantly, although the brand is defined more widely than its legally defensible elements, brand values are attributable only to the owner of those legal elements (ISO, 2010). This points to a core conflict in the politics of brands, namely that they are co-produced by firms and consumers, but the financial and economic benefits flow to their legal owners. This contradiction is central to the productive nature and function of brands.

Already by the early 1900s, goodwill and trademarks were recognised as productive assets. New York attorney Frank Schechter argued for extending trademark protection on the basis that the mark itself 'actually *sells* the goods' and rather than just being a 'symbol of goodwill', the most 'potent aspect of the nature of a trademark' is its capacity 'for the actual creation and perpetuation of goodwill' (Schechter, 1927: 818, emphasis in original). Around the same time, economist John Commons pointed out that the value of a firm's goodwill can exceed the value of its tangible property, and that 'without goodwill, tangible property is a liability rather than an asset' (Commons, 1919: 26). Here Commons, writing at the time when trademarks and goodwill merged into the early stages of modern branding, was implicitly referring to the dual commodity function of brands. First, they are balance sheet assets, commodities in themselves that can be traded between firms in the context of mergers and acquisitions. Second, they are amorphous vehicles of the intangible value that is distributed to consumers through trade in the goods and services to which they attach.

For firms, brands are a use value because they increase the price and the volume of goods and services traded, they facilitate opening new markets, and they provide efficiencies in communication. These economic benefits are the basis of brand valuation (ISO, 2010) as stipulated by the International Organization for Standardization (ISO) and operationalised by various brand valuation agencies. In addition to mediating relations between a firm and its consumers, brands also condition relations between a firm and its other stakeholders. This is particularly the case in a highly networked economy where production relations become more complex and brands are split from manufacturers. Andrew Griffiths (2018) shows that brands are core to the organisation of global production relations, using the three examples of Apple, Clark's shoes and fast fashion. Brands enable the separation of marketing and production activity, but with brand holders maintaining the position of power (Griffiths, 2018). Examples of this kind of brand power in action include Google's payments to Apple to maintain its position as the default search engine on Apple devices. In 2019, for example, it was estimated that Google paid almost USD 10 billion in these 'traffic acquisition costs' (Salinas, 2019).

Brands also deliver use value to consumers. When people buy branded goods or services, they purchase not only the commodity itself but also the benefit of the brand. In many cases, people purchase results, experiences, ways of being and images, rather than products themselves: 'Consumers buy holes, not drills' (Gundlach and Phillips, 2015: 124). As the ISO puts it, stakeholders 'value the functional/emotional/social benefits and experiences they associate with the brand' (ISO, 2019: v). Brands are one of the primary vehicles for delivering intangible value to consumers, and are part of a consumer's calculation of the value of a good or service.

In order for brands to be able to deliver these intangible use values, the brand becomes a relationship between firms and consumers, which 'mediates the supply and demand of products through the organisation, co-ordination and integration of the use of information' (Lury, 2004: 3). While trademarks historically functioned as an indicator of origin and of quality, the brand is an increasingly dialogic communication between firms and consumers. Brands are cultural artefacts to which many consumers feel a sense of connection and ownership. This understanding is common to marketing scholars who explore the ways in which brands can leverage their relationships with consumers (Prahalad and Ramaswamy, 2004; Ramaswamy and Ozcan, 2014, 2016; Sheth and Uslay, 2007), cultural economy scholars who are interested in the exploitative elements of this process and what it reveals about the nature of contemporary capitalism (Arvidsson, 2005, 2013; Foster, 2013), and intellectual property law-makers who recognise the dependence of brand values on consumers' behaviour (Fhima, 2015).

Brands, then, are commodities in a dual sense, with independent use and exchange values for consumers and for brand owners. They are vehicles for the intangible value they attach to goods and services, which are use values to consumers and increase exchange values consumers pay to brand owners. They are also corporate balance sheet assets with an independent use and exchange value from the brand owner's perspective. Indeed, brands are typically much more valuable than the commodities they sell. Multifaceted commodities, with several intersecting use values and exchange values, brands are produced through the co-creative activities of capital and labour-as-consumer. This crucial co-productive relation is the vehicle for ethical capital production through brands.

Measuring brand value

The co-production of brands by labour-as-consumer and capital is one avenue through which affective labour is productive in the contemporary economy (Arvidsson, 2005, 2013; Foster, 2007, 2008; Willmott, 2010). This work builds on Maurizio Lazzarato's theorisation of 'immaterial labour' as a way of understanding the production of value in an economy, which he describes as a 'production of worlds' (Lazzarato, 2004: 187). Through processes of co-creation, brands render human relationships, behaviour and sentiments productive for capital. They are a mechanism that 'enable a direct valorization (in the form of share prices, for example) of people's ability to create trust, affect and shared meanings' (Arvidsson, 2005: 236). Robert Foster argues that 'brand valuation translates or gives expression to the value of consumption work by bringing the brand into relation with the universal equivalent of money' (Foster, 2013: 57). This is one instance of how people's productive activity outside of the wage relation, the agency of brand users, has been 'harnessed to the interests of capital' (Foster, 2013:

58). Foster (2013) also points out that this is the case regardless of the nature of the consumer's relationship with the brand, giving the example of brands that co-opt protest by counter-cultural activists to transform their image, thus rendering even this kind of oppositional activity productive for the firm.

Practices of brand valuation, comparable to social accounting standards which are finding new ways to measure capital (see Chapter 4), offer a useful perspective on the productive relation between capital, labour, ethics and risk. The brand valuation industry was established in the 1980s when corporate raiders, paying high price premia for intangible assets like goodwill (brands), needed to account for this part of a company's assets (Blackett, 1991). The question of how to value brands is a knotty one, which remains unresolved. Leading brand valuation agencies include Interbrand, Eurobrand, BrandZ and Brand Finance, all of which use different methodologies and generate different figures (Seddon, 2015). Similar to the case of ESG risk analysis for investors, brand valuation is plagued by a lack of transparency and wildly different valuation figures, which lead to a lack of confidence in valuations. As Joanna Seddon explains, '[i]naccuracies ... bedevil brand-valuation rankings. Differences in valuations included in rankings published by BrandZ, Interbrand, Brand Finance, and Eurobrand range from a minimum of 30 per cent (HP and American Express) to a factor of more than four (McDonald's and Shell)' (Seddon, 2015: 151). Despite these inconsistencies, an analysis of brand valuation schemes reveals the important co-productive contributions of labour and the role of qualitative claims (including claims about ethics and ESG risk) in the value of brands.

The ISO released a standard to guide monetary valuations of brands in 2010 (ISO 10668), and for non-financial evaluations of brands in 2019 (ISO 20671). They state that brand values comprise financial as well as legal and behavioural dimensions (ISO, 2010). The ISO's standard 10668 stipulates that the 'core of the brand value lies in the asset's associated meaning(s) among stakeholders' (ISO, 2010: 8), demonstrating that labour-as-consumer is essential to building and maintaining the shared meanings that lend brands their economic value. In its 2019 standard, the ISO reiterates this essential role for labour-as-consumers when it states that '[b]rands ultimately exist *in the minds of stakeholders* as the impressions, benefits, and experiences that they associate with a good or service' (ISO, 2019: v, emphasis added).

Drivers of brand strength identified by the ISO include 'changes in consumer behaviour and trends, brand investment, competitive activity and trademark enforcement protection programmes' (ISO, 2010: 8). According to the ISO's guidance, the firm invests in its brand strength through marketing activity, and consumers participate (or not) in that activity through purchasing choices, engagement on social media and other brand-building activity. These are the processes through which consumers' experiences are 'harvested' (Foster, 2007) and put into the service of capital.

Brand valuation also depends on assessments of image and reputation. In relation to both sales revenues and share prices, corporate reputation – a core part of the brand – has become a valuable asset (Kirsch, 2014: 208). For companies whose brand makes up a substantial percentage of their market capitalisation, the risk of scandals and similar impacting reputation is a significant one (Foster, 2013). As the responsible capital imaginary becomes more prevalent, qualitative claims about ethics or ESG issues create both reputational opportunities and risks for brand owners.

Brands in the speculative moral economy

Marketing scholars and practitioners have long debated whether corporate responsibility is a sufficiently powerful motivating factor for consumers (Carrington et al., 2016; Coffin and Egan-Wyer, 2022; Page and Fearn, 2006). A range of mainstream publications, including *Forbes* (Scott, 2019; Townsend, 2018) and the *Financial Times* (Bounds, 2019; Hancock, 2017), refer to consumer surveys and related evidence that reinforce the responsible capital imaginary. According to this evidence, a significant majority of people believe that it is possible to take meaningful action through consumption practices and are motivated to do so in relation to a range of social, political and environmental issues. A 2015 global survey of over 30,000 consumers in sixty countries found that two thirds of people were willing to pay more for sustainable brands (up from 55 per cent the year before), and that the figure was nearly three quarters for people born after 1980 (Neilsen IQ, 2015). Global consumer goods firm Unilever claims that its ethical brands, those that 'combine a strong purpose delivering a social or environmental benefit', grew 40 per cent faster than the rest of the business in 2016 (Hancock, 2017). Research by the New York University Stern Center for Sustainable Business found that 50 per cent of growth in consumer packaged goods markets from 2013 to 2018 came from sustainably marketed products (Kronthal-Sacco and Whelan, 2019). Marketing agency Havas (2019a) has claimed that the majority of people expect brands to play a more significant role than governments in improving society.

Leading brand valuation agencies and standards recognise the significance of sustainability or ESG issues for building and maintaining brand value and managing risk. The ISO 20671 standard (ISO, 2019) notes that brand valuation may include the firm's position on sustainable development, and social and ecological responsibility. Paula Oliveira and Andrea Sullivan

(2015) from Interbrand have issued guidance to clients explaining the role of sustainable practices and images in increasing the firm's value, building sales and strengthening relationships with consumers. Interbrand links sustainability and branding directly to reducing ESG risks. Oliveira and Sullivan (2015) give examples of firms which have led their industry sectors in proactive renewable energy and clean tech investments, creating a 'halo' effect on other product offerings within their brand. On-going research by the Stern Center for Sustainable Business at New York University aims to measure the return on sustainable investment, measuring benefits to consumer-facing brands and multinational firms as well as those further down the supply chain. Recent research from Brand Finance claims that the largest brands stand to lose billions as a result of poor ESG management (Brand Finance Institute, 2023b). Corporations reflect their understanding of the importance of the responsible capital imaginary through innumerable appeals to "wokeness", such as Dove's campaign for inclusive beauty, Gillette's posturing against toxic masculinity, Qantas's support for equal marriage and Nike's collaboration with Colin Kaepernick to comment on police brutality and racism.

As is the case with responsible investment, the substance of ethical consumption is weakly defined. Christine Vallaster and her co-authors claim that 'consumers yearn for something meaningful in their consumption' (Vallaster et al., 2012: 34). Marketing agency Havas releases a bi-annual report entitled *Meaningful Brands* highlighting successful efforts by firms to develop brands that consumers identify with and consider socially beneficial. The 2019 study claims that 'consumers will reward brands who want to make the world a better place and who reflect their values. A massive 77% of consumers prefer to buy from companies who share their values. Brand activism will become a crucial part of a brand's strategy' (Havas, 2019b). Havas bases this claim on evidence that meaningful brands are able to command high premium prices, are more likely to maintain consumer loyalty, and have higher scores for brand awareness and strength.

Andy Milligan and Simon Bailey (2019) make similar arguments about brand purpose and the importance of meaningful consumption. While brand purpose is not necessarily synonymous with CSR, the authors give examples that imply value judgements whereby brands might 'improve the lives of customers or consumers and the world in which they live' or create 'a better everyday life for as many people as possible' (Milligan and Bailey, 2019: 78, 54). As brands increasingly trade on their capacity to generate emotional and affective connections with consumers, not only to deliver particular goods and services, many of these connections rely on ethical claims or offers. The reference to brand or corporate purpose also mirrors recent claims by business leaders, as discussed in Chapter 2, to centre 'purpose' in business management (Edgecliffe-Johnson and Mooney, 2019; US BRT, 2019b). More recent marketing research reveals a growing scepticism of firms' behaviour in relation to sustainability claims: '72 percent [of consumers surveyed] are tired of brands pretending they want to help society when they just want to make money' (Havas, 2023: 4; see also Havas, 2021). Despite this lack of trust, the same research shows that consumers surveyed are insistent that global business must act in the best interests of 'the planet and society' (Havas, 2023: 2), reflecting the persistence of the responsible capital imaginary in an age of escalating and overlapping crises.

Many sensible objections are raised against the proposition of ethical consumption as a vehicle for social change, including the problem of differing ethical preferences, consumers' differential willingness or capacity to pay more for ethical products, and the quality of information that is available to support consumers in making decisions (Iredale, 2018; Singer, 2019). Celia Lury cautions that though brands may facilitate a relationship between consumers and firms, they limit us to communicating 'using a very small part of who we are' (Lury, 2004: 13). Robbie Fordyce and Luke van Ryn (2014) suggest that while ethical branding may not offer a way out of capitalism, it perhaps points to alternative ways of producing. Reviewing the practices of several European supermarkets and food retailers, Matthias Lehner and Sue Vaux Halliday (2014) find consumers' concerns are captured and translated into production processes and branding strategies. They raise some concerns about the anti-democratic implications of corporate domination of sustainability discourse, allowing capital to define sustainability.

All of these raise valid concerns about CSR and corporate power, and about the nature of the ethics that can be practised through the vehicle of a brand. But understanding ethical consumption and branding through the derivative logic reveals more about the productive nature of this kind of activity. The narrative about brands becoming "more ethical" and firms making ethical claims is only part of the story. While community concerns about ethical issues may be driving the responsible capital imaginary, what makes this form of engagement profitable or facilitates the creation of value for capital is the integration of those ethical issues into a derivative logic. Put another way, firms are able to capitalise on their speculations about which ethical risks to hedge, or to be exposed to, and which ethical opportunities to prioritise. This was revealed in relation to climate action, discussed in Chapter 3. While many financial institutions, insurance companies and others are succumbing to public pressure to divest from fossil fuels, it is clear that there is still a profitable schism in the market to be exploited. This was observed by a portfolio manager for the BlackRock World Mining Trust in 2018, who made clear that ESG risk, while dynamic and politically shaped, is balanced against a financial trade-off: 'There's a bifurcation in the market. There is a growing pressure from the investor base and that voice is going to grow stronger over time. But if you've got a high-quality coal product — that's quite a nice area to be in the market' (Sanderson, 2018).

Sustainable market offerings are hedged by conventional or unethical counterparts. The decisions about which sustainable goods and services to offer in the market are informed by an assessment of which ESG risks and opportunities are financially material and market-compatible. Decisions about when to assert a political position are measured up against the risk of doing so. Investors profit on the spread between one ethical position and another, between the time when a human rights breach is profitable and the time when it is costly, between a place where ecological costs must be recognised and a place where they can be ignored. As was explored in Chapters 3 and 4, the boundaries of financially material ESG risk are dynamic and contested, requiring investors to continually update and revise their assessments about the likely impact of particular social, environmental and political issues on an investee firm or portfolio.

The backlash against sustainability and ESG investing which has developed since 2022, particularly in the US, implies not that business is likely to be less politicised, but rather that the spread of ethical possibilities available in the marketplace is likely to widen. Brand managers can also engage in this kind of calculation about how to speculate on ethical risk. Joachim Scholz and Andrew Smith (2019) offer a case study of a brand fighting back against a 'firestorm' on social media. The approach of the protein shake brand in that case was to defend its own 'core values' of discipline and achievement against a body-shaming critique. Protein World's brand managers calculated that their own customer base was more likely to respond positively to its aggressive defence than an approach that sought to placate critics. The facility to negotiate and leverage the qualitative and affective dimensions of production and distribution is a core element of how brands become productive through the derivative logic in a speculative moral economy, and of how ethics become a form of capital. What is particularly troublesome for firms is that brand and reputation are 'at the limits of managerial control' (Foster, 2013: 57).

Quality control: managing the affective associations of brands

A necessary requirement for activating the derivative logic and enabling firms to leverage the affective associations and qualitative claims associated with their products is control over the brand image. Developments in intellectual property law, and trademarks, in particular, reflect the ways in which the law accommodates this economic necessity.

Brands and the (re)production of ethics 129

As the economic significance of branding and consumer behaviour has grown (Cohen, 2003; Schwarzkopf, 2010), courts have shown increasing willingness to protect brand values. This has comprised extending the range of what can be included as registrable subject matter for trademarks (Davis, 2002; Fhima, 2015),[1] as well as expanding protection against uses of a mark which degrade the qualitative associations through which it builds its relationship with labour-as-consumer (Bone, 2006; Davis and Maniatis, 2010; Dogan and Lemley, 2012; Neuberger, 2015; Potočnik, 2019).

The expansion of trademark and branding protection that underpins Lizabeth Cohen's 'consumer republic' (2003) included the 1946 Lanham Act and the UK's Trade Marks Act 1938. While capital's development had previously relied on encouraging the values of thrift and prudence among poorly paid workers (see Chapter 2), over-accumulation required greater levels of consumption, and therefore a spendthrift labouring class (Beder, 2004; Cleaver, 2005). Along with other public policies of the New Deal era that supported higher levels of discretionary spending, at least for some fractions of the working class, these developments used consumption as a bulwark against both economic crisis and the threat of communism.

The consumer republic was 'founded upon a shared world of signs, symbols and products' (Wilf, 2008: 143), and changes in spending habits were driven, in part, by the adoption of new marketing tactics, like emotional and psychological advertising (Bone, 2006; Schwarzkopf, 2010). This approach to advertising shifted its focus from descriptive, detailing the features of the commodity being sold, to psychological, generating an emotional response in the consumer. Advertisers linked their products to sentiments, such as motherly love or prestige, and sought to generate a relationship between the consumer and the mark. As these qualitative claims have become more integral to branding strategies, the capacity of firms to protect and control those qualities has become more important.

One of the earliest cases dealing with the legal protection of brand image was a 1980s Australian matter relating to soft drinks.[2] The plaintiff sought protection when a competitor launched a similar product using a similar marketing campaign. The UK's Privy Council, hearing an appeal from the New South Wales Supreme Court, found that the law had expanded from protection of goodwill anchored in a name or trademark to become 'wide enough to encompass other descriptive material, such as slogans or visual images'.[3] While the court decided on the facts of the case not to protect the plaintiff's property in the abstract image (brand image) that it sought to sell, the court acknowledged that such protection was possible. Mark Davison (2009) has hypothesised that the decision may have been made differently sometime in the future.

130 *Producing ethical capital*

Since then, protection for brand image has been extended in common law jurisdictions such as the UK and the US, as well as in the combined civil and common law jurisdictions of the EU. Ilanah Fhima (2015) details a series of European cases. In *Bristol-Myers Squibb*, the Court of Justice of the European Union (CJEU) imposed restrictions to protect the image of the trademark owner (senior user) whose goods were being imported and re-sold.[4] The limitations required on-sellers (junior users) to package the goods in such a way that did not undermine their image. In *Copad*, the CJEU held that action of the junior user impaired the 'aura of luxury' of the goods and was 'likely to affect the actual quality of the goods'.[5] This highlighted the importance of social reputation to the value of a brand and its associated branded goods, which the court equated to physical damage. Similarly, in *Hollywood*, the trademark owner was entitled to protection of an 'image of health, dynamism and youth' connected to its mark.[6]

In *Intel*, the court recognised a right to protection of a mark against blurring of its image, but required the owner to show that such blurring led to a change in consumer behaviour, or the likelihood of such a change.[7] Importantly, this element of the *Intel* decision illustrates the function of labour-as-consumer and that the value of the trademark depends on consumer behaviour. Other intellectual property law scholars have also highlighted the important function of labour-as-consumer. Jennifer Davis and Spyros Maniatis (2010) rely on evidence of consumer behaviour to show that people are often more influenced by brand than they are by actual quality or specifications of a product. As a result, corporate strategies that rely on acquiring successful brands tend to be more profitable than those which innovate and compete with successful brands. Jessica Litman (1999) has made a similar argument about the possibility of competing on image, showing that persuasive advertising undermines investment in innovation, allowing firms to address niche markets without having to change anything but their marketing campaigns.

The extension of protection for brand owners is becoming increasingly controversial as courts adopt what Fhima calls a 'branding perspective' (Fhima, 2015: 235). The 2009 case of *L'Oréal* in the European Court of Justice attracted widespread criticism.[8] The claim was based on the defendant's use of a comparative marketing strategy. A perfume retailer (Bellure) produced fragrances that imitated those produced by L'Oréal and packaged them in a similar fashion. It was agreed that there was little prospect of confusion in the minds of consumers, but the trademark owner argued that Bellure was taking 'unfair advantage' of its property. The European Court's decision in favour of L'Oréal created a new source of protection for brand owners in trademark law. Dilution of trademarks by confusion or by tarnishment of the mark's reputation was already recognised. *L'Oréal* added a prohibition on 'freeriding' on the value of the mark.

A similar expansion took place in the US in 2006, when Congress passed the Trademark Dilution Revision Act (TDRA). This legislation revised and clarified the law regarding dilution to more closely align trademarks and brands (Mittelstaedt, 2015). The TDRA provides 'famous' marks with protection against blurring or loss of distinctiveness, and tarnishment, or loss of reputation. These changes facilitate greater control by brand owners over the destiny and value of their marks, and how they are used by others (Mittelstaedt, 2015).

The expansion of anti-dilution doctrine points to an important contradiction in trademark law, with respect to the co-productive relation between capital and labour-as-consumer. Lux (2011: 1079) argues that the only logical jurisprudential basis for expanding anti-dilution doctrine is to protect the financial investments made by brand owners. This Lockean defence of trademarks is flawed, according to Lux (2011), because the value of contemporary brands is as much dependent on the contribution of consumers as it is on brand owners. Luke McDonagh (2015) similarly argues that the strong protection of brand value and image ignores their heavy reliance on consumers. What this tension in the law reveals is that even though a brand is a relationship between a firm and its stakeholders, intellectual property law facilitates the brand owner's control of that relationship. Such control over the deployment of a brand's image and affective associations is necessary for owners to optimise their use, including activation of the derivative logic.

The tension between brand owners and other users of marks or brands becomes even more apparent in the law's treatment of parody and satirical uses. Trademark owners often argue that the reputations of their marks are undermined by parody and satire. The fervour with which brand owners defend their marks against these uses highlights the importance of their reputation.

In the US, Stacey Dogan and Mark Lemley observe a trend towards litigation 'against parodies that serve as brands, logos, or taglines for commercial products' (Dogan and Lemley, 2012: 99). Given the inconsistent judicial treatment of parody that the authors identify, this leaves open the possibility of actions for dilution of trademarks. There are similar ambiguities elsewhere. In England, although trademarks are protected from infringement by dilution only in the course of trade, some recent cases suggest a move towards a tendency to privilege the rights of intellectual property owners over free speech rights (Neuberger, 2015). One example is the divergent decisions on the satirical use of the UK Miss World trademark in cases between the early 1980s and the mid-2000s.[9] Lord Neuberger (2015) argues that courts in

132 *Producing ethical capital*

the UK are more inclined to protect the interests of famous marks (or brands) today than they have been in the past.

While the South African *Laugh It Off* case was decided in favour of the junior users (those engaging in parody) rather than the intellectual property owners,[10] Neuberger (2015) has expressed concern that this case may be decided differently in Europe. At issue in this matter was the junior user's production of t-shirts featuring Carling Black Label beers with 'Black labour' on the front and 'White guilt' on the back. The court found that this was a satirical and political use and found no infringement because there was no economic prejudice. Neuberger argued that that in the EU, particularly following *L'Oréal*, the case may be decided in favour of the trademark owners because a European court would be required to protect against this type of freeriding on the brand, regardless of economic prejudice.

The court's reasoning in *Laugh It Off* reveals the politics of branding in the context of a speculative moral economy. Sachs J observed that 'trademarks represent highly visible and immediately recognisable symbols of societal norms and values. The companies that own famous trademarks exert substantial influence over public and political issues, making them and their marks ripe and appropriate targets for parody and criticism' (*Laugh It Off* at para. 105).

Firms participate in public conversations and take positions on social issues, and make qualitative assertions about their organisations and their products, for the purpose of increasing sales of their products and/or to increase the value of the firm. The controversies regarding expansion of protection for trademarks demonstrate that the productive nature of the brand depends on a firm's capacity to engage in public discourse and to evoke qualitative and affective associations with consumers, and the extent of the firm's capacity to control the brand's image and qualitative associations.

Intensification of ethical capital production

The utility of thinking brands and ethical capital production through the lens of value theory becomes even more clear in considering recent developments in ICT that are intensifying the productive relation between capital, labour, ethics and risk.

The "labour processes" at work in the production of brands are intensified through these new technologies as information about consumers' priorities and preferences comes from a wider range of sources, including conversations online, purchasing decisions, travel routes, weekend activities, group memberships and more. As Brian Massumi has argued, 'we are hard at "work," even in leisure, for the production of capitalist surplus-value, all the while absorbed in our real-life process and its intensifying relational reticulation through ever-densifying social media' (Massumi, 2018: 30). Rather than relying only on what consumers tell them directly, firms are able to find out much more about labour-as-consumer's thoughts, feelings, opinions and desires through social media and other online behaviour. This increased capacity to monitor different elements of consumer behaviour renders the management of ESG risk increasingly productive of ethical capital.

Evolutions in marketing practice and research reflect the dependence on consumer participation observed above, and demonstrate an on-going process of finding new ways to learn about consumer behaviour and optimise the relationship between firm and labour-as-consumer. Interbrand, describing the strategy of 2018's most successful brands and, in particular, Amazon, says that '[b]eing truly customer-centric today means going deeper than just offering a product or service that the customer wants, and truly recognizing *how* customers think, feel and behave, and then delivering the most optimized experience possible across each and every customer touchpoint' (Interbrand, 2018). What is reflected in this approach is an effort to cultivate a deeper relationship with consumers and to develop a massified and personalised corporate strategy that leverages observations of consumer preferences and desires, both in relation to consumption (what people want to buy) and in relation to non-market activity (what people want to be or experience) (Havas, 2019a). Branding strategies are oriented around a 'promise' to consumers, and corporations organise their delivery of 'products, services and experiences' around this 'promise' (for example, Disney's magic, Amazon's fulfilment and Apple's empowerment) (Interbrand, n.d.a).

User-generated content on social media and other forms of surveillance technologies permit firms to obtain much more information about labour-as-consumer, facilitating a more fine-grained delivery of "mass individualised" products and services. Emerging methodologies and data sources used by brand valuation agencies reveal this expansive approach to acquiring information. In addition to corporate financial reports, investor presentations, analyst reports and data regarding trade in consumer goods, Interbrand's annual branding research process relies on text analytics and 'social listening'. Similarly, Brand Finance's annual review of leading brands includes social listening and data mining for analysing conversations about brands online, for understanding consumer sentiment, 'buzz' issues and how to most effectively drive consumer behaviour. One of many firms that provides these kinds of analytics for brand valuation is Infegy, which includes among its techniques analysis of 'billions of online conversations about topics most important to you', 'in-depth text analysis', machine learning and artificial intelligence, and real-time dashboards for continually updated analysis (Infegy, n.d.).

Measures of brand equity increasingly rely on observations of people's engagement with brands through online communications and retail platforms. Techniques like sentiment analysis and network analysis on social media provide a basis for measuring this value. Given the increasing capacity of ICT and surveillance capital to monitor and observe human behaviour, firms have ever-greater capacity to determine consumer preferences and likely behaviour based on conversations with friends, groups they are affiliated with, activities they engage in, places they travel to, and many more characteristics and behaviours (Manwaring, 2018; Zuboff, 2019).

The shift in how brand owners obtain information about labour-as-consumer represents a shift in the capital–labour relation analogous to the transition that Marx identified from absolute surplus value production to relative surplus value production. One of the earliest instances of the dialogic relation between consumers and brand owners is described by Schwarzkopf in the 1930s. Lux soap flakes pioneered affective advertising through its offer of an escape from the drudgery of domestic labour through personification of its brand identity. A copywriter for the advertising agency explained in the 1920s, 'I think of Lux as a member of the lesser nobility. She is probably a Marquise. She is gay, spontaneous, care-free. If you met her in the flesh she would greet you with squeals of delight and trills of laughter' (Schwarzkopf, 2010: 180).

In 1924, the marketers demonstrated their understanding of the dialogic nature of this relationship by directly contacting Lux consumers and requesting testimonials. The advertising firm received over 53,000 letters from women in the US, which revealed that users had begun to develop a range of alternate uses for the product, paving the way for brand extensions into new product lines (Schwarzkopf, 2010: 178). Firms were beginning to directly subsume labour-as-consumer into the process of producing brand values.

Modern ICT means that firms no longer need to rely on direct communications from consumers about their brands. Firms are able to find out much more about labour-as-consumer's thoughts and preferences. The emergence of more powerful and pervasive ICT is facilitating an acceleration of brand co-creation in two key ways, one active and the other passive. First, ICT makes direct communication between people and institutions possible (and easy). Internet-based communication technologies which enable individuals to generate and publish content, as well as social media platforms like X (formerly Twitter), Facebook and Instagram, facilitate consumers' active engagement with brands. By generating and sharing content, engaging with a brand online, and raising its profile through 'likes' and 'shares', consumers build brand equity (Gielens and Steenkamp, 2019; Quesenberry and Coolsen, 2019; Yuki, 2015). As the digital economy becomes more prevalent and

Brands and the (re)production of ethics   135

interactive, the opportunities for labour-as-consumer to participate in brand-building processes expand. Through social media and other platforms that allow users to generate content, labour-as-consumer has immense capacity to convey information about their emotions, preferences, political tendencies, relationships and much more. As Kylie Jarrett (2015) has shown with the concept of the digital housewife, participatory media and consumer culture is comparable to social reproductive labour in its contribution to value creation. Jarrett (2015) highlights the fact that capital has long relied on unpaid and affective labour in the home. People engage in digital prosumer or consumption labour for similar reasons: to build relationships, to enrich their own lives, to support and care for one another, to communicate and coordinate with one another. While social reproductive labour subsidises capital's costs of production by reducing labour costs, digital labour boosts the values of ICT firms, and the value of branded goods and services.

Firms recognise the significance of active consumer co-creation through online interaction and the user-generated content. Social media spending by brands is increasing and is the fastest growing channel for marketing spend (Carlson et al., 2019). Brand managers understand that social media is a crucial point of engagement with consumers, and that this is essential to increasing brand value in an era when consumers are part of the value co-creation process through 'sharing their knowledge, ideas, and preference information to support and collaborate with the brand' (Carlson et al., 2019: 1734). Firms undertake granular analysis of social media dynamics in order to maximise consumer engagement (Carlson et al., 2019; Kannan and Li, 2017; Quesenberry and Coolsen, 2019; Yuki, 2015).

While co-creative relationships between consumers and firms have been developing for a long time, interactive media engagement and increased opportunities for users and consumers to generate content are changing media practice. There are more opportunities for widely dispersed consumers to talk among themselves, and a much greater capacity to collect data about individuals for 'mass personalization of product offerings' (Gielens and Steenkamp, 2019: 368). Online and social media provide a wealth of tools and information for marketing. Text data provides extensive consumer insights, using techniques like sentiment analysis and machine learning to constantly improve and hone these techniques (Verhoef and Bijmolt, 2019). User-generated content is a valuable source of big data for these kinds of analyses (Liu et al., 2017). Artificial intelligence, big data and, in particular, machine learning technologies present further potential for optimisation of branding strategies (Fulgoni, 2013; Liu et al., 2017; Vermeer et al., 2019; Voorveld, 2019; Voorveld et al., 2018; Wiencierz and Röttger, 2017).

136 *Producing ethical capital*

This leads to the second, passive contribution that labour-as-consumer makes to generating brand value through new ICT. This is characterised as passive because there is not necessarily any direct or intentional engagement with a brand, but rather this kind of data is generated from incidental activity in an individual's daily life. Almost any kind of data can be used to develop what Lizzie O'Shea (2019: 21–22) has described as an 'abstract identity'. This abstract identity can be filtered, fused and sold for the purposes of firms developing more effective strategies to "centre" consumers within their organisations. As O'Shea puts it, 'our social, political and economic preferences as determined by the data collected about us, are generated and then repeatedly refined and used to determine advertising for us' (O'Shea, 2019: 21–22). Through the use of extensive data collection, artificial intelligence and cognitive computing, firms aim to use mass personalisation to structure their marketing plans to maximise "customer life-time value".

The generation of O'Shea's 'abstract identities' takes place through the observation of people in their daily lives. Zuboff (2019) argues that surveillance capitalists, such as Google and Facebook, use their observations of people in daily life as a source of raw material for creating what she calls behavioural surplus. These observations include scanning the content of emails and other messages; collecting personal information such as credit details; internet browsing histories; medical information; location data; photos; and group affiliations. The Internet of Things (IoT), or the networking of more and more objects from telephones to watches to fridges to fitness trackers, expands the possibilities for data mining and increases opportunities for this kind of digital consumer manipulation (Manwaring, 2018). The information gathered is bundled, analysed and traded as a commodity to customers such as advertisers (but also others, including political campaign strategists), enabling predictions of how people will behave and how people's behaviour can be manipulated, constituting a market in 'behavioural futures' (Zuboff, 2019: 100). In this way, Zuboff argues that 'surveillance capitalism feeds on every aspect of every human's experience' (Zuboff, 2019: 9). Digital technologies enable firms to capture an increasingly wide range of data about consumers, their preferences, vulnerabilities and cognitive biases (Manwaring, 2018). While marketing has always sought to influence consumer behaviour, these kinds of digital consumer manipulation are more pervasive, insidious and personalised than marketing practices in the past. Developments in ICT and the observations that they facilitate mean that whether or not an individual has an intentional relationship with a brand, they can be drawn into these processes of value creation, co-opted into building brand values. The processes by which labour-as-consumer is subsumed into the production of brand values have expanded and intensified,

Brands and the (re)production of ethics 137

and part of that intensification is a greater capacity for producing ethics as capital.

Conclusion

Commons wrote in the early 1900s that '[t]he corporation has no soul. Goodwill is its soul' (Commons, 1919: 20). Almost a century later, Lazzarato (2004) observed that immaterial production incorporates the worker's soul, along with their personality and subjectivity. The transformation of production and consumption practices which render image, information and affect so much more significant creates conditions in which capital grows through subsumption of labour in different ways: capital 'feeds off life itself' (Arvidsson, 2005: 252). The above analysis of brands and the relation between capital, labour, ethics and risk through which they are produced, exposes the ghoulish manner in which contemporary firms create a human face for themselves based on information generated by labour-as-consumers. The ethical component of the brand is generated by the hopes, preferences and outrages expressed by billions of people online and through the activity of their daily lives, which is subject to surveillance capital. Firms minimise their exposure to reputational and operational risks and maximise their opportunities to profit through leveraging a spread of ethical possibilities and positions. Through these interactions, ethics become a form of capital.

While brands are not exclusively vehicles for ethical capital or the management of ESG risks, as the responsible capital imaginary becomes increasingly prevalent, the opportunities to boost brand values through the production of ethics expand. The increased capacity to leverage different elements of consumer behaviour that is generated by the active and passive intensifications of the relation between capital and labour-as-consumer renders the management of ESG risk increasingly productive of ethical capital (and other forms of capital). As people become more willing to consider taking social or political action through consumption, or perhaps see consumption as one of the only vehicles available for action, ethics becomes a point of competition for firms and a point of comparison for investors. As financialised firms are increasingly configured and managed as a 'bundle of risks', ESG risk is the avenue through which ethics become productive. Brand valuation and social accounting standards provide a framework through which to assess those risks. As ICT develops, it expands the possibilities of learning about which particular ESG issues present financially material risks to hedge or lucrative opportunities to pursue, in which markets and consumer groups, intensifying the production of ethics as capital. At the same time, increasing disillusionment and disappointment in the practical realities of ethical capital in action are

138   *Producing ethical capital*

reflected in escalating claims of greenwashing and other forms of deceptive corporate conduct.

Notes

1 Case C-353/03 *Société des Produits Nestlé SA v Mars UK Ltd* [2005] ECR I-6135; *Colloseum Holding AG v Levi Strauss & Co.* [2013] EUECJ C-12/12 (18 April 2013); Case C-252/12 *Specsavers International Healthcare Ltd v Asda Stores Ltd* [2013] ETMR 46.
2 *Cadbury Schweppes v The Pub Squash Co Ltd* ('*Pub Squash*') (1980) 2 NSWLR 851.
3 *Pub Squash* at 22.
4 Case C-436/93 *Bristol-Myers Squibb v Paranova A/S C. H. Boehringer Sohn, Boehringer Ingelheim KG and Boehringer Ingelheim A/S v Paranova A/S; Bayer Aktiengesellschaft and Bayer Danmark A/S v Paranova A/S* ('*Bristol-Myers Squibb*') [1996] ECR I-3457.
5 Case C-59/08 *Copad SA v Christian Dior couture SA, Vincent Gladel and Société industrielle lingerie (SIL)* ('*Copad*') [2009] ECR I-3421.
6 *Hollywood S.A.S. v Souza Cruz S.A.R. 283/1999-3* ('*Hollywood*') [2002] ETMR 64.
7 Case C-252/07 *Intel Corp. Inc v CPM United Kingdom Ltd* ('*Intel*') [2008] ECR I-8823.
8 *L'Oréal SA v. Bellure NV* (C-487/07) [2009] ECR I-5185.
9 *Miss World (Jersey) Ltd v James Street Productions Ltd* [1981] F.S.R. 309; *Miss World Ltd v Channel 4 Television Corp.* [2007] EWHC 982.
10 *Laugh It Off Promotions CC v South African Breweries International (Finance) BV t/a Sabmark International and Another* (CCT42/04) [2005] ZACC 7; 2006 (1) SA 144 (CC); 2005 (8) BCLR 743 (CC) (27 May 2005).

Chapter 6

ESG information as an ethical capital asset

ESG is a pernicious strategy, because it allows the left to accomplish what it could never hope to achieve at the ballot box or through competition in the free market. ESG empowers an unelected cabal of bureaucrats, regulators and activist investors to rate companies based on their adherence to left-wing values. (Pence, 2022)

Gosh, it's nothing nearly as exciting as that. It's simply about companies and investors managing material risk factors to ensure long-term value creation. (Eccles, 2022, responding to Pence, 2022)

Introduction

As ESG edges into the mainstream of financial markets, political tensions are escalating. Mike Pence's comments in the *Wall Street Journal*, above, reflected similar sentiments to those of many, primarily Republican, politicians in the US who have been part of the recent "ESG backlash". ESG is positioned, by its detractors, as an anti-democratic strategy for forcing firms and financial markets to adopt progressive approaches to environmental and social issues. While Harvard Business School professor and leading expert on ESG Robert Eccles and many other experienced ESG advocates insist that ESG integration is value-free and objective, simply expanding the realm of financial risk management to include a wider range of issues, there is extensive confusion about what ESG is and does.

This chapter sets out the contours of the private and public sector response to this problem. The private sector response comprises the consolidation and growth of the ESG information industry. This industry is built around identifying and assessing ESG risks and opportunities and using that information to the advantage of investors. As well as providing a service to investors, the ESG information industry is a vehicle for profit among the information producers themselves. The production and exchange of ESG information is a nascent but rapidly growing segment in the financial services sector.

This generates revenue and profit for the firms that produce this information and is also a vector for increasing the profitability of asset managers and investment advisors which create financial products based on ESG ratings, indices and analyses.

The ESG information industry is also a space in which contestation is building from both progressive and conversative angles. Progressive social movements are contesting the accumulation of ethical capital which is based on groundless claims about ESG performance which have little connection to meaningful social change. These claims are contested through assertions of greenwashing and demands for higher standards of corporate accountability on ESG issues (Agnew et al., 2022; Global Witness, 2023). Conservative elements in the financial and political sphere are pushing back against the principle that finance should incorporate ESG considerations at all, or asserting their prerogative to pursue different ethical objectives, for example by prioritising extraction of fossil fuels (Masters and Temple-West, 2023a).

Alongside the expansion of the ESG information industry, public sector regulators have begun setting standards for ESG, which has largely been an unregulated segment of the financial sector to date. The EU has already legislated its sustainable finance disclosure regime, while the UK and the US have proposals afoot. Regulators have also begun taking enforcement action against investors, alleging greenwashing and other forms of misleading or deceptive conduct.

As industry players and regulators battle over the meaning and content of ESG investing, the limits and the contradictions of the responsible capital imaginary are exposed.

The ESG data industry

As ESG investing has become part of mainstream financial markets, the producers of ESG ratings and their underlying data take on a greater influence. ESG ratings and the services and information products associated with them can be thought of as another form of "ethical capital". These commodities, bought and sold in financial markets, are a source of profits to the firms that generate them and the investment managers who build financial products and indices around them. Whatever its practical impact on environmental and social outcomes, ESG investing and research is an increasingly lucrative and rapidly growing part of the financial services industry.

Estimates vary on revenue and spending in the ESG data industry. The EU's latest research into ESG ratings and data providers found widespread use of ESG ratings among financial market participants and expectations that the market will continue to grow, driven principally by investor demand

(BlackRock and European Commission, 2021; European Commission and ERM, 2020). In 2020, KPMG estimated that there are more than 150 firms worldwide offering ESG data products (KPMG, 2020: 45). Financial consultancy Opimas claims that ESG data spend globally was over USD 1 billion in 2021, comprising 70 per cent on ESG research and analytics, including ratings, raw data and other ESG products; and 30 per cent on ESG indices, which exceeded USD 300 million (Foubert, 2022). The compound annual growth rate for research and analytics was 24 per cent and for ESG indices it was 38 per cent (Foubert, 2022). Meanwhile, UBS already estimated the ESG data industry to be worth more than USD 2 billion in 2020, with potential growth leading to a doubling of revenues by 2025 to more than USD 5 billion (IOSCO, 2021; UBS, 2020).

A 2022 global study of over 1,100 investors found that the growing market for ESG ratings, data and services is supported by widespread investor demand (Capital Group, 2022). The UK Treasury reported that 65 per cent of institutional investors used ESG ratings at least once per week in 2020 (HM Treasury, 2023). In a 2021 report, the Board of IOSCO, the international peak body for securities regulators and the global standard setter for securities regulation, found that most asset managers, pension funds and central banks use ESG ratings regularly (IOSCO, 2021: 24). IOSCO (2021) anticipates that the ESG data industry is likely to grow further given two key drivers: the increasing regulatory attention on ESG and sustainable finance; and the increasing investor demand for sustainable financial products. These two drivers are also connected as financial sector clients increasingly demand more clarity and transparency in ESG ratings and products, and credible research to show a connection between ESG and better financial performance. IOSCO also notes that ESG data products are 'constantly evolving to respond to new topics of interest … and emerging areas of attention' (IOSCO, 2021: 7–8).

Asset managers are a crucial client to the ESG industry, responsible for around 60 per cent of the spend on ESG data (European Commission and ERM, 2020: 16). In addition, some of the products they offer, such as ESG-based index funds, are co-designed with ESG data providers and are central to deploying ESG strategies (Capital Group, 2022: 26). ESG is a key driver of building market share for asset managers courting investors' appetite for sustainable finance (Flood, 2023a). The world's three largest asset managers, BlackRock, Vanguard and State Street, manage enormous investment portfolios on behalf of their clients. The business model of asset managers differs slightly from that of institutional investors and other financial market participants (Braun, 2021). Financial returns for asset managers are driven by fees on their assets under management (AUM), in contrast to other investors who are motivated by investee company profits and distributions to shareholders. This means that asset managers are motivated to attract and retain client funds, and to maximise the management and performance fees they are able to charge on those funds. Part of the pitch by asset managers to their potential clients is that astute integration of ESG risks improves their investment performance, particularly for BlackRock.

BlackRock is a publicly traded firm which provides investment management services to institutional and retail clients. It had USD 8.6 trillion under management as at December 2022, up from USD 6 trillion in 2018. BlackRock booked revenue at USD 17.8 billion in 2022, with USD 5.1 billion profit. Consistent with Braun's (2021) analysis, revenue for BlackRock is comprised primarily of investment management fees, which are typically a percentage of AUM. Base fees accounted for approximately USD 14 billion in 2022, or 80 per cent of total revenue (BlackRock, 2023). Vanguard, the world's second largest asset manager after BlackRock, does not report its financial results publicly due to its ownership structure, but State Street reported total 2022 revenue at USD 12.1 billion, of which USD 9.6 billion (79 per cent) was investment management fees (State Street Global Advisors, 2022: 34).

Geographically, the majority of the ESG data spend is in Europe (over 60 per cent) and one third in North America. This regional breakdown is consistent with the locations of most ESG data providers, which are in Europe and North America, as well as key sites for institutional investors and asset managers. It is anticipated that Europe's share of the ESG data market will continue to grow due to compliance requirements under the new sustainable finance disclosure regime (European Commission and ERM, 2020: 7).

Key products and services offered by the ESG data industry include both ratings or scores and other data products. Ratings, rankings and scores provide an 'assessment of an entity, an instrument or an issuer exposure to ESG risks and/or opportunities' (IOSCO, 2021: 10). Providers use different information sources and proprietary methodologies to develop these assessments. ESG scores tend to be based on quantitative analysis while ratings are more likely to be a mix of quantitative and qualitative analysis, accompanied by a discursive report by an analyst. In addition to these assessments of risk, ESG data products include raw data that clients can manipulate themselves, screening tools to support investment decisions, controversy alerts for particular issues, indices for investment benchmarking, consulting services, certification and third-party opinions.

IOSCO has found that the most popular ESG product offerings include ESG scores; daily monitoring and alerts; corporate scores for climate physical and transition risk; and various forms of investment screening, including norm-based, sector-based and controversy-based (IOSCO, 2021: 13). There is a geographic influence on the popularity of ESG products. Screening

ESG data providers

The growing economic significance of the ESG data industry as a site of accumulation is reflected in its concentration and expansion. In the 2010s–20s, the industry has undergone a phase of consolidation with traditional credit rating agencies, exchanges and index providers acquiring smaller boutique ESG firms. MSCI, Institutional Shareholder Services (ISS) (a subsidiary of Deutsche Börse) and Sustainalytics (a subsidiary of Morningstar) are estimated to control around 60 per cent of the ESG data market (HM Treasury, 2023). Other key firms in the sector include Moody's, S&P, Bloomberg and London Stock Exchange Group (LSEG) (in particular, its subsidiaries FTSE Russell and Refinitiv). In addition to these, the large asset managers like BlackRock, State Street, UBS and JP Morgan are also investing heavily in their own in-house ESG teams (Morningstar, 2023: 20).

Early in the recent phase of consolidation, KLD, a leading ESG player, was acquired by MSCI via its 2010 purchase of RiskMetrics. More recently, MSCI's traditional financial ratings competitors have also sought a stake in the industry. Moody's acquired Vigeo EIRIS, which was itself a merger of a British boutique firm and a Franco-Belgian sustainable investment research agency. Morningstar acquired Sustainalytics, a Dutch firm, which had previously acquired the Swedish research and advisory firm GES International. S&P acquired Trucost and later CICERO, which provides evaluations of green bonds and sustainable finance, as well as RobecoSAM, an ESG research firm. Refinitiv has been purchased by LSEG (Table 6.1). The outcome of these mergers and acquisitions is that there is now a mix of large international providers alongside smaller ESG rating agencies. The smaller firms tend to have a particular geographic or industry focus or a speciality in particular data sets or issues. In addition, there are fintech firms which focus on the application of big data and artificial intelligence in their offerings.

Analysis of the business models and financial results of these firms reveals the increasingly lucrative contribution made by ESG information products and services. Firms in the ESG data industry offer similar services, but with wide variations in rating outcomes, often due to their differing choice and weighting of indicators. Indeed, for some time, this differentiation was a key part of their pitch to different potential clients, 'proprietary scoring methodologies and unique metrics' that claim to offer the most compelling research and prescient interpretation of the data (Brackley et al., 2022).

144 *Producing ethical capital*

Table 6.1 Some acquisitions in the ESG data industry

Year of acquisition	ESG firm	Acquired by
2009	KLD	RiskMetrics
2009	Innovest	RiskMetrics
2010	RiskMetrics	MSCI
2010	ISS	MSCI
2014	FTSE Russell	LSEG
2016	EIRIS	Vigeo
2016	Trucost	S&P
2017	Sustainalytics (40 per cent)	Morningstar
2019	Vigeo EIRIS	Moody's
2019	GES International	Sustainalytics
2019	RobecoSAM	S&P
2020	Sustainalytics (60 per cent)	Morningstar
2020	ISS	Deutsche Börse
2021	Refinitiv	LSEG
2022	CICERO	S&P

MSCI, for example, offers ratings on 8,500 companies globally, and uses its data to generate MSCI indices, many of which have an ESG component. While it is a generalist investment advisory and services firm, MSCI aims to position itself as a niche provider and a 'thought leader' (MSCI, 2023: 4) in relation to ESG-specific services and data products. Demonstrating the strong connection between the ESG data industry and asset managers, MSCI's largest single client is asset manager BlackRock, which accounted for 10.3 per cent of its revenues in 2022; over 95 per cent of the revenue from BlackRock was based on fees paid on assets invested in BlackRock's ETFs, which are themselves based on MSCI indexes (MSCI, 2023: 2).

MSCI reports its revenue in four segments, including ESG and Climate, which represented 10 per cent of total revenue in 2022, compared with 58 per cent for Index, 25 per cent for Analytics and 6 per cent for All Other (MSCI, 2023). Although ESG and Climate is reported separately, it is also integrated into other segments. Specifically, MSCI provides data, ratings, research and tools for investors to manage regulation around ESG issues, to meet client expectations regarding ESG performance and to integrate management of ESG risk into their portfolios. In the Index segment, MSCI offers many ESG-based Index funds which screen or manage for ESG risk. In Analytics, the firm offers advice to investors about risk/return calculations on a range of issues, including climate, and supports investor clients to meet regulatory and reporting requirements.

ESG information as an ethical capital asset   145

MSCI describes ESG as a growing market for the firm, and it is a fast-growing contributor to its financial results. In 2022, MSCI's overall operating revenues grew by 16 per cent, with the majority of growth in ESG and Climate, which was up by USD 60 million or 37 per cent (MSCI, 2023: 37). Operating profit (EBITDA) in the ESG and Climate segment increased by 105 per cent to USD 32 million. ESG and Climate represents 18 per cent of the firm's adjusted EBITDA, which is an over-representation in relation to revenue (at only 10 per cent). The ESG and Climate run rate is fastest growing among all MSCI segments at 33 per cent, and ESG and Climate has exceptionally high client retention rates (MSCI, 2023).

Competitor Sustainalytics publishes ratings on more than 13,000 companies. Morningstar provides research, data and analysis on a wide range of issues and since its acquisition of Sustainalytics, now delivers its ESG-specific services through this subsidiary. Its 'ESG Risk Ratings' underpin the Morningstar Sustainability Fund Ratings for a range of mutuals and ETFs, investable indices and several investment platforms. Morningstar Sustainalytics is also the world's largest provider of second party opinions for green bonds (Morningstar, 2023: 19). Morningstar's estimation of ESG's economic value is represented in the purchase price for the Sustainalytics acquisition. In 2017, it acquired 40 per cent of the ESG specialist firm, valued at USD 75 million with a book value of USD 25 million. In 2020, Sustainalytics purchased the remaining 60 per cent stake, resulting in a total book value of assets at USD 49 million and USD 134 million in goodwill.

As in the case of MSCI, ESG is a growth market for Morningstar. The firm derives revenue from licences to its data products (approximately 70 per cent); fees for managing assets (approximately 15 per cent); and transaction-based revenue for credit ratings and ad sales (approximately 15 per cent) (Morningstar, 2023: 11). Sustainalytics was one of its main drivers of revenue growth in 2022, as well as growth in staff. The ESG business generated USD 103 million in revenue in 2022, growing by 30.5 per cent, or 41.0 per cent on an organic basis, which was driven by demand for compliance and reporting support from clients regarding changes in the EU (Morningstar, 2023: 59). In 2022, Morningstar Sustainalytics expanded its ratings coverage universe by around 30 per cent, in particular growing its coverage of Chinese companies in Shanghai and Shenzhen (Morningstar, 2023: 20).

ISS, the world's largest proxy advisory firm and a majority-owned subsidiary of Deutsche Börse, publishes ratings on almost 12,000 firms and 25,000 funds through ISS ESG. Deutsche Börse defines its net revenues from ESG activities as those revenues from products 'related to the transformation of the real and/or financial economy in terms of environmental, social and governance aspects' (Deutsche Börse, 2023: 39). Key consumers of its ESG information products are investors, asset managers and market participants.

Deutsche Börse reports its revenue in four segments: Data and Analytics, Trading and Clearing, Funds Services and Securities Services. ESG activity is primarily located within its Data and Analytics segment, and includes sales of 'ESG data, ratings, scores, and reporting' (Deutsche Börse, 2023: 40). The firm also recognises revenue from ESG activities in Trading and Clearing (trading in ESG-based ETFs, ESG indices and fixed income indices), Fund Services (revenue linked to ESG funds) and Securities Services (proxy voting services) (Deutsche Börse, 2023: 40).

In 2022, Deutsche Börse earned around 10 per cent of its net revenue from ESG activities, and these revenues grew by 31 per cent (Deutsche Börse, 2023: 28). In addition, it reported net ESG revenue within its Data and Analytics segment at EUR 250 million for 2022 (Deutsche Börse, 2023: 158). This accounted for more than one third of revenue in the Data and Analytics segment. Like other financial market participants, Deutsche Börse anticipates strong growth in the ESG data industry.

Moody's is a traditional credit rating agency which offers ratings on nearly 34,000 organisations and structured deals. It has diversified its business by acquiring ESG specialist firms, notably Vigeo EIRIS, and integrating their ESG data products into its existing offerings. It frames its services and products as tools to support investor decision-making, and organises its business into two segments: Analytics and Investor Services. Each of Moody's business segments generates around half of the firm's total revenue of USD 5.4 billion (Moody's, 2023). Moody's does not report its ESG segment revenue separately from its investor services and analytics businesses, but it has reported that it attributed USD 90 million in goodwill related to proprietary models for its ESG analysis business (Moody's, 2023: 93).

LSEG delivers ESG data services and products primarily through its subsidiaries Refinitiv and FTSE Russell. Refinitiv, previously known as Thomson Reuters, offers ESG scores on 11,800 companies. FTSE Russell primarily derives revenue from the sale of licences for its market indices. LSEG reports that it provides ESG data and scores for more than 15,000 companies, which can be used for individual investment analysis as well as for benchmarking ETFs and mutuals, and delivers ESG indices through FTSE Russell which comprise USD 296 billion in AUM (LSEG, 2022: 27).

Bloomberg is also a major provider of ESG data products, as well as a broader range of investment analytics, tools and news. With a long-standing position as a provider of data and analysis to financial markets, Bloomberg has positioned itself as a leader in relation to ESG. Its offerings to clients include financial products (analytics, data, indices and scores), as well as research and news media, and specific services for legal and tax professionals.

ESG information as an ethical capital asset   147

Given the firm is privately held, it does not report its ESG data revenues separately, but some estimations can be drawn from what is known about Bloomberg's revenue and business model.

In 2022, Bloomberg's revenue was USD 12.2 billion and the company's CEO, who owns 88 per cent of its stock, is estimated to have a net worth of USD 82 billion (Forbes, n.d.). The company's Terminals, which also offer ESG data, generate around 75 per cent of its revenue (Milton, 2019). Bloomberg's own ESG data products cover over 14,000 companies. In addition, Bloomberg sells access to third-party ESG scores for MSCI, Sustainalytics, ISS and RobecoSAM. Bloomberg also offers index products, many of which are co-branded with other ESG data providers. These include the Bloomberg SASB ESG Indices, which have been developed with SASB and State Street Global Advisors, and the Bloomberg MSCI ESG Fixed Income Indices (Bloomberg, 2022).

Like its collaborators and competitors, Bloomberg observes that ESG is a growth market. The ESG issues 'that have the most impact on [Bloomberg's] business' (Bloomberg, 2022: 16) include opportunities in relation to offering new or enhanced ESG products and services, developing news media that focuses on ESG issues, and integration of ESG into non-ESG focused products and services. The company has also identified that its clients seek more high-quality ESG data sets, decision support tools that incorporate ESG factors, analytics that enable peer benchmarking of sustainability initiatives, and research on emerging trends. In line with this, Bloomberg is increasing its capacity in news reporting and analysis on ESG issues. Bloomberg's media team comprises 2,700 journalists and analysts in 120 countries, who deliver over 5,000 stories a day to the company's subscribers (Bloomberg, 2022: 38). In 2021, Bloomberg expanded its ESG reporting team and published 53 per cent more stories on ESG issues and 78 per cent more stories on climate (Bloomberg, 2022: 30).

Some of the ESG data products Bloomberg generates for investors include ESG data for around 12,000 companies, Scope 1 and 2 emissions data for more than 50,000 companies, and Bloomberg's proprietary ES scores for more than 2,500 companies. In addition to these, Bloomberg produces climate transition scores, carbon emissions performance scores and clean energy data sets, data on environmental exposures, including physical risk (such as extreme weather events) as well as transition risks (regulatory changes), and guidance on sustainability-linked debt. Bloomberg has also developed products in relation to new regulatory regimes such as the EU's sustainable finance taxonomy, including a reporting tool with coverage of 45,000 companies and services to support clients' disclosure and compliance with the EU regime. Consistent with this new product development, some of Bloomberg's strongest client demand is in the legal and regulatory domain.

148 *Producing ethical capital*

Bloomberg Law clients have extensive ESG advisory businesses. Nearly 40 per cent of its law clients have a dedicated ESG risk group, while 62 per cent of firms report that they had advised on corporate ESG risk strategy during the past 12 months; 42 per cent on ESG regulatory compliance; 40 per cent on environmental compliance; 38 per cent on ESG disclosure requirements; and 35 per cent on renewable energy (Bloomberg, 2022: 37). As the regulatory landscape develops further, this is expected to provide further impetus for growth in ESG data and information products and services.

Regulation and standardisation of the ESG data industry

The publication of ESG information and ratings was largely unregulated until the early 2020s. As discussed in relation to debates about sustainability accounting (see Chapter 4), there have long been calls for standardisation and harmonisation of sustainability disclosure and corporate reporting. The European regulator, European Securities and Markets Authority (ESMA), has expressed frustration due to the lack of consistency and transparency regarding ESG rating methodologies (Andrew, 2022) as have the users of ESG data products and ratings, who also identify bias and conflicts of interest, weak correlation of ratings and reliability as common issues (European Commission, 2022; European Commission and ERM, 2020). Others have observed the uneven distribution of ESG ratings due to the exclusion of many privately held companies, and companies listed on smaller exchanges or in emerging markets (Brackley et al., 2022). The lack of regulation, standardisation and consistency in corporate reporting on ESG issues has driven growth in the private market for ESG data products and services, as well as driving the establishment of private sector standardisation initiatives like those offered by SASB and Integrated Reporting, discussed in Chapter 5.

Recent rapid growth of ESG funds along with political controversy regarding ESG investing (Agnew et al., 2022; Hancock and Bryan, 2023; Miller, 2022; Politi and Fedor, 2023) are accelerating regulatory moves towards standardising ESG investing practices and the information underlying them. Escalating concerns and scandals about greenwashing, and the exposure of contradictions between sustainability claims and practice, are generating chaotic conditions in the ESG investing market. Politicians in the US, in particular, are in conflict over the integration of ESG issues into investment decisions (Politi and Fedor, 2023). Florida Governor Ron DeSantis has banned the consideration of ESG issues in investment decisions relating to the state's pension fund (DeSantis, 2022). Attorneys-General in nineteen Republican-governed states have accused BlackRock of climate activism in its investment practices (Masters, 2022), while Democrat-governed states such as Maryland and Illinois have legislated to require state investment funds to consider ESG (Ropes & Gray, n.d.).

Much of the controversy surrounding ESG integration relates to the variability of ESG ratings, the opacity of investment decision-making based on ESG criteria and the weak definition of ESG as a practice. These criticisms are not only made by politicians but have also been a staple of the academic and popular discourse about ESG in recent years. A 2021 report by IOSCO revealed many limitations to ESG data, which have also been cited in the European Commission's work on regulating the sustainable finance market (European Commission, 2022; IOSCO, 2021). Some of the problems identified include considerable variation in ESG ratings and products, due to differences in geographic and industry coverage as well as differences in the criteria on which they are based. There is also limited transparency about how ESG ratings agencies and analysts make their decisions, little communication between ratings agencies and the companies they assess, and high risks of conflicts of interest. These concerns have spurred regulators, especially in Europe, to standardise ESG metrics and disclosures by rating agencies (Fisher and Bryan, 2023).

ESG ratings providers occupy an ambiguous space between the roles of traditional financial credit rating agencies (and many of the major players are traditional credit rating agencies, including MSCI, Moody's and S&P) and investment research services. Craig Coben (2023) sets out the contours of current debates about how to standardise and regulate ESG data products, and how to categorise these firms and the services they provide. Coben argues that there are two options for regulators. One is to treat ESG data providers as investment researchers or brokers with idiosyncratic approaches based on different theories about what will drive a firm's performance. This would only require regulations ensuring that ESG providers are not subject to conflicts of interest. The second option for regulators is to treat ESG data providers like credit rating agencies. These agencies are required to meet standards both for registration and for credibility of their ratings. This regulatory model would require managing conflicts as well as transparency, standards for data collection, demonstrating the materiality of data used, methodology for analysis and objectives underlying the analysis. In line with the second of these approaches, IOSCO recommends that securities regulators require ESG data providers to disclose their data sources and their methodologies, and describe how conflicts of interest and confidential information are managed. It also recommends that ESG data providers be subject to due diligence reviews and that information gathering and communication processes be improved (IOSCO, 2021). ESG ratings users have expressed similar preferences for increased standardisation and transparency

150   *Producing ethical capital*

to promote greater consistency and comparability of ratings and data products (European Commission, 2022).

Regulators in various jurisdictions, notably the European Union as well as the United States federal securities regulator and the UK's Financial Conduct Authority (FCA), are in the process of tightening regulation of the ESG sector and self-described sustainable finance markets. The regulations vary significantly but share prohibitions on greenwashing, broadly require more stringent disclosures by ESG data providers, and restrict marketing of financial products which claim green or ethical credentials. There are already several regulations in force in the EU regarding disclosures by financial market participants on sustainable finance, along with a taxonomy which provides a definition of environmentally sustainable investment. The EU is in an on-going process of research, consultation and revision, with new regulations coming into force, such as the Corporate Sustainability Reporting Directive, which firms will need to report against from 2024 (European Commission, n.d.). In September 2023, the US SEC finalised new regulations for naming of investment funds, with the objective to 'ensure that a fund's portfolio aligns with a fund's name' (Gensler, 2023). Rules proposed in March 2022 to regulate disclosure and marketing of ESG funds are yet to be finalised (SEC, 2022). The UK FCA began consultation in relation to climate change and green finance in 2018 and has since developed more targeted consultation, research and regulatory proposals in relation to specific aspects of ESG information. The UK Treasury announced in December 2022 that it would consult on a regulatory regime for ESG ratings providers. It further announced in late 2023 that it plans to introduce more stringent regulation of ESG ratings agencies as early as January 2024, following the announcement by the European Commission in June 2023 that it would require more careful management of conflicts of interest by ratings firms and greater transparency (Fisher and Bryan, 2023). These moves suggest that regulators are likely to treat ESG data and ratings providers in a similar manner to traditional credit rating agencies, rather than allowing for more idiosyncratic approaches which have prevailed to date.

EU Sustainable Finance Regulation

As part of its sustainable finance strategy, the EU Commission has enacted a series of regulations regarding disclosure and marketing of financial products that include some reference to environmental or social characteristics, or 'sustainable finance'. These include the Sustainable Finance Disclosure Regulation (SFDR), enacted in 2019,[1] and the EU Taxonomy Regulation, which is an amendment to the SFDR, enacted in June 2020.[2] In addition, in early 2023, the EU's Corporate Sustainability Reporting Directive (CSRD) entered into force. The CSRD introduces more stringent standards for corporate reporting on a range of ESG issues, with which around 50,000 firms will need to comply from 2024.

The SFDR mandates different levels of disclosure depending on how financial products are marketed. Products which promote 'environmental or social characteristics' (Article 8 products) must include information on how those characteristics are met. For products which explicitly have 'sustainable investment' as an objective (Article 9 products), disclosures should explain how that objective is attained, with reference to the EU's definition of sustainable investment. In addition to these disclosure requirements, the SFDR also requires certain disclosures from financial market participants, regardless of whether they promote an ESG or sustainability focus. Financial institutions are required to publicly disclose their policies about the integration of sustainability risks into their investment decision-making and advice at the entity level (Article 3); and descriptions of how sustainability risks are integrated into their investment decisions for particular products (Article 6). Where financial institutions decide sustainability risks are not relevant, Article 6 requires that they explain why. Given that 'sustainability risk' is defined as 'an environmental, social or governance event or condition that, if it occurs, could cause an actual or a potential material negative impact on the value of the investment' (Article 2), the SFDR effectively requires financial market participants to integrate ESG risks into their financial products or to defend their decision not to do so.

The Taxonomy Regulation is a key element of the EU's anti-greenwashing provisions. It provides four criteria for determining what constitutes an 'environmentally sustainable investment'. First, the investment must contribute substantially to one or more of the six environmental objectives set out in the EU taxonomy. Second, the investment must not significantly harm any of those environmental objectives. Third, the investment must be carried out in compliance with the 'minimum safeguards' on labour rights (ILO), human rights (UN Guiding Principles) and the OECD Guidelines for Multinational Enterprises. Finally, the investment must comply with 'technical screening criteria', as established by the European Commission. The six allowable environmental objectives for establishing an environmentally sustainable investment include climate change mitigation; climate change adaptation; the sustainable use and protection of water and marine resources; the transition to a circular economy; pollution prevention and control; and the protection and restoration of biodiversity and ecosystems.

US SEC proposals regarding ESG labelling and disclosure

The SEC Climate and ESG taskforce is proposing a range of regulatory changes which will be relevant to ESG investing. In September 2023, the SEC finalised a change to the Names Rule which will require investment managers to ensure that the name of a fund is reflected in the portfolio. That is, a manager of a fund that is named with a term such as 'ESG', 'green' or 'sustainable' will need to define the fund's investment approach, in accordance with the name, and ensure that 80 per cent of the portfolio is consistent with that approach (Gensler, 2023).

In addition to this change, the SEC has proposed several rules regarding climate disclosure and ESG disclosures. The May 2022 proposal for new labelling and disclosure requirements for ESG does not prescribe what ESG investing is but asks investors to define their own approach, consistent with the derivative logic of ethics that permeates responsible investment. The SEC proposes three types of funds for the purposes of these disclosure rules. The first is an Integration fund which would 'consider one or more ESG factors alongside other, non-ESG factors in investment decisions' (SEC, 2022: 14). The second is an ESG-focused fund which would 'focus on one or more ESG factors by using them as a significant or main consideration in selecting investments or in engaging with portfolio companies' (SEC, 2022: 14). The SEC states that ESG-focused strategies would involve screening investments based on ESG criteria, such as excluding or including companies based on carbon emissions, workforce diversity or other issues; or they would involve engaging with corporate managers on ESG issues through direct engagement or proxy voting (SEC, 2022: 14). The third category, Impact Funds, are a subset of ESG-focused funds. These have a specific ESG impact or objective, comprising targeted portfolio investments to achieve measurable ESG outcomes (SEC, 2022: 14). The SEC proposes a layered disclosure framework which becomes more stringent and onerous according to the degree of the product's claims to promote sustainability.

UK proposals regarding ESG and sustainable investment

In addition to the UK Treasury's declaration that ESG credit ratings will soon be subject to new regulatory requirements (Fisher and Bryan, 2023), the FCA has indicated its intention to introduce new rules on labelling, marketing and disclosure for financial products with an 'ESG' or 'sustain-ability' dimension. The draft rules have been released for comment but are yet to be finalised. Proposals indicate that financial institutions will not be permitted to promote investments with sustainability-type labels unless they fall into one of the FCA's new categories. Proscribed descriptors include but are not limited to 'ESG', 'environmental', 'social', 'governance', 'climate', 'impact', 'sustainable', 'sustainability', 'responsible', 'green', 'SDG' (sustainable development goals), 'Paris-aligned' and 'net zero'.

The FCA's proposed new categories for sustainable investments include 'sustainable focus', 'sustainable improver' and 'sustainable impact'. Sustainable focus products will be those with an objective to maintain a high standard of sustainability in the profile of assets by investing to either meet a credible standard of environmental and/or social sustainability or align with a specified environmental and/or social sustainability theme. Sustainable improvers will be products that may not qualify as sustainable now but have an objective to deliver measurable improvements in the sustainability profile of assets over time. Sustainable impact products are those with an explicit objective to achieve a positive, measurable contribution to sustainable outcomes. These are invested in assets that provide solutions to environmental or social problems, often in underserved markets, or aim to address observed market failures (FCA, 2022: 31).

Disclosure and reporting requirements attached to each of these product lines incorporate stipulations that sustainability impacts and standards be 'credible' and 'measurable', meaning 'robust, independently assessed, evidence-based and transparent' (FCA, 2022: 41). In addition to the category-specific disclosures, the FCA requires financial institutions to meet disclosure requirements on five over-arching principles regarding governance, policy, strategy, key performance indicators and stewardship. The UK proposal also imposes an explicit prohibition on greenwashing, which stipulates that information communicated to clients must be clear, fair and not misleading. The FCA argues that this anti-greenwashing rule reiterates existing rules rather than imposing a new obligation, but is indicative of an intention on the part of the regulator to be more active in enforcement.

Exposing the limits of ethical capital

The concerns expressed by securities regulators in proposing or legislating these new requirements for disclosure and labelling primarily relate to safeguarding investors' financial interests, the proper pricing of risks, transparency and efficiency of markets, and appropriate capital allocation (European Commission, 2019; FCA, 2022; IOSCO, 2021; SEC, 2022). That is, the approaches of securities regulators remain embedded in assumptions about properly functioning, competitive financial markets and a certain confidence in the market's capacity to price ESG risk. While the impacts of these regulations remain to be seen, there are already indications that the imperative to meet credible, robust standards of environmental and social performance is exposing the contradictions embedded in the responsible capital imaginary.

The rapid growth of "ethical capital" production is increasingly accompanied by frustration with firms that make unsubstantiated green or sustainability claims while making few meaningful or material changes in their operations. This frustration is being channelled into litigation and other complaints of greenwashing and corporate misconduct. Much of this action has focused on breaches of consumer law and requirements regarding misleading or deceptive business practices in commerce and finance. In August 2021, the Australasian Centre for Corporate Responsibility (ACCR) brought claims against gas company Santos, alleging misleading or deceptive conduct under the Australian Corporations Act and the Australian Consumer Law, relating to Santos's net zero and clean energy claims in its 2020 annual report. The litigation was expanded in August 2022 to include allegations of greenwashing in the company's 2020 Investor Day Briefing and 2021 Climate Change Report (ACCR, 2022). In 2022, Greenpeace France, Friends of the Earth France and Notre Affaire à Tous, along with lawyers at ClientEarth, launched a greenwashing complaint in the French courts, arguing that TotalEnergies is defying EU consumer law with misleading claims about its net zero strategy (Jessop et al., 2022). NGO Zero Waste France filed a complaint in Strasbourg and Paris against Adidas and New Balance, under the French consumer code. The companies' false environmental claims, the NGO alleges, are likely to mislead consumers about the environmental impacts of fast fashion, which is estimated to contribute 2 per cent to global greenhouse gas emissions (Mathews, 2022; *Time News*, 2022).

Several organisations have sought to use consumer law in the US against fossil fuel firms. Earthworks, Global Witness and Greenpeace have collaborated on their complaint to the Federal Trade Commission that Chevron undermines consumer interests by presenting itself as 'climate-friendly' though fossil fuels are at the core of its business (McCormick, 2021). The government of New York City used consumer protection law to sue several energy firms and the American Petroleum Institute in relation to greenwashing claims. The lawsuit, filed in the Supreme Court of the State of New York, alleged that Big Oil companies use their promotional activities to imply purchase and use of their products is beneficial in addressing climate change, failing to disclose the impacts of those products. The suit also alleged greenwashing advertising campaigns enable Big Oil to present themselves as corporate champions of the transition to a low carbon economy while profiting from the sale of damaging fossil fuels (New York City Government, 2021).

Other activists have sought to use international standards for responsible corporate conduct as a vehicle for greenwashing claims. In December 2019, action against BP in the UK alleged that the company had breached its obligations under the OECD's Guidelines for Multinational Enterprises. Legal advocacy group ClientEarth argued that BP's advertising implied it is a renewable energy company, when 96 per cent of its investments related to oil and gas. BP discontinued its advertising campaign before the complaint could be mediated (UK National Contact Point, 2020). Another complaint filed at the UK National Contact Point for the OECD Guidelines has been accepted for mediation (UK National Contact Point, 2022). A coalition of NGOs acting under the umbrella name 'Forest Litigation Collaborative' has argued that UK wood-burning electricity generator Drax misleads consumers about its climate impacts. Drax's power plant burns millions of tonnes of wood pellets each year. Wood pellets emit more carbon pollution than coal. Despite this, Drax earned GBP 982.5 million in ratepayer-funded renewable energy subsidies in 2021, over GBP 2.68 million every day, for generating electricity by burning wood.

In line with the flurry of activity around regulating the labelling, marketing and disclosure requirements for ESG investment funds, regulators are also showing a greater appetite for enforcement action. In May 2022, authorities in Germany took action against a subsidiary of Deutsche Bank in relation to misleading statements about its ESG investments (Miller et al., 2022). The UK's FCA has publicly criticised ESG credit rating providers for providing misleading information (Flood, 2023b). The US SEC established its Climate and ESG taskforce in early 2021 (SEC, 2021). The taskforce has since brought actions against financial institutions such as BNY Mellon and Goldman Sachs, as well as mining, healthcare and insurance companies (SEC, n.d.; Barton, 2022). Both BNY Mellon and Goldman Sachs settled the claims with payments of USD 1.5 million and USD 4 million, respectively.

The Australian Securities and Investments Commission (ASIC) took its first enforcement actions regarding greenwashing in October 2022. ASIC issued four infringement notices against Tlou Energy alleging the company made false or misleading sustainability-related statements via the Australian Securities Exchange (ASX) in October 2021. Tlou's statements included claims regarding carbon neutrality, 'low emissions', 'clean energy' and the company's capacity to generate electricity from solar power (ASIC, 2022). In January 2023, ASIC issued three more infringements against Black Mountain Energy in relation to its 'net zero' claims and other statements regarding its greenhouse gas emissions (ASIC, 2023).

In addition to consumer protection law, the emerging regulation of disclosures related to ESG investing also seems to provide avenues for contestation. In early 2023, the US-based NGO Mighty Earth filed a whistle-blower complaint with the SEC in relation to a sustainability-linked bond for Brazilian agrifood company JBS (Mitchell, 2023). Mighty Earth relies on a second party opinion about the bond written by ISS's ESG division. The complaint highlights the discrepancy between JBS's claims to achieve net zero by 2040 and the reality that its emissions have increased in recent years, as well as its exclusion of scope 3 emissions from the analysis.

Shortly after, NGO Global Witness lodged a complaint with the SEC against Shell, claiming the company had misled the market in relation to its 'net zero' strategy (Global Witness, 2023). Global Witness alleges that Shell has overstated its renewable energy investments in its disclosures to the US regulator, and requests that the SEC open an investigation to determine whether the company has violated US securities law. Shell's US disclosures claim that 12 per cent of capital expenditure is invested in 'Renewables and Energy Solutions'. By contrast, the company's EU disclosures, which are governed by the new taxonomy for sustainable finance, were more restricted. In those documents, Shell revealed only USD 288 million, or 1.5 per cent of capex, invested in renewables, including 'electricity generation using solar voltaic energy', 'electricity generation from wind power', and 'installation, maintenance & repair of renewable energy technologies' (Global Witness, 2023: 9–10). A core element of the dispute turns on the definition of renewable energy and the classification of gas investments, among other things. The more specific and stringent requirements of the EU taxonomy elicited a more specific and restrained disclosure by Shell, revealing the limitations of its sustainability claims in its US reports. This action by Global Witness suggests that there may be productive tensions between disclosure requirements and definitions of ESG and sustainability in different jurisdictions. These contradictions may facilitate greater scrutiny of ESG claims and exposing the fallacies of ethical capital.

Conclusion

A burgeoning industry has emerged to meet the needs of investors for information and analysis about ESG risks. As the responsible capital imaginary has taken hold, and institutional investors have assumed for themselves the quasi-regulatory role of managing systemic or ESG risks across the economy, a frontier of accumulation has emerged. While investors and asset managers are able to generate market share and grow their AUM based on a promise of prescient analysis of ESG risk, providers of ESG data and related services are generating revenue by servicing this market. Assessments of the ESG risks and opportunities for investee companies are built into ESG ratings, scores and discursive analysis, screening tools and investment indices. As the ESG investing sector grows and consolidates, so too does the industry providing the data underpinning it. Firms like MSCI, Morningstar Sustainalytics and ISS are demonstrating that this is an increasingly lucrative growth area in finance.

Underlying the ESG investing and data industry is the promise – or illusion – that the social, ecological and political contradictions of capital accumulation can be managed to the point that there is no conflict between profitability and sustainability. Political struggles over greenwashing contest this responsible capital imaginary by exposing its contradictions. Recent and anticipated regulation of ESG standards and disclosures is likely to expose more of the gaps between corporate claims of sustainability and public expectations about what sustainable economic activity should comprise. Major asset managers and investors have already recognised the recent political turmoil over ESG investing as a material financial risk in itself (Masters and Temple-West, 2023b). At the same time, as demonstrated above, these new regulations are also creating growth opportunities for capital in the ESG data sector, which is developing new tools to support investors and their advisors in meeting disclosure requirements.

Notes

1 Regulation (EU) 2019/2088 of the European Parliament and of the Council of 27 November 2019.
2 Regulation (EU) 2020/852 of the European Parliament and of the Council of 18 June 2020 on the establishment of a framework to facilitate sustainable investment, and amending Regulation (EU) 2019/2088.

Conclusion: risky politics

It is easy to dismiss ethical capital as meaningless and "not really ethical". But stopping at this point fails to engage with what ethical capital does.

In striving to identify the function that the phenomenon of ethical capital plays in contemporary accumulation, this book has traversed three interlocking themes: use of the moral economy concept to understand how ethics are mobilised at different times and places; reconceptualising Marxian value in the context of finance and intangible assets; and understanding the treatment of ethical issues as risks and how this relates to the production of ethical capital.

As a conceptual tool, the moral economy reveals the particular ways in which ethics support, constrain and structure economic activity. This book contributed to recent developments in the moral economy literature by providing an exemplar of its use in practice. Framing capital's history and present through the moral economy lens has shown how ethics have been mobilised at different times, for different purposes, in contradictory ways, as the institutions of capital developed. This approach looks beyond superficial moral claims to understand what lies beneath them and the role they are playing. As applied here, the moral economy concept aims not to privilege one moral code over another, but to tease out the ways in which certain philosophies and structures hide their inherent morality, much as Thompson aimed to do in relation to laissez-faire doctrine. Although Thompson's conceptualisation was restricted to a particular time and place, the argument here extends his application of the moral economy as a vehicle for legitimating political and economic action, and as a product of class conflict and evolutionary economic processes (Thompson, 1971, 1991).

Applying the moral economy concept in this fashion exposes a speculative moral economy in operation today. This moral economy comprises a responsible capital imaginary, as its superficial public face, while the practical functions of responsible or ethical capitalism reveal quite a different reality. The responsible capital imaginary that insists ethical conduct is as profitable as, if not more profitable than, other ways of doing business has created a

Conclusion   159

basis on which ethical capital can be built. This book has developed an understanding of ethical capital, not as objectively ethical (whatever that might mean), but as capital that is produced by speculating on the spread between different ethical claims and positions. Ethical capital is measured through ESG risk analyses and credit ratings (Chapters 2 and 3), according to social accounting standards (Chapter 4) and manifests in intangible corporate assets such as brands (Chapter 5) and ESG information products (Chapter 6). It is monetised through corporate stock prices as well as price premia and volume premia on sales revenue.

Labour plays an important role in co-producing ethical capital assets in two important ways. One is the social and political process by which ethical debates are translated into financial risks – ESG metrics – by investment professionals. This process is informed by social movements and political work that reflects pressing ethical concerns like those associated with climate change and human rights abuse. The second vector through which labour co-produces ethical capital is marketing and branding. Corporations shape their product offerings and images according to their speculations about what matters to labour-as-consumers. Firms offer a range of ethical realities that aim to maximise the opportunities and minimise the risks associated with prominent ethical issues and debates. Through each of these vectors, ethics – a fundamental aspect of the human being – are alienated from their human source and reduced to quantifiable metrics, illustrating another instance of capital's tendency to grow through its creeping subsumption of all areas of life and labour to processes of accumulation.

None of this activity necessarily means that capital is becoming *more ethical* in a normative sense. Overall levels of carbon emissions, corruption, ecological devastation and human rights abuse may or may not change as a result of the production of ethical capital. But capital grows by leveraging different ethical possibilities and by commodifying and profiting from ESG risk and opportunities.

The derivative logic of ethics that prevails in the contemporary moral economy is most clearly revealed in the practice of ESG integration, which presents itself as "responsible" investment, at the same time as recognising that the only ESG issues it must integrate are financially material ones. ESG integration does not take an absolute position on the ethical quality of economic activity. It demands management of ethical risks, and an appropriate risk/return trade-off. Ethics have been mobilised in an elastic fashion throughout capitalism's history. But in the speculative moral economy, ethics become capital through the prism of risk, and speculation shifts from being an object of ethical critique to becoming a vehicle for the practice of ethics.

This points to the contribution this book makes to a conceptualisation of Marxian value in the context of finance and intangible assets. There are

160 *False profits of ethical capital*

lively debates regarding the form and measure of value in contemporary capitalism (see Chapter 3) to which this book aims to modestly contribute. Specifically, it has demonstrated one way in which value is produced outside the wage relation. In doing so, it has offered some clarification about the role of abstract risk as a means of connecting people and institutions, and shows how abstract risk operates as a measure of value.

As intangible assets and finance play increasingly significant roles in capital accumulation, it becomes more difficult to understand and measure value in relation to socially necessary labour time. On the basis that value is the particular form of connectivity that prevails in a capitalist economy, by rendering commensurate the incommensurable, this book has suggested an alternative measure of value. Empirical evidence from interviews with key informants in the ESG research and advice sector reveals that dynamic assessments of the possible costs and profits associated with ethical risks is relevant to the credit ratings and advice given by these firms to their investor clients. Capital's value is adjusted according to assessments of risks through ESG ratings processes. The abstract risks represented by concrete forms of ESG risk connect investors to workers, communities and the biosphere as economic performance incorporates social and ecological issues.

The identification, measurement and assessment of ESG risks depends on the specification of standards for social and environmental accounting (SEA). The analysis in Chapter 4 aimed to move beyond a discussion of the limitations of SEA in order to understand what SEA does. I have argued that SEA renders ethics legible for capital accumulation. Using the examples of SASB and Integrated Reporting, Chapter 4 demonstrates how these practices codify ethics for commodification and speculation. These developments, analogous to historical examples of rationalisation, standardisation and metricisation, establish a foundation on which ethical capital can be produced.

The final observations the book makes relate to the realisation of ethical capital in intangible corporate assets, and the role of labour in producing these. Chapter 5 has extended debates regarding the co-production of brands in marketing, cultural economy and legal theory, to identify how ethical debates and priorities, expressed by labour-as-consumer, become a source of information for ethical capital production. Particularly as digital technologies accelerate in their capacity to collect and analyse all manner of data, firms have access to increasing possibilities to identify profitable spreads between different ethical positions, minimising their exposure to reputational and operational ESG risks. Chapter 6 explores the most recent growth and concentration of the ESG information industry and the emerging regulation of that industry, which is providing further impetus for growth at the same time as exposing the contradictions of ethical capital.

In closing, a few further implications arise from the overview of this book. One is of a theoretical or scholarly nature, and others have a political,

Conclusion   161

strategic nature. First, the book contributes to the critical literature on financialisation and the social studies of finance. In particular, it advocates the value of thinking social and economic phenomena financially, of seeing financialisation as a transformation of thinking and being. The derivative logic of ethics is the frame through which this is most clearly observed. By treating ESG integration as the derivative position on ethics, the productive nature of the practice becomes clear. Thinking about ESG integration without this financial lens, one simply observes that ESG integration is ethically anaemic; it lacks substance or meaning. This supports an interpretation of the practice that it is grounded by a liberal notion of ethics, in which there are no universal principles, rather each individual chooses their own. But seeing ESG integration through the derivative logic reveals that it offers an infinite range of ethical realities, enabling investors to speculate on which will be the most profitable. This leveraging of the ethical spread is the vehicle through which ethics become productive for capital.

Second, from a political or strategic perspective, the book raises several problems or challenges for those engaging directly with the phenomenon of ethical capital. Given that sites of accumulation are sites of struggle, ethical capital may present opportunities for social and labour movements. However, recalling Harvie's (2005) crucial contribution to the discussion about productive and unproductive labour, it is necessary to reflexively examine whether our interventions challenge capital accumulation or reinforce it. Similarly, Massumi argues that while our complicity with capital accumulation is an 'ontological condition', this is not 'all-defining' and the imperative for anti-capitalist movements is to increase 'the ratio of escape over capture' (Massumi, 2018: 81).

One conundrum for activists working with investee politics (Feher, 2018) and pushing the 'boundaries of ESG risk' (Chapter 3) may be the question of how to contest the production and realisation of ethical capital. Chapter 4 observed that SASB and the IIRC are holding back from fully quantifying social and environmental costs in their schemas. Should activists contest this and drive towards a more comprehensive quantification to expose how capital becomes unprofitable when all social and ecological externalities are internalised? This is the nature of the approach already being taken by groups like Global Witness, as discussed in Chapter 6. Alternatively, critical thinkers and practitioners might refuse to price social and ecological 'values' (Hines, 1991; Lehman, 1999), taking a position that certain values are beyond the market. This tension between quantification and incommensurability is central to the struggle against ethical capital.

The key contribution this book makes to these debates about political strategy is that we can struggle over the limits of ethical capital, as we do with other sites of accumulation. We can – and should – simultaneously reject the reduction of ethics to generalisable quantities and the many violences of that abstraction *and* argue for an expansion of what is included in ethical or ESG risk to include more of the complexity that is stripped out by quantification and financial calculation. Movements, like fossil fuel divestment, that aim to expand what counts as financially material risk by materialising formerly immaterial risks are engaging in that struggle. Similarly, movements that aim to expand the definition of ESG risks to include more complexity, to include more of what might be thought of as a human-centred understanding of ethical or ESG risk, are both pushing back against the accumulation of ethical capital and perhaps pushing ESG investing to the brink of collapsing under the weight of its own contradictions.

Risks that at one time appear to be only qualitative and financially immaterial can be transformed into financially material risks through political action. The boundaries of ethical risk are mobile. Risks associated with climate change and fossil fuels are politically, economically and ecologically dynamic. Risks associated with human rights abuse can be materialised through social movements. Chapters 4 and 6 noted recent developments in which civil society organisations have sought to use regulation of the ESG to expose its limitations and push for a different, more expansive definition of sustainability. Other initiatives include collaborations between trade unions and non-profit ESG advocacy organisations that connect investor pressure to workplace organising strategies, aiming to build the power of labour through various channels concurrently (Hepworth and Kennedy, 2019; Hepworth and Newman, 2019). These efforts are a practical application of a Marxian value theory that grapples seriously with the proposition that labour is productive not only in the workplace but also through finance and in the social factory. While detailing myriad examples of financial campaigning by trade unions, this is an approach Alice Martin and Annie Quick describe as 'joining the dots between the financial protagonists who dominate our working [waged] and non-working lives' (Martin and Quick, 2020: 78). They argue that financial campaigning is one way to 'expand the bargaining unit' and to expand the scope of bargaining outside the workplace, drawing on a broader pool of collective power and action (Martin and Quick, 2020: 74–104).

This book aims to provide those engaged in such strategic debates with a framework through which to reflect on how ethical capital is being produced in the particular context of their struggle and what is the most useful way of contesting it. It is possible to hold the position that capital is not (and cannot be) objectively ethical while engaging in a meaningful struggle over the limits of its (un)ethicalness.

References

ACCR (2022) Australasian Centre for Corporate Responsibility expands landmark Federal Court case against Santos. Available at: https://www.accr.org.au/news/australasian-centre-for-corporate-responsibility-expands-landmark-federal-court-case-against-santos/ (accessed 25 April 2023).

Adams, C.A. (2015) The International Integrated Reporting Council: a call to action. *Critical Perspectives on Accounting* 27: 23–28. DOI: https://doi.org/10.1016/j.cpa.2014.07.001.

Aglietta, M. (2000) Shareholder value and corporate governance: some tricky questions. *Economy and Society* 29(1): 146–159. DOI: https://doi.org/10.1080/030851400360596.

Agnew, H., Klasa, A. and Mundy, S. (2022) How ESG investing came to a reckoning. *Financial Times*, 6 June. Available at: https://www.ft.com/content/5ec1dfcf-eea3-42af-aea2-19d739ef8a55 (accessed 1 April 2023).

Alessandrini, D. (2016) *Value Making in International Economic Law and Regulation: Alternative Possibilities*. New York: Routledge.

Alessandrini, D. (2018) Of value, measurement and social reproduction. *Griffith Law Review* 27(4): 393–410. DOI: https://doi.org/10.1080/10383441.2018.1548332.

Allen, J. and Pryke, M. (2013) Financializing household water: Thames Water, MEIF, and 'ring-fenced' politics. *Cambridge Journal of Regions, Economy and Society* 6(3): 419–439.

Allon, F. (2010) Speculating on everyday life: the cultural economy of the quotidian. *Journal of Communication Inquiry* 34(4): 366–381. DOI: https://doi.org/10.1177/0196859910383015.

Amoore, L. (2013) *The Politics of Possibility: Risk and Security Beyond Probability*. Durham, NC: Duke University Press.

Anderson, G. (2019) *Want to Get Serious about Sustainability? Use SASB's Standards to Inform ERM*. Available at: https://www.sasb.org/knowledge-hub/want-to-get-serious-about-sustainability-use-sasbs-standards-to-inform-erm/ (accessed 12 February 2020).

Andrew, J. and Cortese, C. (2013) Free market environmentalism and the neoliberal project: the case of the Climate Disclosure Standards Board. *Critical Perspectives on Accounting* 24(6): 397–409. DOI: https://doi.org/10.1016/j.cpa.2013.05.010.

Andrew, T. (2022) ESMA calls for regulation of ESG rating providers as shortfalls exposed. ETF Stream. Available at: https://www.etfstream.com/articles/

esma-calls-for-regulation-of-esg-rating-providers-as-shortfalls-exposed (accessed 9 April 2023).

Arvidsson, A. (2005) Brands: a critical perspective. *Journal of Consumer Culture* 5(2): 235–258.

Arvidsson, A. (2011) Ethics and value in co-production. *Marketing Theory* 11(3): 261–278. DOI: https://doi.org/10.1177/1470593111408176.

Arvidsson, A. (2013) The potential of consumer publics: the politics of consumption. *ephemera* 13(2): 367–391.

Arvidsson, A. and Peitersen, N. (2013) *The Ethical Economy: Rebuilding Value after the Crisis*. New York: Columbia University Press.

ASIC (2022) Media release (22-294MR) ASIC acts against greenwashing by energy company. Available at: https://asic.gov.au/about-asic/news-centre/find-a-media-release/2022-releases/22-294mr-asic-acts-against-greenwashing-by-energy-company/ (accessed 22 April 2023).

ASIC (2023) Media release (23-001MR) ASIC issues infringement notices to energy company for greenwashing. Available at: https://asic.gov.au/about-asic/news-centre/find-a-media-release/2023-releases/23-001mr-asic-issues-infringement-notices-to-energy-company-for-greenwashing/ (accessed 22 April 2023).

Australian Financial Review (2019) Ethical investment: how green is my fund really? 17 April. Available at: https://www.afr.com/personal-finance/specialist-investments/ethical-investment-how-green-is-my-fund-really-20190417-p51ey7 (accessed 24 May 2019).

Axtle-Ortiz, M.A. (2013) Perceiving the value of intangible assets in context. *Journal of Business Research* 66(3): 417–424. DOI: https://doi.org/10.1016/j.jbusres.2012.04.008.

Bair, J., Anner, M. and Blasi, J. (2020) The political economy of private and public regulation in post-Rana Plaza Bangladesh. *ILR Review* 73(4): 969–994. https://doi.org/10.1177/0019793920925424.

Baker, T. and Simon, J. (2004) *Embracing Risk*. Chicago, IL: University of Chicago Press.

Barkan, J. (2013) Plutocrats at work: how big philanthropy undermines democracy. *Social Research: An International Quarterly* 80(2): 635–652.

Barton, R.E. (2022) The greenwashing wave hits securities litigation. *Reuters*, 22 September. Available at: https://www.reuters.com/legal/legalindustry/greenwashing-wave-hits-securities-litigation-2022-09-22/ (accessed 22 April 2023).

Bathurst, T.F. (2013) The historical development of corporations law. *Australian Bar Review* 37(3): 217–230.

Bebbington, J., Gray, R. and Owen, D. (1999) Seeing the wood for the trees: taking the pulse of social and environmental accounting. *Accounting, Auditing & Accountability Journal* 12(1): 47–52. DOI: https://doi.org/10.1108/09513579910259906.

Beder, S. (2004) Consumerism: an historical perspective. *Pacific Ecologist* 9: 42–48.

Berle, A.A. (1954) *The 20th Century Capitalist Revolution*. New York: Harcourt, Brace.

Berle, A.A. (1959) Foreword. In: Mason, E. (ed.) *The Corporation in Modern Society*. Cambridge, MA: Harvard University Press, pp. ix–xv.

References

Bernstein, P.L. (1993) *Capital Ideas: The Improbable Origins of Modern Wall Street*. New York: Free Press.

Bigger, P. and Robertson, M. (2017) Value is simple. Valuation is complex. *Capitalism Nature Socialism* 28(1): 68–77. DOI: https://doi.org/10.1080/10455752.2016.1273962.

Blackburn, R. (2004) *Banking on Death: Or, Investing in Life: The History and Future of Pensions*. London: Verso.

Blackett, T. (1991) The valuation of brands. *Marketing Intelligence & Planning* 9(1): 27–35. DOI: https://doi.org/10.1108/02634509110135442.

BlackRock (2020) FAQs. Making sustainability our standard. Available at: https://www.blackrock.com/corporate/literature/investor-education/sustainability-faqs-global.pdf (accessed 3 May 2020).

BlackRock (2023) *BlackRock, Inc. Section 10k Report to the US SEC*. Washington, DC: US Securities and Exchange Commission.

BlackRock and European Commission (2021) *Development of Tools and Mechanisms for the Integration of ESG Factors into the EU Banking Prudential Framework and into Banks' Business Strategies and Investment Policies*. May. European Commission, Directorate-General for Financial Stability, Financial Services and Capital Markets Union. Luxembourg: Publications Office of the European Union.

Bloomberg (2022) *Impact Report*. Available at: https://assets.bbhub.io/company/sites/56/2022/04/Impact-Report-2021.pdf (accessed 19 January 2024).

Bogle, J. (2009) Building a fiduciary society. IA Compliance Summit, Washington, DC.

Böhm, S. and Land, C. (2012) The new 'hidden abode': reflections on value and labour in the new economy. *The Sociological Review* 60(2): 217–240. DOI: https://doi.org/10.1111/j.1467-954X.2012.02071.x.

Boiral, O. (2013) Sustainability reports as simulacra? A counter-account of A and A+ GRI reports. *Accounting, Auditing & Accountability Journal* 26(7): 1036–1071. DOI: https://doi.org/10.1108/AAAJ-04-2012-00998.

Boiral, O. and Henri, J.-F. (2017) Is sustainability performance comparable? A study of GRI reports of mining organizations. *Business & Society* 56(2): 283–317. DOI: https://doi.org/10.1177/0007650315576134.

Boltanski, L. and Chiapello, E. (2005) *The New Spirit of Capitalism*. London: Verso.

Bolton, P., Despres, M., Pereira Da Silva, L., et al. (2020) *The Green Swan: Central Banking and Financial Stability in the Age of Climate Change*. Bank of International Settlements. Available at: https://www.bis.org/publ/othp31.pdf (accessed 3 May 2020).

Bond, S.R. and Cummins, J.G. (2003) The stock market and investment in the new economy: some tangible facts and intangible fictions. In: Hand, J.R.M. and Lev, B. (eds) *Intangible Assets: Values, Measures, and Risks*. Oxford: Oxford University Press, pp. 95–119.

Bone, R.G. (2006) Hunting goodwill: a history of the concept of goodwill in trademark law. *Boston University Law Review* 86(3): 547–622.

Bounds, A. (2019) Ethical sales rise as UK consumers go sustainable. *Financial Times*, 30 December. Available at: https://www.ft.com/content/5272ea7e-2336-11ea-92da-f0c92e957a96 (accessed 27 July 2020).

Bowen, H. (1953) *Social Responsibilities of the Businessman*. 2nd edition. Iowa City, IA: University of Iowa Press.

Boyd, E. (2023) ESG accounts for 65% of all flows into European ETFs in 2022. *Financial Times*, 13 January. Available at: https://www.ft.com/content/a3e9d87f-fa6f-4e5e-be6e-e95b42af2fec (accessed 18 January 2024).

Brackley, A., Brock, E.K. and Nelson, J. (2022) Rating the raters yet again: six challenges for ESG ratings. Available at: https://www.sustainability.com/thinking/rating-the-raters-yet-again-six-challenges-for-esg-ratings/ (accessed 19 January 2024).

Braithwaite, J. and Drahos, P. (2000) *Global Business Regulation*. Cambridge: Cambridge University Press.

Brand Finance Institute (2023a) *Global Intangible Finance Tracker—An Annual Review of the World's Intangible Value*. Available at: https://brandirectory.com/reports/gift-2023 (accessed 19 January 2024).

Brand Finance Institute (2023b) World's biggest brands could stand to lose billions from poor management of ESG. Available at: https://brandfinance.com/press-releases/worlds-biggest-brands-could-stand-to-lose-billions-from-poor-management-of-esg-perceptions (accessed 13 March 2023).

Braun, B. (2021) Asset manager capitalism as a corporate governance regime. In: Hertel-Fernandez, A., Hacker, J.S., Thelen, K., et al. (eds) *The American Political Economy: Politics, Markets, and Power. Cambridge Studies in Comparative Politics*. Cambridge: Cambridge University Press, pp. 270–294. DOI: https://doi.org/10.1017/9781009029841.010.

Braun, B. (2022) Fueling financialization: the economic consequences of funded pensions. *New Labor Forum* 31(1): 70–79. DOI: https://doi.org/10.1177/10957960211062218.

Brejning, J. (2012) *Corporate Social Responsibility and the Welfare State: The Historical and Contemporary Role of CSR in the Mixed Economy of Welfare*. Farnham: Ashgate.

Bridle, J. (2018) *New Dark Age: Technology and the End of the Future*. London: Verso.

Bryan, D., Martin, R. and Rafferty, M. (2009) Financialization and Marx: giving labor and capital a financial makeover. *Review of Radical Political Economics* 41(4): 458–472. DOI: https://doi.org/10.1177/0486613409341368.

Bryan, D. and Rafferty, M. (2006a) Can financial derivatives inform HRM? Lessons from *Moneyball*. *Human Resource Management* 45(4): 667–671. DOI: https://doi.org/10.1002/hrm.20139.

Bryan, D. and Rafferty, M. (2006b) *Capitalism with Derivatives*. London: Palgrave Macmillan.

Bryan, D. and Rafferty, M. (2013) Fundamental value: a category in transformation. *Economy and Society* 42(1): 130–153. DOI: https://doi.org/10.1080/03085147.2012.718625.

Bryan, D. and Rafferty, M. (2014) Financial derivatives as social policy beyond crisis. *Sociology* 48(5): 887–903.

Bryan, D. and Rafferty, M. (2018) *Risking Together: How Finance Is Dominating Everyday Life in Australia*. Sydney: Sydney University Press.

Bryan, D., Rafferty, M. and Jefferis, C. (2015) Risk and value: finance, labor, and production. *South Atlantic Quarterly* 114(2): 307–329.

References

Bryer, R. (2000a) The history of accounting and the transition to capitalism in England. Part one: theory. *Accounting, Organizations and Society* 25(2): 131–162. DOI: https://doi.org/10.1016/S0361-3682(99)00032-X.

Bryer, R. (2000b) The history of accounting and the transition to capitalism in England. Part two: evidence. *Accounting, Organizations and Society* 25(4–5): 327–381. DOI: https://doi.org/10.1016/S0361-3682(99)00033-1.

Bryer, R. (2005) A Marxist accounting history of the British industrial revolution: a review of evidence and suggestions for research. *Accounting, Organizations and Society* 30(1): 25–65. DOI: https://doi.org/10.1016/j.aos.2003.11.002.

Bryer, R. (2015) For Marx: a critique of Jacques Richard's 'The dangerous dynamics of modern capitalism (from static to IFRS' futuristic accounting)'. *Critical Perspectives on Accounting* 30: 35–43. DOI: https://doi.org/10.1016/j.cpa.2014.09.004.

Buller, A. (2022) *The Value of a Whale: On the Illusions of Green Capitalism.* Manchester: Manchester University Press.

Burchell, G., Gordon, C. and Miller, P. (eds) (1991) *The Foucault Effect: Studies in Governmentality.* Chicago, IL: University of Chicago Press.

Capital Group (2022) *ESG Global Study.* Available at: https://www.capitalgroup.com/content/dam/cgc/tenants/eacg/esg/global-study/esg-global-study-2022-full-report(en).pdf (accessed 9 April 2023).

Carlson, J., Gudergan, S.P., Gelhard, C., et al. (2019) Customer engagement with brands in social media platforms. *European Journal of Marketing* 53(9) 1733–1758. DOI: https://doi.org/10.1108/EJM-10-2017-0741.

Carney, M. (2014) Inclusive capitalism – creating a sense of the systemic. Available at: https://www.bis.org/review/r140528b.htm (accessed 12 April 2019).

Carrington, M.J., Zwick, D. and Neville, B. (2016) The ideology of the ethical consumption gap. *Marketing Theory* 16(1): 21–38. DOI: https://doi.org/10.1177/1470593115595674.

Carroll, A.B., Lipartito, K., Post, J., et al. (2012) *Corporate Responsibility: The American Experience.* Cambridge: Cambridge University Press.

Carruthers, B.G. and Espeland, W.N. (1991) Accounting for rationality: double-entry bookkeeping and the rhetoric of economic rationality. *American Journal of Sociology* 97(1): 31–69.

Castree, N., Kitchin, R. and Rogers, A. (2013) *A Dictionary of Human Geography.* Oxford: Oxford University Press.

Çelik, S. and Isaksson, M. (2014) Institutional investors and ownership engagement. *OECD Journal: Financial Markets Trends* 2013(2): 93–114.

CFA Institute (2022) *Guidance for Integrating ESG Information into Equity Analysis and Research Reports.* Available at: https://www.cfainstitute.org/en/research/industry-research/guidance-for-integrating-esg-information-into-equity-analysis-and-research-reports (accessed 8 February 2023).

Chalmers, J. (2023) Capitalism after the crises. *The Monthly*, 1 February. Available at: https://www.themonthly.com.au/issue/2023/february/jim-chalmers/capitalism-after-crises (accessed 2 February 2023).

Chamberlain, N.W. (1959) The corporation and the trade union. In: Mason, E. (ed.) *The Corporation in Modern Society*. Cambridge, MA: Harvard University Press, pp. 122–140.

References

Chayes, A. (1959) The modern corporation and the rule of law. In: Mason, E. (ed.) *The Corporation in Modern Society*. Cambridge, MA: Harvard University Press, pp. 25–45.

Chiapello, E. (2007) Accounting and the birth of the notion of capitalism. *Critical Perspectives on Accounting* 18(3): 263–296. DOI: https://doi.org/10.1016/j.cpa.2005.11.012.

Cho, C.H. and Giordano-Spring, S. (2015) Critical perspectives on social and environmental accounting. *Critical Perspectives on Accounting* 33: 1–4. DOI: https://doi.org/10.1016/j.cpa.2015.09.001.

Cho, C.H. and Patten, D.M. (2013) Green accounting: reflections from a CSR and environmental disclosure perspective. *Critical Perspectives on Accounting* 24(6): 443–447. DOI: https://doi.org/10.1016/j.cpa.2013.04.003.

Chowdhury, R. (2017) The Rana Plaza disaster and the complicit behavior of elite NGOs. *Organization* 24(6): 938–949. DOI: https://doi.org/10.1177/1350508417699023.

Christophers, B. (2015) Value models: finance, risk, and political economy. *Finance and Society* 1(2): 1. DOI: https://doi.org/10.2218/finsoc.v1i2.1381.

Christophers, B. (2016a) Risking value theory in the political economy of finance and nature. *Progress in Human Geography* 42(3): 330–349. DOI: https://doi.org/10.1177/0309132516679268.

Christophers, B. (2016b) *The Great Leveler: Capitalism and Competition in the Court of Law*. Cambridge, MA: Harvard University Press.

Christophers, B. (2017) Climate change and financial instability: risk disclosure and the problematics of neoliberal governance. *Annals of the American Association of Geographers* 107(5): 1108–1127. DOI: https://doi.org/10.1080/24694452.2017.1293502.

Christophers, B. (2019) Environmental beta or how institutional investors think about climate change and fossil fuel risk. *Annals of the American Association of Geographers* 109(3): 754–774. DOI: https://doi.org/10.1080/24694452.2018.1489213.

Christophers, B., Bigger, P. and Johnson, L. (2018) Stretching scales? Risk and sociality in climate finance. *Environment and Planning A: Economy and Space* 52(1): 88–110. DOI: https://doi.org/10.1177/0308518X18819004.

Chung, J. and Cho, C.H. (2018) Current trends within social and environmental accounting research: a literature review. *Accounting Perspectives* 17(2): 207–239. DOI: https://doi.org/10.1111/1911-3838.12171.

Clark, G.L. and Dixon, A.D. (2023) Legitimacy and the extraordinary growth of ESG measures and metrics in the global investment management industry. *Environment and Planning A: Economy and Space*. DOI: https://doi.org/10.1177/0308518X231155484.

Cleaver, H. (2001) *Reading Capital Politically*. 2nd edition. Edinburgh: Antithesis.

Cleaver, H. (2005) Work, value and domination. *The Commoner* 10(Spring/Summer): 115–131. Available at: https://thecommoner.org/back-issues/issue-10-spring-summer-2005/ (accessed 9 January 2024).

Coase, R.H. (1937) The nature of the firm. *Economica* 4(16): 386–405. DOI: https://doi.org/10.2307/2626876.

Coben, C. (2023) How should we regulate ESG research? *Financial Times*, 6 April. Available at: https://www.ft.com/content/e1cd27c0-aec0-4c44-8d9f-64bef387a576 (accessed 9 April 2023).

References

Coffin, J. and Egan-Wyer, C. (2022) The ethical consumption cap and mean market morality. *Marketing Theory* 22(1): 105–123. DOI: https://doi.org/10.1177/14705931211058772.

Cohen, L. (2003) *A Consumers' Republic: The Politics of Mass Consumption in Postwar America*. New York: Vintage Books.

Cojoianu, T.F., Ascui, F., Clark, G.L., et al. (2021) Does the fossil fuel divestment movement impact new oil and gas fundraising? *Journal of Economic Geography* 21(1): 141–164. DOI: https://doi.org/10.1093/jeg/lbaa027.

Commons, J.R. (1919) *Industrial Goodwill*. New York: McGraw-Hill.

Cooper, M. (2015) Shadow money and the shadow workforce: rethinking labor and liquidity. *South Atlantic Quarterly* 114(2): 395–423.

Crosland, C.A.R. (1959) The public and private corporation in Great Britain. In: Mason, E. (ed.) *The Corporation in Modern Society*. Cambridge, MA: Harvard University Press, pp. 260–276.

Dahmash, F.N., Durand, R.B. and Watson, J. (2009) The value relevance and reliability of reported goodwill and identifiable intangible assets. *The British Accounting Review* 41(1): 120–137.

Daum, J.H. (2002) *Intangible Assets and Value Creation*. Hoboken, NJ: Wiley.

Davis, J. (2002) European trade mark law and the enclosure of the commons. *Intellectual Property Quarterly* 4: 342–367.

Davis, J. and Maniatis, S. (2010) Trademarks, brands, and competition. In: da Silva Lopes, T. and Duguid, P. (eds) *Trademarks, Brands, and Competitiveness*. New York: Routledge, pp. 119–137.

Davison, M.J. (2009) *Cadbury Schweppes v Pub Squash*: what is all the fizz about? In: Kenyon, A.T., Richardson, M. and Ricketson, S. (eds) *Landmarks in Australian Intellectual Property Law*. Melbourne: Cambridge University Press, pp. 126–141.

De Angelis, M. (2005) Value(s), measure(s) and disciplinary markets. *The Commoner* 10(Spring/Summer): 66–86. Available at: https://thecommoner.org/back-issues/issue-10-spring-summer-2005/ (accessed 9 January 2024).

De Angelis, M. (2007) *The Beginning of History: Value Struggles and Global Capital*. London: Pluto Press.

De La Cruz, A., Medina, A. and Tang, Y. (2019) *Owners of the World's Listed Companies*. OECD Capital Markets Series. Paris: OECD.

de Villiers, C. and Sharma, U. (2017) A critical reflection on the future of financial, intellectual capital, sustainability and integrated reporting. *Critical Perspectives on Accounting* 70: 101999. DOI: https://doi.org/10.1016/j.cpa.2017.05.003.

Deegan, C. (2013) The accountant will have a central role in saving the planet … really? A reflection on 'green accounting and green eyeshades twenty years later'. *Critical Perspectives on Accounting* 24(6): 448–458. DOI: https://doi.org/10.1016/j.cpa.2013.04.004.

Deegan, C. (2017) Twenty five years of social and environmental accounting research within *Critical Perspectives of Accounting*: hits, misses and ways forward. *Critical Perspectives on Accounting* 43: 65–87. DOI: https://doi.org/10.1016/j.cpa.2016.06.005.

170 *References*

Del Bello, A. (2008) Credit rating and intangible assets: a preliminary inquiry into current practices. In: Zambon, S. and Marzo, G. (eds) *Visualising Intangibles: Measuring and Reporting in the Knowledge Economy*. Aldershot: Ashgate, pp. 165–190.

Deloitte (2018) *Overview of Integrated Reports Published by SBF 120 Companies in 2018*. Paris: Deloitte Touche Tohmatsu. Available at: https://integratedreporting.org/wp-content/uploads/2018/10/Deloitte-study-integrated-report-SBF120_0918_vDEF_ENG.pdf (accessed 6 November 2020).

DeSantis, R. (2022) Governor Ron DeSantis eliminates ESG considerations from state pension investments. Available at: https://www.flgov.com/2022/08/23/governor-ron-desantis-eliminates-esg-considerations-from-state-pension-investments/ (accessed 26 April 2023).

Deutsche Börse (2023) *Annual Report*. Corporate report. Available at: https://www.deutsche-boerse.com/dbg-en/investor-relations/financial-reports/annual-reports/annual-report-2022 (accessed 26 April 2023).

Djelic, M.-L. (2013) When limited liability was (still) an issue: mobilization and politics of signification in 19th-century England. *Organization Studies* 34(5–6): 595–621. DOI: https://doi.org/10.1177/0170840613479223.

Dobb, M. (1976) A reply. In: Sweezy, P., Dobb, M., Hill, C., et al. *The Transition from Feudalism to Capitalism*. London: NLB, pp. 57–67.

Dogan, S.L. and Lemley, M.A. (2012) Parody as brand. ID 2170498, SSRN Scholarly Paper, 2 November. Rochester, NY: Social Science Research Network. Available at: https://papers.ssrn.com/abstract=2170498 (accessed 3 October 2019).

Dowling, E. (2017) In the wake of austerity: social impact bonds and the financialisation of the welfare state in Britain. *New Political Economy* 22(3): 294–310. DOI: https://doi.org/10.1080/13563467.2017.1232709.

Dowling, E. and Harvie, D. (2014) Harnessing the social: state, crisis and (big) society. *Sociology* 48(5): 869–886.

Draaijer, A. de (2014) A new vision of value: connecting corporate and societal value creation – KPMG Global. Available at: https://home.kpmg/xx/en/home/insights/2014/09/a-new-vision-connecting-corporate.html (accessed 22 July 2020).

Eccles, N. (2011) New values in responsible investment. In: Vandekerckhove, W., Leys, J., Alm, K., et al. (eds) *Responsible Investment in Times of Turmoil*. Issues in Business Ethics. Dordrecht: Springer, pp. 19–34.

Eccles, R.G. (2022) ESG is not about ethical standards and ethical values. *Forbes*, 29 December. Available at: https://www.forbes.com/sites/bobeccles/2022/12/29/esg-is-not-about-ethical-standards-and-ethical-values/ (accessed 17 January 2024).

Eccles, R.G. and Klimenko, S. (2019) The investor revolution. *Harvard Business Review*, 1 May. Available at: https://hbr.org/2019/05/the-investor-revolution (accessed 12 March 2020).

Eccles, R.G., Lee, L.-E. and Stroehle, J.C. (2019) The social origins of ESG? An analysis of Innovest and KLD. ID 3318225, SSRN Scholarly Paper, 20 August. Rochester, NY: Social Science Research Network. Available at: https://papers.ssrn.com/abstract=3318225 (accessed 19 February 2020).

References

171

Eccles, N. and Viviers, S. (2011) The origins and meanings of names describing investment practices that integrate a consideration of ESG issues in the academic literature. *Journal of Business Ethics* 104(3): 389–402. DOI: https://doi.org/10.1007/S10551-011-0917-7.

Edgecliffe-Johnson, A. and Mooney, A. (2019) The year capitalism went cuddly. *Financial Times*, 20 December. Available at: https://www.ft.com/content/da1d824a-1bd4-11ea-97df-cc63de1d73f4 (accessed 6 March 2020).

Eekelen, B.F. van (2015) Accounting for ideas: bringing a knowledge economy into the picture. *Economy and Society* 44(3): 445–479.

Elson, D. (1979) *Value: The Representation of Labour in Capitalism: Essays*. London: CSE Books.

El-Tawy, N. and Tollington, T. (2013) Some thoughts on the recognition of assets, notably in respect of intangible assets. *Accounting Forum* 37(1): 67–80. DOI: https://doi.org/10.1016/j.accfor.2012.10.001.

Engels, F. (1947) *Anti-Dühring: Herr Eugen Dühring's Revolution in Science* (trans. E. Burns). Moscow: Progress Publishers. Available at: https://www.marxists.org/archive/marx/works/1877/anti-duhring/ (accessed 25 May 2015).

Ernst and Young and AHRC (2017) *Human Rights in Investment: The Value of Considering Human Rights in ESG Due Diligence*. Canberra: Ernst and Young; Australian Human Rights Commission.

European Commission (n.d.) *Corporate Sustainability Reporting*. Available at: https://finance.ec.europa.eu/capital-markets-union-and-financial-markets/company-reporting-and-auditing/company-reporting/corporate-sustainability-reporting_en (accessed 9 November 2023).

European Commission (2019) Regulation (EU) 2019/2088 of the European Parliament and of the Council. Available at: https://eur-lex.europa.eu/legal-content/EN/TXT/?uri=celex%3A32019R2088 (accessed 21 January 2024).

European Commission (2022) *Summary Report: Targeted Consultation on the Functioning of the ESG Ratings Market in the EU and on the Consideration of ESG Factors in Credit Ratings*. 3 August. Directorate-General for Financial Stability, Financial Services and Capital Markets Union. Available at: https://finance.ec.europa.eu/regulation-and-supervision/consultations/finance-2022-esg-ratings_en (accessed 20 April 2023).

European Commission and ERM (2020) *Study on Sustainability-Related Ratings, Data and Research*. November. Directorate-General for Financial Stability, Financial Services and Capital Markets Union.

Fancy, T. (2021) The secret diary of a 'sustainable investor', part 3. *Medium*. Available at: https://medium.com/@sosofancy/the-secret-diary-of-a-sustainable-investor-part-3-3c238cb0dcbf (accessed 8 November 2023).

FCA (2022) Sustainability Disclosure Requirements (SDR) and investment labels. Consultation Paper 22/20, October. London: Financial Conduct Authority. Available at: https://www.fca.org.uk/publication/consultation/cp22-20.pdf (accessed 9 April 2023).

Federici, S. (2004) *Caliban and the Witch*. New York: Autonomedia.

Feher, M. (2018) *Rated Agency: Investee Politics in a Speculative Age* (trans. G. Elliott). New York: Zone Books.

References

Fhima, I.S. (2015) Trade mark law meets branding? In: Desai, D.R., Lianos, I. and Waller, S.W. (eds) *Brands, Competition and IP Law*. Cambridge: Cambridge University Press, pp. 217–237.

Fink, L. (2020) BlackRock client letter. Available at: https://www.blackrock.com/corporate/investor-relations/blackrock-client-letter (accessed 19 February 2020).

Fink, L. (2022) BlackRock CEO letter. Available at: https://www.blackrock.com/corporate/investor-relations/larry-fink-ceo-letter# (accessed 23 November 2023).

Fink, L. (2023) BlackRock chairman's letter to investors. Available at: https://www.blackrock.com/corporate/investor-relations/larry-fink-annual-chairmans-letter (accessed 23 November 2023).

Fisher, L. and Bryan, K. (2023) UK set to unveil regulatory regime for ESG ratings industry. *Financial Times*, 8 November. Available at: https://www.ft.com/content/61a61fc5-fedd-4c01-bb24-99c1606d446d (accessed 8 November 2023).

Fisher, M. (2009) *Capitalist Realism: Is There No Alternative?* Winchester: Zero Books.

Flood, C. (2023a) Investors warned of 'greenwashing' risk as ESG-labelled funds double. *Financial Times*, 24 April. Available at: https://www.ft.com/content/79772342-d260-4dd5-b943-5e75bc27878c (accessed 1 May 2023).

Flood, C. (2023b) UK regulator takes aim at index providers over greenwashing. *Financial Times*, 22 March. Available at: https://www.ft.com/content/0ea165df-6e5f-4c2a-b780-17ef5aa123f7 (accessed 1 April 2023).

Flower, J. (2015) The International Integrated Reporting Council: a story of failure. *Critical Perspectives on Accounting* 27: 1–17. DOI: https://doi.org/10.1016/j.cpa.2014.07.002.

Forbes (n.d.) Bloomberg: company overview & news. Available at: https://www.forbes.com/companies/bloomberg/ (accessed 21 April 2023).

Ford, J. and Nolan, J. (2020) Regulating transparency on human rights and modern slavery in corporate supply chains: the discrepancy between human rights due diligence and the social audit. *Australian Journal of Human Rights* 26(1): 27–45. DOI: https://doi.org/10.1080/1323238X.2020.1761633.

Fordyce, R. and van Ryn, L. (2014) Ethical commodities as exodus and refusal. *ephemera* 14(1): 35–55.

Fortunati, L. (2007) Immaterial labor and its machinization. *ephemera* 7(1): 139–157.

Foster, R.J. (2007) The work of the new economy: consumers, brands, and value creation. *Cultural Anthropology* 22(4): 707–731. DOI: https://doi.org/10.1525/can.2007.22.4.707.

Foster, R.J. (2008) Commodities, brands, love and kula: comparative notes on value creation in honor of Nancy Munn. *Anthropological Theory* 8(1): 9–25. DOI: https://doi.org/10.1177/1463499607087492.

Foster, R.J. (2013) Things to do with brands: creating and calculating value. *Journal of Ethnographic Theory* 3(1): 44–63.

Foubert, A.-L. (2022) ESG data is now worth it. Opimas, 19 April. Available at: https://www.opimas.com/research/742/detail/ (accessed 21 April 2023).

Fourcade, M. and Healy, K. (2007) Moral views of market society. *Annual Review of Sociology* 33(1): 285–311.

References

Fransen, L. and LeBaron, G. (2019) Big audit firms as regulatory intermediaries in transnational labor governance. *Regulation & Governance* 13(2): 260–279. DOI: https://doi.org/10.1111/rego.12224.

Freeman, R.E. (1984) *Strategic Management: A Stakeholder Approach*. Cambridge: Cambridge University Press.

Friedman, M. (1970) The social responsibility of business is to increase its profits. *New York Times Magazine*, 13 September.

Friedman, M. and Friedman, R. (1980) *Free to Choose*. Harmondsworth: Penguin.

Friedman, T. (1999) *The Lexus and the Olive Tree*. London: HarperCollins.

Froud J., Haslam C., Johal S., et al. (2000) Shareholder value and financialization: consultancy promises, management moves. *Economy and Society* 29(1): 80–110. DOI: https://doi.org/10.1080/030851400360578.

FT Editorial Board (2019) Responsible capitalism requires new standards. *Financial Times*, 27 October. Available at: https://www.ft.com/content/8a719968-f666-11e9-a79c-bc9acae3b654 (accessed 5 June 2020).

FT Editorial Board (2023) Joe Biden's ESG rule is sound risk management. *Financial Times*, 7 March. Available at: https://www.ft.com/content/4dc4d7b2-ecd5-4c32-9552-be1c94e0545e (accessed 1 April 2023).

Fuchs, C. (2014) Theorising and analysing digital labour: from global value chains to modes of production. *The Political Economy of Communication* 1(2): 3–27.

Fuchs, C. (2015) Against divisiveness: digital workers of the world unite! A rejoinder to César Bolaño and Eloy Vieira. *Television & New Media* 16(1): 62–71. DOI: https://doi.org/10.1177/1527476414528053.

Fulgoni, G. (2013) Big data: friend or foe of digital advertising? Five ways marketers should use digital big data to their advantage. *Journal of Advertising Research* 53(4): 372–376. DOI: https://doi.org/10.2501/JAR-53-4-372-376.

Galbraith, J. (1952) *American Capitalism: The Concept of Countervailing Power*. Boston, MA: Houghton Mifflin.

Galbraith, J. (1967) *The New Industrial State*. Princeton, NJ: Princeton University Press.

Gardberg, N.A. and Fombrun, C.J. (2006) Corporate citizenship: creating intangible assets across institutional environments. *Academy of Management Review* 31(2): 329–346. DOI: https://doi.org/10.5465/amr.2006.20208684.

Gawne, M. (2014) *Ontology, Composition & Affect: The Political Limits of Post-workerist Thought*. Doctoral thesis, University of Sydney. Available at: http://hdl.handle.net/2123/13004 (accessed 9 January 2024).

Gensler, G. (2023) Statement on updates to the Names Rule. Securities and Exchange Commission. Available at: https://www.sec.gov/news/statement/gensler-statement-names-rule-092023 (accessed 9 November 2023).

George, B. (2019) Forget socialism. The U.S. needs responsible capitalism. *Fortune*, 6 May. Available at: https://fortune.com/2019/05/06/socialism-ceo-leadership-responsible-capitalism/ (accessed 10 May 2020).

Gielens, K. and Steenkamp, J.-B.E.M. (2019) Branding in the era of digital (dis)intermediation. *International Journal of Research in Marketing* 36(3): 367–384. DOI: https://doi.org/10.1016/j.ijresmar.2019.01.005.

Giese, G., Lee, L.-E., Melas, D., et al. (2018) *Foundations of ESG Investing*. MSCI. Available at: https://www.msci.com/documents/10199/206fe4b3-f98 1-f235-ccfe-790d0c1b4bae (accessed 18 March 2019).

Gleeson-White, J. (2014) *Six Capitals: The Revolution Capitalism Has to Have – or Can Accountants Save the Planet?* Crows Nest: Allen & Unwin.

Global Witness (2023) Complaint requesting an investigation into apparent greenwashing by Shell plc. Complaint letter to SEC. Available at: https://www.globalwitness.org/documents/20472/Global_Witness_SEC_Shell_Complaint_-_February_2023.pdf (accessed 22 April 2023).

Götz, N. (2015) 'Moral economy': its conceptual history and analytical prospects. *Journal of Global Ethics* 11(2): 147–162.

Graeber, D. (2005) Value as the importance of actions. *The Commoner* 10(Spring/Summer): 4–65. Available at: https://thecommoner.org/back-issues/issue-10-spring-summer-2005/ (accessed 9 January 2024).

Gray, R. (2013) Back to basics: what do we mean by environmental (and social) accounting and what is it for? – A reaction to Thornton. *Critical Perspectives on Accounting* 24(6): 459–468. DOI: https://doi.org/10.1016/j.cpa.2013.04.005.

Gray, R. and Bebbington, J. (2000) Environmental accounting, managerialism and sustainability: is the planet safe in the hands of business and accounting? In: Freedman, M. and Jaggi, B. (eds) *Advances in Environmental Accounting and Management: Volume 1*. Leeds: Emerald Publishing, pp. 1–44.

Gray, R. and Laughlin, R. (2012) It was 20 years ago today. *Accounting, Auditing & Accountability Journal* 25(2): 228–255. DOI: https://doi.org/10.1108/09513571211198755.

Griffiths, A. (2018) Brands and corporate power. *Journal of Corporate Law Studies* 18(1): 75–112. DOI: https://doi.org/10.1080/14735970.2017.1317131.

Gundlach, G. and Phillips, J. (2015) Brands and brand management. In: Desai, D.R., Lianos, I. and Waller, S.W. (eds) *Brands, Competition Law and IP*. Cambridge: Cambridge University Press, pp. 113–127.

Hacker, J.S. (2008) *The Great Risk Shift: The New Economic Insecurity and the Decline of the American Dream*. Revised edition. Oxford: Oxford University Press.

Hancock, A. (2017) Younger consumers drive shift to ethical products. *Financial Times*, 23 December. Available at: https://www.ft.com/content/8b08bf4c-e5a0-11e 7-8b99-0191e45377ec (accessed 27 July 2020).

Hancock, A. and Bryan, K. (2023) Brussels clamps down on 'greenwashing' in bond market. *Financial Times*, 1 March. Available at: https://www.ft.com/conten t/560f0634-63fd-4f87-a66b-8d74d518f5b6 (accessed 1 April 2023).

Hancox, D. (2019) No logo at 20: have we lost the battle against the total branding of our lives? *The Observer*, 11 August. Available at: https://www.theguardian.com/books/2019/aug/11/no-logo-naomi-klein-20-years-on-interview (accessed 17 August 2020).

Hand, J.R.M. and Lev, B. (eds) (2003) *Intangible Assets: Values, Measures, and Risks*. Oxford: Oxford University Press.

Harding, T. (2022) *White Debt: The Demerara Uprising and Britain's Legacy of Slavery*. London: Weidenfeld & Nicolson.

Hardt, M. and Negri, A. (2000) *Empire*. Cambridge, MA: Harvard University Press.

Hardt, M. and Negri, A. (2004) *Multitude: War and Democracy in the Age of Empire*. New York: Penguin.

Harris, R. (2020) A new understanding of the history of limited liability: an invitation for theoretical reframing. *Journal of Institutional Economics* 16(5): 643–664. DOI: https://doi.org/10.1017/S1744137420000181.

Harvey, D. (2005) *A Brief History of Neoliberalism*. Oxford: Oxford University Press.

Harvie, D. (2005) All labour produces value for capital and we all struggle against value. *The Commoner* 10(Spring/Summer): 132–171. Available at: https://thecommoner.org/back-issues/issue-10-spring-summer-2005/ (accessed 9 January 2024).

Harvie, D. and De Angelis, M. (2009) 'Cognitive capitalism' and the rat-race: how capital measures immaterial labour in British universities. *Historical Materialism* 17(3): 3–30. DOI: https://doi.org/10.1163/146544609X12469428108420.

Harvie, D. and Milburn, K. (2010) Speaking out: how organizations value and how value organizes. *Organization* 17(5): 631–636. DOI: https://doi.org/10.1177/1350508410372620.

Harvie, D. and Milburn, K. (2013) The moral economy of the English crowd in the twenty-first century. *South Atlantic Quarterly* 112(3): 559–567.

Harvie, D. and Ogman, R. (2019) The broken promises of the social investment market. *Environment and Planning A: Economy and Space* 51(4): 980–1004. DOI: https://doi.org/10.1177/0308518X19827298.

Havas (2019a) Meaningful brands. Available at: https://www.meaningful-brands.com/en (accessed 22 October 2019).

Havas (2019b) Building meaningful is good for business. Available at: https://havasmedianetwork.com/building-meaningful-is-good-for-business-77-of-consumers-buy-brands-who-share-their-values/ (accessed 20 November 2023).

Havas (2021) Age of cynicism. Available at: https://www.havas.com/havas-content/uploads/2021/05/press_release_mb21-final.pdf (accessed 20 November 2023).

Havas (2023) *New Havas 2023 Global Meaningful Brands*™ *Report*. Available at: https://meaningful-brands.com/assets/docs/HAVAS_MB_WhitePaper2023_FINAL.pdf (accessed 20 November 2023).

Hawley, J.P. (2011) Corporate governance, risk analysis, and the financial crisis: did Universal owners contribute to the crisis? In: Hawley, J.P., Kamath, S.J. and Williams, A.T. (eds) *Corporate Governance Failures: The Role of Institutional Investors in the Global Financial Crisis*. Philadelphia, PA: University of Pennsylvania Press, pp. 97–114.

Hawley, J. and Lukomnik, J. (2018) The third, system stage of corporate governance: why institutional investors need to move beyond modern portfolio theory. ID 3127767, SSRN Scholarly Paper, 21 February. Rochester, NY: Social Science Research Network. DOI: https://doi.org/10.2139/ssrn.3127767.

Hawley, J. and Williams, A. (1997) The emergence of fiduciary capitalism. *Corporate Governance: An International Review* 5(4): 206–213. DOI: https://doi.org/10.1111/1467-8683.00062.

Hawley, J. and Williams, A. (2005) Shifting ground: emerging global corporate-governance standards and the rise of fiduciary capitalism. *Environment and Planning A: Economy and Space* 37(11): 1995–2013. DOI: https://doi.org/10.1068/a3791.

Hawley, J. and Williams, A. (2007) Universal owners: challenges and opportunities. *Corporate Governance: An International Review* 15(3): 415–420. DOI: https://doi.org/10.1111/j.1467-8683.2007.00574.x.

Hepworth, K. and Kennedy, T. (2019) Worker exploitation is a core issue for super funds. *Crikey*, 5 April. Available at: https://www.crikey.com.au/2019/04/05/worker-exploitation-a-core-issue-for-super-funds/ (accessed 18 April 2019).

Hepworth, K. and Newman, F. (2019) Trade unions v. social audits: addressing labour exploitation in Woolworths domestic food supply chain. *Human Rights Defender* 28(1): 14–17.

Herman, L. (2020) Neither takers nor makers: the Big-4 auditing firms as regulatory intermediaries. *Accounting History* 25(3): 349–374. DOI: https://doi.org/10.1177/1032373219875219.

Hines, R. (1988) Financial accounting: in communicating reality, we construct reality. *Accounting, Organizations and Society* 13(3): 251–261. DOI: https://doi.org/10.1016/0361-3682(88)90003-7.

Hines, R. (1991) On valuing nature. *Accounting, Auditing & Accountability Journal* 4(3): 27–29. DOI: https://doi.org/10.1108/09513579110144802.

Hiss, S. (2013) The politics of the financialization of sustainability. *Competition & Change* 17(3): 234–247. DOI: https://doi.org/10.1179/1024529413Z.00000000035.

HM Treasury (2023) Future regulatory regime for environmental, social, and governance (ESG) ratings providers. Consultation Paper, March. Available at: https://www.gov.uk/government/consultations/future-regulatory-regime-for-environmental-social-and-governance-esg-ratings-providers (accessed 9 April 2023).

Hobsbawm, E.J. and Wrigley, C. (1999) *Industry and Empire: From 1750 to the Present Day*. New York: New Press.

Hoegh-Krohn, N. and Knivflsa, K. (2000) Accounting for intangible assets in Scandinavia, the UK, the US, and by the IASC: challenges and a solution. *The International Journal of Accounting* 35(2): 243–265.

Holloway, J. (1996) The rise and fall of Keynesianism. In: Bonefeld, W. and Holloway, J. (eds) *Global Capital, National State and the Politics of Money*. London: Palgrave Macmillan, pp. 7–34.

Hook, L. (2023) Spotlight turns to coal at Glencore as pressure mounts on climate plans. *Financial Times*, 24 May. Available at: https://www.ft.com/content/3ef4a51e-f209-4fd5-9084-f029723bae3c (accessed 6 June 2023).

Hopwood, A.G. (1976) Editorial. *Accounting, Organizations and Society* 1(1): 1–4. DOI: https://doi.org/10.1016/0361-3682(76)90002-7.

Hu, H.T.C. and Black, B. (2006) Empty voting and hidden (morphable) ownership: taxonomy, implications and reforms. *The Business Lawyer* 61(3): 1011–1070.

Hu, H.T.C. and Black, B. (2008) Debt, equity and hybrid decoupling: governance and systemic risk implications. *European Financial Management* 14(4): 663–709.

Huber, M.T. (2017) Value, nature, and labor: a defense of Marx. *Capitalism Nature Socialism* 28(1): 39–52. DOI: https://doi.org/10.1080/10455752.2016.1271817.

References

177

Hutley, N.C. and Mack, J.E. (2021) Superannuation trustees and climate change: memorandum of opinion. Equity Generation Lawyers. Available at: https://equitygenerationlawyers.com/opinions/trustee-duties/ (accessed 1 May 2023).

IIRC (2013) IIRC Framework. Available at: https://integratedreporting.org/wp-content/uploads/2013/12/13-12-08-THE-INTERNATIONAL-IR-FRAMEWORK-2-1.pdf (accessed 22 July 2020).

IIRC (2015) *Creating Value: Value to Investors*. Available at: https://integratedreporting.org/wp-content/uploads/2015/04/Creating-Value-Investors.pdf (accessed 22 July 2020).

IIRC (2018) Investors support integrated reporting as a route to better understanding of performance. Available at: https://integratedreporting.org/wp-content/uploads/2018/12/Investor-statement-2018.pdf (accessed 22 July 2020).

Infegy (n.d.) Text analytics + social listening. Available at: http://infegy.com/ (accessed 31 October 2019).

Interbrand (n.d.a) Brands are replacing sectors (and what this means). Available at: https://www.interbrand.com/views/brands-replacing-sectors-means/ (accessed 25 October 2019).

Interbrand (n.d.b) What is a brand? Available at: https://www.interbrand.com/views/what-is-a-brand/ (accessed 31 October 2019).

Interbrand (2018) Hallmarks of the 2018 top growing brands. Available at: https://www.brandknewmag.com/hallmarks-of-the-2018-top-growing-brands/ (accessed 19 January 2024).

International Energy Agency (2022) *World Energy Outlook 2022*. Available at: https://www.iea.org/topics/world-energy-outlook (accessed 24 May 2023).

IOSCO (2021) *Environmental, Social and Governance (ESG) Ratings and Data Products Providers*. FR09/21, November. Available at: https://www.iosco.org/library/pubdocs/pdf/IOSCOPD690.pdf (accessed 9 April 2023).

Iredale, A. (2018) Do consumers really care about ethical products? *Choice*. Available at: https://www.choice.com.au/shopping/everyday-shopping/ethical-buying-and-giving/articles/do-consumers-care-about-ethical-products (accessed 30 October 2019).

ISO (2010) ISO 10668 – Brand valuation: requirements for monetary brand valuation. Geneva: International Organization for Standardization.

ISO (2019) ISO 20671 – Brand evaluation: principles and fundamentals. Geneva: International Organization for Standardization.

James, C.L.R. (1938) *The Black Jacobins: Toussaint L'Ouverture and the San Domingo Revolution*. 2nd edition. New York: Vintage.

Jarrett, K. (2015) *Feminism, Labour and Digital Media: The Digital Housewife*. New York: Routledge.

Jensen, M.C. (2002) Value maximization, stakeholder theory, and the corporate objective function. *Business Ethics Quarterly* 12(2): 235–256. DOI: https://doi.org/10.2307/3857812.

Jensen, M.C. and Meckling, W.H. (1976) Theory of the firm: managerial behavior, agency costs and ownership structure. *Journal of Financial Economics* 3(4): 305–360. DOI: https://doi.org/10.1016/0304-405X(76)90026-X.

Jessop, J., Dickie, G. and Mallet, B. (2022) Environmental groups sue TotalEnergies over climate marketing claims. *Reuters*, 3 March. Available at: https://www.reuters.com/business/sustainable-business/environmental-groups-sue-totalenergies-over-climate-marketing-claims-2022-03-03/ (accessed 21 April 2023).

Johns, F. (2011) Financing as governance. *Oxford Journal of Legal Studies* 31(2): 391–415. DOI: https://doi.org/10.1093/ojls/gqr005.

Johnson, L. (2013) Catastrophe bonds and financial risk: securing capital and rule through contingency. *Geoforum* 45: 30–40. DOI: https://doi.org/10.1016/j.geoforum.2012.04.003.

Kannan, P.K. and Li, A. (2017) Digital marketing: a framework, review and research agenda. *International Journal of Research in Marketing* 34(1): 22–45. DOI: https://doi.org/10.1016/j.ijresmar.2016.11.006.

Kaplan, R. (2015) Who has been regulating whom, business or society? The mid-20th-century institutionalization of 'corporate responsibility' in the USA. *Socio-Economic Review* 13(1): 125–155.

Kaysen, C. (1959) The corporation: how much power? What scope? In: Mason, E. (ed.) *The Corporation in Modern Society*. Cambridge, MA: Harvard University Press, pp. 85–105.

Kennedy, L. (2019) Top 400: cultures change. *IPE Magazine*. Available at: https://www.ipe.com/top-400-cultures-change/10031470.article (accessed 12 March 2020).

Keynes, J.M. (1921) *A Treatise on Probability*. London: Macmillan.

Keynes, J.M. (1926) *The End of Laissez-Faire*. London: Hogarth Press.

Keynes, J.M. (1936) *The General Theory of Employment, Interest, and Money*. London: Macmillan.

Kiernan, M.J. (2007) Universal owners and ESG: leaving money on the table? *Corporate Governance: An International Review* 15(3): 478–485. DOI: https://doi.org/10.1111/j.1467-8683.2007.00580.x.

Kindleberger, C.P. and Aliber, R.Z. (2005) *Manias, Panics and Crashes: A History of Financial Crises*. 5th edition. London: Palgrave Macmillan. DOI: https://doi.org/10.1057/9780230628045.

Kirsch, S. (2014) Imagining corporate personhood. *Political and Legal Anthropology Review* 37(2): 207–217.

Knafo, S. (2007) Political Marxism and value theory: bridging the gap between theory and history. *Historical Materialism* 15(2): 75–104. DOI: https://doi.org/10.1163/156920607X192084.

Knaus, C. and Davidson, H. (2019) Paladin controversy prompts renewed scrutiny of $591m Nauru deal. *The Guardian*, 18 February. Available at: https://www.theguardian.com/australia-news/2019/feb/19/paladin-controversy-prompts-renewed-scrutiny-of-591m-nauru-deal (accessed 24 May 2019).

Knight, F.H. (2014) *Risk Uncertainty and Profit*. Eastford, CT: Martino Fine Books.

Konings, M. (2018) *Capital and Time: For a New Critique of Neoliberal Reason*. Stanford, CA: Stanford University Press.

KPMG (2020) *Sustainable Investing: Fast-Forwarding Its Evolution*. Available at: https://assets.kpmg.com/content/dam/kpmg/xx/pdf/2020/02/sustainable-investing.pdf (accessed 19 January 2024).

References

Kristoffersen, I., Gerrans, P. and Clark-Murphy, M. (2005) The corporate social responsibility and the theory of the firm. Finance and Economics & FIMARC Working Paper Series. Joondalup: Edith Cowan University.

Kronthal-Sacco, R. and Whelan, T. (2019) Research on IRI purchasing data 2013–2018. NYU Stern Center for Sustainable Business. Available at: https://www.stern.nyu.edu/experience-stern/about/departments-centers-initiatives/centers-of-research/center-sustainable-business/research/internal-research (accessed 30 October 2019).

Lagarde, C. (2014) Economic inclusion and financial integrity: an address to the Conference on Inclusive Capitalism. *International Monetary Fund*. Available at: https://www.imf.org/en/News/Articles/2015/09/28/04/53/sp052714 (accessed 12 April 2019).

Lagarde, C. (2019) The financial sector: redefining a broader sense of purpose. *International Monetary Fund*. Available at: https://www.imf.org/en/News/Articles/2019/02/21/sp022819-md-the-financial-sector-redefining-a-broader-sense-of-purpose (accessed 12 March 2020).

Lampert, M. (2016) Corporate social responsibility and the supposed moral agency of corporations. *ephemera* 16(1): 79–105.

Langley, P. (2018) The folds of social finance: making markets, remaking the social. *Environment and Planning A: Economy and Space* 52(1): 130–147. DOI: https://doi.org/10.1177/0308518X17752682.

Lapavitsas, C. (2014) *Profiting Without Producing: How Finance Exploits Us All.* London: Verso.

Lazonick, W. and O'Sullivan, M. (2000) Maximizing shareholder value: a new ideology for corporate governance. *Economy and Society* 29(1): 13–35. DOI: https://doi.org/10.1080/030851400360541.

Lazzarato, M. (2004) From capital-labour to capital-life. *ephemera* 4(3): 187–208.

LeBaron, G., Edwards, R., Hunt, T., et al. (2022) The ineffectiveness of CSR: understanding garment company commitments to living wages in global supply chains. *New Political Economy* 27(1): 99–115. DOI: https://doi.org/10.1080/13563467.2021.1926954.

LeBaron, G., Lister, J. and Dauvergne, P. (2017) Governing global supply chain sustainability through the ethical audit regime. *Globalizations* 14(6): 958–975. DOI: https://doi.org/10.1080/14747731.2017.1304008.

Lee, L.-E. and Moscardi, M. (2019) *2019 ESG Trends to Watch*. MSCI. Available at: https://www.msci.com/documents/10199/239004/MSCI-2019-ESG-Trends-to-Watch.pdf (accessed 8 January 2024).

Lee, L.-E., Thwing-Eastman, M. and Marshall, R. (2020) *2020 ESG Trends to Watch*. MSCI. Available at: https://www.msci.com/documents/10199/02f6473f-6fd8-aa8f-be72-443196478ec3 (accessed 8 January 2024).

Lehman, G. (1999) Disclosing new worlds: a role for social and environmental accounting and auditing. *Accounting, Organizations and Society* 24(3): 217–241. DOI: https://doi.org/10.1016/S0361-3682(98)00044-0.

Lehman, G. and Kuruppu, S.C. (2017) A framework for social and environmental accounting research. *Accounting Forum* 41(3): 139–146. DOI: https://doi.org/10.1016/j.accfor.2017.07.001.

180 *References*

Lehner, M. and Halliday, S.V. (2014) Branding sustainability: opportunity and risk behind a brand-based approach to sustainable markets. *ephemera* 14(1): 13–34.

Leins, S. (2020) 'Responsible investment': ESG and the post-crisis ethical order. *Economy and Society* 49(1): 71–91. DOI: https://doi.org/10.1080/03085147.2020.1702414.

Lev, B. (2018) The deteriorating usefulness of financial report information and how to reverse it. *Accounting and Business Research* 48(5): 465–493. DOI: https://doi.org/10.1080/00014788.2018.1470138.

Lev, B. and Gu, F. (2016) *The End of Accounting and the Path Forward for Investors and Managers*. Hoboken, NJ: Wiley.

Levy, J. (2014) Accounting for profit and the history of capital. *Critical Historical Studies* 1(2): 171–214.

Lhaopadchan, S. (2010) Fair value accounting and intangible assets: goodwill impairment and managerial choice. *Journal of Financial Regulation and Compliance* 18(2): 120–130. DOI: https://doi.org/10.1108/13581981011033989.

Lipton, P. (2018) The introduction of limited liability into the English and Australian colonial Companies Acts: inevitable progression or chaotic history? *Melbourne University Law Review* 41(3): 1278–1323. DOI: https://doi.org/10.3316/informit.750659270648905.

Lipton, P. (2020) The utilisation of evolutionary concepts in legal history: company law as a case study. *Monash University Law Review* 46(1): 58–58.

LiPuma, E. (2017) *The Social Life of Financial Derivatives*. Durham, NC: Duke University Press.

Litman, J. (1999) Breakfast with Batman: the public interest in the advertising age. *Yale Law Journal* 108(7): 1717–1735. DOI: https://doi.org/10.2307/797448.

Liu, X., Burns, A.C. and Hou, Y. (2017) An investigation of brand-related user-generated content on Twitter. *Journal of Advertising* 46(2): 236–247. DOI: https://doi.org/10.1080/00913367.2017.1297273.

Locke, J. (1993) *Political Writings of John Locke* (ed. D. Wootton). London: Penguin.

LSEG (2022) *London Stock Exchange Group Annual Report 2022*. Available at: https://www.lseg.com/en/investor-relations/annual-reports (accessed 19 April 2023).

Lury, C. (2004) *Brands: The Logos of the Global Economy*. London: Routledge.

Lux, S. (2011) Evaluating trade mark dilution from the perspective of the consumer. *UNSW Law Journal* 34(3): 1053–1079.

MacKenzie, D. (2009) Making things the same: gases, emission rights and the politics of carbon markets. *Accounting, Organizations and Society* 34(3): 440–455. DOI: https://doi.org/10.1016/j.aos.2008.02.004.

Malinak, S., Du, J. and Bala, G. (2018) Performance tests of Insight, ESG Momentum, and Volume signals. TruValue Labs. Available at: https://www.truvaluelabs.com/wp-content/uploads/2018/05/WP_PerfTest_R1k.pdf (accessed 22 July 2020).

Malsch, B. (2013) Politicizing the expertise of the accounting industry in the realm of corporate social responsibility. *Accounting, Organizations and Society* 38(2): 149–168. DOI: https://doi.org/10.1016/j.aos.2012.09.003.

Manjapra, K. (2018) When will Britain face up to its crimes against humanity? *The Guardian*, 29 March. Available at: https://www.theguardian.com/news/2018/

mar/29/slavery-abolition-compensation-when-will-britain-face-up-to-its-crimes-against-humanity (accessed 13 March 2019).

Manjoo, F. (2022) What BlackRock, Vanguard and State Street are doing to the economy. *New York Times*, 12 May. Available at: https://www.nytimes.com/2022/05/12/opinion/vanguard-power-blackrock-state-street.html (accessed 15 April 2023).

Mann, G. (2010) Value after Lehman. *Historical Materialism* 18(4): 172–188. DOI: https://doi.org/10.1163/156920610X550640.

Mann, G. (2017) *In the Long Run We Are All Dead: Keynesianism, Political Economy and Revolution*. London: Verso.

Manwaring, K. (2018) Will emerging technologies outpace consumer protection law? The case of digital consumer manipulation. *Competition and Consumer Law* 26(2): 141–181.

Marazzi, C. (2015) Money and financial capital. *Theory Culture & Society* 32(7–8): 39–50. DOI: https://doi.org/10.1177/0263276415598213.

Marcuse, H. (1964) *One-Dimensional Man: Studies in the Ideology of Advanced Industrial Society*. Boston, MA: Beacon Press.

Marshall, A. (2009) *Principles of Economics: Unabridged Eighth Edition*. New York: Cosimo Classics.

Mårtensson, M. (2009) Recounting counting and accounting: from political arithmetic to measuring intangibles and back. *Critical Perspectives on Accounting* 20(7): 835–846. DOI: https://doi.org/10.1016/j.cpa.2008.09.006.

Martin, A. and Quick, A. (2020) *Unions Renewed: Building Power in an Age of Finance*. Cambridge: Polity Press.

Martin, R. (2002) *Financialization of Daily Life*. Philadelphia, PA: Temple University Press.

Martin, R. (2013) After economy? Social logics of the derivative. *Social Text* 31(1): 83–106. DOI: https://doi.org/10.1215/01642472-1958908.

Martin, R. (2014) What difference do derivatives make? From the technical to the political conjuncture. *Culture Unbound* 6(1): 189–210.

Martin, R. (2015) *Knowledge LTD: Toward a Social Logic of the Derivative*. Philadelphia, PA: Temple University Press.

Marx, K. (1990) *Capital: Volume 1: A Critique of Political Economy* (trans. B. Fowkes). Reprint edition. London: Penguin.

Marx, K. and Engels, F. (2018) *The Communist Manifesto*. New York: Vintage.

Mason, E. (1959) Introduction. In: Mason, E. (ed.) *The Corporation in Modern Society*. Cambridge, MA: Harvard University Press, pp. 1–24.

Mason, P. (2007) *Live Working or Die Fighting: How the Working Class Went Global*. London: Vintage.

Massumi, B. (2018) *99 Theses on the Revaluation of Value: A Postcapitalist Manifesto*. Minneapolis, MN: University of Minnesota Press.

Masters, B. (2022) BlackRock denies Republican claims of climate 'activism'. *Financial Times*, 7 September. Available at: https://www.ft.com/content/a4af6919-b1cc-4c1 5-b17c-46186fddbd4c (accessed 9 January 2024).

Masters, B. and Temple-West, P. (2023a) Vivek Ramaswamy's fund manager Strive sticks to its 'anti-woke' mission. *Financial Times*, 24 February. Available at:

https://www.ft.com/content/c7ccc5ea-3e8f-49a1-b250-31365f4f33e0 (accessed 1 April 2023).

Masters, B. and Temple-West, P. (2023b) Wall Street titans confront ESG backlash as new financial risk. *Financial Times*, 1 March. Available at: https://www.ft.com/content/f5fe15f8-3703-4df9-b203-b5d1dd01e3bc (accessed 1 May 2023).

Mata, C., Fialho, A. and Eugénio, T. (2018) A decade of environmental accounting reporting: what do we know? *Journal of Cleaner Production* 198: 1198–1209. DOI: https://doi.org/10.1016/j.jclepro.2018.07.087.

Mathews, B. (2022) French NGO files court complaint over Adidas, New Balance greenwashing. *Apparel Insider*. Available at: https://apparelinsider.com/french-ngo-files-court-complaint-over-adidas-new-balance-greenwashing/ (accessed 21 April 2023).

McCormick, M. (2021) Chevron accused of 'greenwashing' in complaint lodged with FTC. *Financial Times*, 16 March. Available at: https://www.ft.com/content/2985e18a-fdcb-4cd2-aee3-d5a0fe4cdab2 (accessed 21 April 2023).

McDonagh, L. (2015) From brand performance to consumer performativity: assessing European trade mark law after the rise of anthropological marketing. *Journal of Law and Society* 42(4): 611–636. DOI: https://doi.org/10.1111/j.1467-6478.2015.00727.x.

McGoey, L. (2015) *There's No Such Thing as a Free Gift: The Gates Foundation and the Price of Philanthropy*. London: Verso.

McPhail, K. (2009) Where is the ethical knowledge in the knowledge economy? Power and potential in the emergence of ethical knowledge as a component of intellectual capital. *Critical Perspectives on Accounting* 20(7): 804–822. DOI: https://doi.org/10.1016/j.cpa.2008.09.004.

McQueen, R. (2009) *A Social History of Company Law: Great Britain and the Australian Colonies 1854–1920*. Farnham: Ashgate.

Megaw, N., Masters, B. and Darbyshire, M. (2023) BlackRock hit by backlash after fall in environmental and social votes. *Financial Times*, 23 August. Available at: https://www.ft.com/content/dfc22003-93cc-4a4a-bb94-ac80fa6a84d5 (accessed 23 November 2023).

Mercer, J. (2010) A mark of distinction: branding and trade mark law in the UK from the 1860s. *Business History* 52(1): 17–42. DOI: https://doi.org/10.1080/00076790903281033.

Miller, J. (2022) Corporate America gears up for a new wave of investigations by Congress. *Financial Times*, 7 November. Available at: https://www.ft.com/content/aa5237ab-0646-4e26-bd15-74bbe10e9783 (accessed 1 April 2023).

Miller J., Klasa, A. and Walker, O. (2022) Deutsche banker takes over asset manager in the eye of an ESG storm. *Financial Times*, 2 June. Available at: https://www.ft.com/content/9ad68424-231b-4edc-9d88-d29ceebd4db0 (accessed 1 April 2023).

Milligan, A. and Bailey, S. (2019) *Myths of Branding: A Brand Is Just a Logo, and Other Popular Misconceptions*. London: Kogan Page.

Milton, G. (2019) Bloomberg revenue continues to diversify. Available at: https://www.linkedin.com/pulse/bloomberg-revenue-continues-diversify-jennifer-milton/ (accessed 21 April 2023).

Mitchell, C. (2023) Mighty Earth files complaint with US Securities and Exchange Commission against JBS 'green bonds'. Mighty Earth. Available at: https://www.mightyearth.org/whistleblower-complaint-to-the-securities-and-exchange-commission-against-jbs/ (accessed 22 April 2023).

Mittelstaedt, J. (2015) Trademark dilution and the management of brands. In: Desai, D.R., Lianos, I. and Waller, S.W. (eds) *Brands, Competition Law and IP*. Cambridge: Cambridge University Press, pp. 203–216.

Mizruchi, M.S. (2013) *The Fracturing of the American Corporate Elite*. Cambridge, MA: Harvard University Press.

Moody's (2023) *Moody's Section 10k Report*. Washington, DC: US Securities and Exchange Commission.

Moore, J.W. (2015) *Capitalism in the Web of Life: Ecology and the Accumulation of Capital*. London: Verso.

Morningstar (2023) *Morningstar Section 10k Report*. Washington, DC: US Securities and Exchange Commission.

MSCI (2020) Climate value-at-risk. Available at: https://www.msci.com/documents/1296102/16985724/MSCI-ClimateVaR-Introduction-Feb2020.pdf/f0ff1d77-3278-e409-7a2a-bf1da9d53f30?t=1580472788213 (accessed 17 August 2020).

MSCI (2023) *MSCI Section 10k Report*. Washington, DC: US Securities and Exchange Commission.

Munro, K. (2019) 'Social reproduction theory,' social reproduction, and household production. *Science & Society* 83(4): 451–468.

Nakamura, L. (2003) A trillion dollars a year in intangible investment and the new economy. In: Hand, J.R.M. and Lev, B. (eds) *Intangible Assets: Values, Measures, and Risks*. Oxford: Oxford University Press, pp. 19–47.

Negri, T. (1988) *Revolution Retrieved: Writings on Marx, Keynes, Capitalist Crisis and New Social Subjects*. London: Left Bank Books.

Neilsen IQ (2015) The sustainability imperative. Available at: https://nielseniq.com/global/en/insights/analysis/2015/the-sustainability-imperative-2/ (accessed 18 January 2024).

Nelson, J.A. (2011) Does profit-seeking rule out love? Evidence (or not) from economics and law. *Washington University Journal of Law and Policy* 35: 69–107.

Neuberger, Lord (2015) Harold G. Fox Memorial Lecture 2015: Trade-mark dilution and parody. *Intellectual Property Journal* 28(1): 1–20.

New York City Government (2021) New York City sues ExxonMobil, Shell, BP, and the American Petroleum Institute for systematically and intentionally deceiving New Yorkers. Available at: http://www.nyc.gov/office-of-the-mayor/news/293-21/new-york-city-sues-exxonmobil-shell-bp-the-american-petroleum-institute-systematically (accessed 21 April 2023).

NPR (2019) Facebook pays $643,000 fine for role in Cambridge Analytica scandal. Available at: https://www.npr.org/2019/10/30/774749376/facebook-pays-643-000-fine-for-role-in-cambridge-analytica-scandal (accessed 9 July 2020).

O'Connor, J. (1998) *Natural Causes: Essays in Ecological Marxism*. New York: Guilford Press.

Odier, P. (2017) Why lack of data is the biggest hazard in 'green investing'. *Financial Times*, 6 March. Available at: https://www.ft.com/content/be8e5db2-0249-11e7-aa5b-6bb07f5c8e12 (accessed 29 January 2019).

OECD (2013) *Supporting Investment in Knowledge Capital, Growth and Innovation*. Paris: OECD Publishing.

OECD (2017) *Investment governance and the integration of environmental, social and governance factors*. Available at: https://www.oecd.org/finance/Investment-Governance-Integration-ESG-Factors.pdf (accessed 20 April 2020).

Oliveira, P. and Sullivan, A. (2015) *Sustainability and Its Impact on Brand Value*. Interbrand. Available at: https://www.interbrand.com/wp-content/uploads/2015/10/3.-Sustainabilityand-its-impact-in-BV.pdf (accessed 14 May 2020).

Olusoga, D. (2018) The Treasury's tweet shows slavery is still misunderstood. *The Guardian*, 12 February. Available at: https://www.theguardian.com/commentisfree/2018/feb/12/treasury-tweet-slavery-compensate-slave-owners (accessed 13 March 2019).

ONS (2022) Investment in intangible assets in the UK: 2020. Available at: https://www.ons.gov.uk/economy/economicoutputandproductivity/productivitymeasures/articles/experimentalestimatesofinvestmentinintangibleassetsintheuk2015/2020 (accessed 18 January 2024).

Orsagh, M., Allen, J., Sloggett, J., et al. (2018) *Guidance and Case Studies for ESG Integration: Equities and Fixed Income*. New York: CFA Institute; UNPRI.

O'Shea, L. (2019) *Future Histories: What Ada Lovelace, Tom Paine, and the Paris Commune Can Teach Us about Digital Technology*. London: Verso.

Ouma, S. (2018) This can('t) be an asset class: the world of money management, 'society', and the contested morality of farmland investments. *Environment and Planning A: Economy and Space* 52(1): 66–87. DOI: https://doi.org/10.1177/0308518X18790051.

Page, G. and Fearn, H. (2006) Corporate reputation: what do consumers really care about? *Journal of Advertising Research* 45(3): 305–313. DOI: https://doi.org/10.1017/S0021849905050361.

Palan, R. (2012) The financial crisis and intangible value. *Capital & Class* 37(1): 65–77.

Palomera, J. and Vetta, T. (2016) Moral economy: rethinking a radical concept. *Anthropological Theory* 16(4): 413–432. DOI: https://doi.org/10.1177/1463499616677.

Partnoy, F. (2000) Adding derivatives to the corporate law mix. *Georgia Law Review* 34: 599–629.

Pedrini, M. (2007) Human capital convergences in intellectual capital reporting and sustainability reports. *Journal of Intellectual Capital* 8(2): 346–366.

Pence, M. (2022) Republicans can stop ESG political bias. *Wall Street Journal*, 26 May. Available at: https://www.wsj.com/articles/only-republicans-can-stop-the-esg-madness-woke-musk-consumer-demand-free-speech-corporate-america-11653574189 (accessed 17 January 2024).

Perry, J. (2009) *Goodwill Hunting: Accounting and the Global Regulation of Economic Ideas*. Vrije Universiteit Amsterdam. Available at: https://research.cbs.dk/en/publications/goodwill-hunting-accounting-and-the-global-regulation-of-economic (accessed 21 July 2020).

References

185

Polanyi, K. (1945) *Origins of Our Time: The Great Transformation*. London: Victor Gollancz.

Politi, J. and Fedor, L. (2023) Joe Biden expected to issue first presidential veto in anti-ESG vote. *Financial Times*, 1 March. Available at: https://www.ft.com/content/ba4d0028-eaec-47df-82c4-2c8d9298e9be (accessed 1 April 2023).

Ponte, S., Richey, L. and Baab, M. (2009) Bono's product RED initiative: corporate social responsibility that solves the problems of 'distant others'. *Third World Quarterly* 30(2): 307–317.

Pope Francis (2015) *Encyclical on Capitalism and Inequality: On Care for Our Common Home* (ed. S. Lavigne). London: Verso.

Postone, M. (1996) *Time, Labor, and Social Domination: A Reinterpretation of Marx's Critical Theory*. Cambridge: Cambridge University Press.

Potočnik, M. (2019) *Arbitrating Brands: International Investment Treaties and Trade Marks. Northampton*: Edward Elgar.

Prahalad, C.K. and Ramaswamy, V. (2004) Co-creation experiences: the next practice in value creation. *Journal of Interactive Marketing* 18(3): 5–14. DOI: https://doi.org/10.1002/dir.20015.

Quattrocchi, A. and Nairn, T. (1998) *The Beginning of the End*. London: Verso.

Quesenberry, K.A. and Coolsen, M.K. (2019) What makes Facebook brand posts engaging? A content analysis of Facebook brand post text that increases shares, likes, and comments to influence organic viral reach. *Journal of Current Issues & Research in Advertising* 40(3): 229–244. DOI: https://doi.org/10.1080/10641734.2018.1503113.

Quigley, E. (2019) Universal ownership in the Anthropocene. ID 3457205, SSRN Scholarly Paper, 13 May. Rochester, NY: Social Science Research Network. DOI: https://doi.org/10.2139/ssrn.3457205.

Radin, M. (1996) *Contested Commodities*. Cambridge, MA: Harvard University Press.

Rafferty, M. and Yu, S. (2010) *Shifting Risk Work and Working Life in Australia: A Report for the Australian Council of Trade Unions*. Sydney: Workplace Research Centre.

Ramaswamy, V. and Ozcan, K. (2014) *The Co-Creation Paradigm*. Stanford, CA: Stanford University Press.

Ramaswamy, V. and Ozcan, K. (2016) Brand value co-creation in a digitalized world: an integrative framework and research implications. *International Journal of Research in Marketing* 33(1): 93–106. DOI: https://doi.org/10.1016/j.ijresmar.2015.07.001.

Reinecke, J. and Donaghey, J. (2015) After Rana Plaza: building coalitional power for labour rights between unions and (consumption-based) social movement organisations. *Organization* 22(5): 720–740. DOI: https://doi.org/10.1177/1350508415585028.

Richardson, B. (2015) Financial markets and socially responsible investing. In: Sjåfjell, B. and Richardson, B. (eds) *Company Law and Sustainability: Legal Barriers and Opportunities*. Cambridge: Cambridge University Press, pp. 226–273.

Richardson, B. and Cragg, W. (2010) Being virtuous and prosperous: SRI's conflicting goals. *Journal of Business Ethics* 92(1): 21–39. DOI: https://doi.org/10.1007/s10551-010-0632-9.

Richardson, B. and Peihani, M. (2015) Universal investors and socially responsible finance: a critique of a premature theory. *Banking and Finance Law Review* 30: 405–455.

Robertson, M. (2012) Measurement and alienation: making a world of ecosystem services. *Transactions of the Institute of British Geographers* 37(3): 386–401. DOI: https://doi.org/10.1111/j.1475-5661.2011.00476.x.

Rodriguez, E., Nauman, B., Tett, G., et al. (2020) Covid-19 shows why ESG matters; Barclays' big climate vote; UK impact investors' legal hurdle; your questions answered. *Financial Times*, 8 May. Available at: https://www.ft.com/content/7a94521 9-bd89-450d-9ec8-fdeb8ba3a0da (accessed 10 May 2020).

Ropes & Gray (n.d.) Navigating state regulation of ESG. Available at: https://www.ropesgray.com/en/navigating-state-regulation-of-esg (accessed 26 April 2023).

Rose, S. (2016) Gillian Triggs urges super funds to take up the fight on human rights. *Australian Financial Review*, 10 May. Available at: http://www.afr.com/news/policy/gillian-triggs-urges-super-funds-to-take-up-the-fight-on-human-rights-20160509-gopw7d.

Rostow, E. (1959) To whom and for what ends is corporate management responsible? In: Mason, E. (ed.) *The Corporation in Modern Society*. Cambridge, MA: Harvard University Press, pp. 46–71.

Ruggie, J.G. (1982) International regimes, transactions, and change: embedded liberalism in the postwar economic order. *International Organization* 36(2): 379–415.

St-Pierre, J. and Audet, J. (2011) Intangible assets and performance. *Journal of Intellectual Capital* 12(2): 202–223.

Salinas, S. (2019) Goldman warns that Apple is too dependent on Google for services revenue, and will need to roll out a 'Prime' bundle. CNBC. Available at: https://www.cnbc.com/2019/02/12/goldman-sachs-apple-dependent-on-google-for-services-revenue.html (accessed 4 November 2019).

Sampford, C. and Ransome, W. (2011) *Ethics and Socially Responsible Investing: A Philosophical Approach*. Farnham: Ashgate.

Sandberg, J. (2014) Moral economy and normative ethics. *Journal of Global Ethics* 11(2): 176–187.

Sandberg, J., Jurvale, C., Hedesstrom, T.M., et al. (2009) The heterogeneity of socially responsible investment. *Journal of Business Ethics* 87(4): 519–533. DOI: https://doi.org/10.1007/s10551-008-9956-0.

Sanders, J. (2019) Facebook data privacy scandal: a cheat sheet. TechRepublic. Available at: https://www.techrepublic.com/article/facebook-data-privacy-scandal-a-cheat-sheet/ (accessed 9 July 2020).

Sanderson, H. (2018) Coal industry between a rock and a hard place. *Financial Times*, 28 August. Available at: https://www.ft.com/content/8c558b40-7863-11e 8-8e67-1e1a0846c475 (accessed 9 January 2024).

SASB (n.d.) Standard-Setting Archive. Available at: https://www.sasb.org/standard-setting-archive/ (accessed 2 March 2020).

SASB (2016a) *Company Case Studies: Unlocking the Value of SASB Standards*. Available at: https://www.sasb.org/knowledge-hub/company-case-studies-1/ (accessed 12 February 2020).

SASB (2016b) *The State of Disclosure: An Analysis of the Effectiveness of Sustainability Disclosure in SEC Filings*. Available at: http://library.sasb.org/wp-content/uploads/2016/11/StateofDisclosure-Report-113016v2.pdf (accessed 12 February 2020).

SASB (2018) *Dead Cobras & Fabergé Eggs: Unlocking The Potential of ESG Data*. Available at: https://www.sasb.org/knowledge-hub/dead-cobras-faberge-eggs/ (accessed 13 February 2020).

SASB (2019) *Annual Report 2018*. https://sasb.org/wp-content/uploads/2019/11/SASB-Annual-Report-2018-w.pdf (accessed 21 January 2024).

Satz, D. (1989) Marxism, materialism and historical progress. *Canadian Journal of Philosophy* 19(sup1): 391–424. DOI: https://doi.org/10.1080/00455091.1989.10716805.

Sayer, A. (2007) Moral economy as critique. *New Political Economy* 12(2): 261–270. DOI: https://doi.org/10.1080/13563460701303008.

Sayer, A. (2015) Time for moral economy? *Geoforum* 65: 291–293. DOI: https://doi.org/10.1016/j.geoforum.2015.07.027.

Schechter, F.I. (1927) The rational basis of trademark protection. *Harvard Law Review* 40(6): 813–833.

Scholz, J. and Smith, A.N. (2019) Branding in the age of social media firestorms: how to create brand value by fighting back online. *Journal of Marketing Management* 35(11–12): 1100–1134. DOI: https://doi.org/10.1080/0267257X.2019.1620839.

Schumpeter, J.A. (1943) *Capitalism, Socialism, and Democracy*. London: George Allen & Unwin.

Schwarzkopf, S. (2010) Turning trade marks into brands: how advertising agencies practiced and conceptualized branding 1890–1930. In: da Silva Lopes, T. and Duguid, P. (eds) *Trademarks, Brands, and Competitiveness*. New York: Routledge, pp. 165–193.

Scott, J.C. (1976) *The Moral Economy of the Peasant: Rebellion and Subsistence in Southeast Asia*. New Haven, CT: Yale University Press.

Scott, M. (2019) Shoppers want more sustainable products, but brands are struggling to keep up. *Forbes*, 26 February. Available at: https://www.forbes.com/sites/mikescott/2019/02/26/shoppers-want-more-sustainable-products-but-brands-are-struggling-to-keep-up/ (accessed 30 October 2019).

SEC (n.d.) Enforcement task force focused on climate and ESG issues. Available at: https://www.sec.gov/securities-topics/enforcement-task-force-focused-climate-esg-issues (accessed 10 November 2023).

SEC (2021) SEC announces enforcement task force focused on climate and ESG issues. Available at: https://www.sec.gov/news/press-release/2021-42 (accessed 22 April 2023).

SEC (2022) *Enhanced Disclosures by Certain Investment Advisers and Investment Companies about Environmental, Social, and Governance Investment Practices*. S7-17-22, Proposed Rule, May. Available at: https://www.sec.gov/rules/proposed/2022/33-11068.pdf (accessed 9 April 2023).

Seddon, J. (2015) The brand in the boardroom: how Ogilvy & Mather reinvented the marketing principles of brand valuation. *Journal of Advertising Research* 55(2): 146–161. DOI: https://doi.org/10.2501/JAR-55-2-146-161.

Sen, A. (1999) *On Ethics & Economics*. New Delhi: Oxford.

Sheth, J.N. and Uslay, C. (2007) Implications of the revised definition of marketing: from exchange to value creation. *Journal of Public Policy & Marketing* 26(2): 302–307. DOI: https://doi.org/10.1509/jppm.26.2.302.

Siddiqi, D. (2015) Starving for justice: Bangladeshi workers in a 'post-Rana Plaza' world. *International Labor and Working-Class History* 87: 165–173. DOI: https://doi.org/10.1017/S0147547915000101.

Singer, M. (2019) Why most consumers are still not buying ethical fashion. *The Sydney Morning Herald*, 7 June. Available at: https://www.smh.com.au/lifestyle/fashion/why-most-consumers-are-still-not-buying-ethical-fashion-20190606-p51v31.html (accessed 30 October 2019).

Sippel, S. (2018) Financialising farming as a moral imperative? Renegotiating the legitimacy of land investments in Australia. *Environment and Planning A: Economy and Space* 50(3): 549–568. DOI: https://doi.org/10.1177/0308518X17741317.

Smith, A. (2009) *The Theory of Moral Sentiments*. London: Penguin.

Smith, A. (1993) *An Inquiry into the Nature and Causes of the Wealth of Nations*. Oxford: Oxford University Press.

Soederberg, S. (2014) *Debtfare States and the Poverty Industry: Money, Discipline and the Surplus Population*. Abingdon: Routledge.

Sparkes, R. (2001) Ethical investment: whose ethics, which investment? *Business Ethics: A European Review* 10(3): 194–205.

Sparkes, R. and Cowton, C.J. (2004) The maturing of socially responsible investment: a review of the developing link with corporate social responsibility. *Journal of Business Ethics* 52(1): 45–57. DOI: https://doi.org/10.1023/B:BUSI.0000033106.43260.99.

Spence, C., Chabrak, N. and Pucci, R. (2013) Doxic sunglasses: a response to 'Green accounting and green eyeshades: twenty years later'. *Critical Perspectives on Accounting* 24(6): 469–473. DOI: https://doi.org/10.1016/j.cpa.2013.05.002.

State Street Global Advisors (2022) *State Street Section 10k Report*. Washington, DC: US Securities and Exchange Commission.

Stolowy, H. and Paugam, L. (2018) The expansion of non-financial reporting: an exploratory study. *Accounting and Business Research* 48(5): 525–548. DOI: https://doi.org/10.1080/00014788.2018.1470141.

Sweezy, P. (1976) A critique. In: Sweezy, P., Dobb, M., Hill, C., et al. *The Transition from Feudalism to Capitalism*. London: NLB, pp. 31–56.

Taleb, N.N. (2010) *The Black Swan: The Impact of the Highly Improbable*. 2nd edition. New York: Random House.

Tan, E.S. (2002) 'The bull is half the herd': property rights and enclosures in England, 1750–1850. *Explorations in Economic History* 39(4): 470–489.

Tawney, R.H. (1926) *Religion and the Rise of Capitalism*. London: Hazell, Watson and Viney.

Temple-West, P. and Liu, N. (2020) Chinese companies get to grips with tougher ESG disclosures. *Financial Times*, 14 January. Available at: https://www.ft.com/content/b06291aa-3251-11ea-9703-eea0cae3f0de (accessed 6 March 2020).

The Investor Agenda (2020) The sustainable recovery from the COVID-19 pandemic. Available at: http://theinvestoragenda.org/wp-content/uploads/2020/05/

THE_INVESTOR_AGENDA_A_SUSTAINABLE_RECOVERY_FROM_
COVID-19.pdf (accessed 6 May 2020).

The Social Dilemma (2020) Film. Directed by Jeff Orlowski. US: Exposure Labs, Argent Pictures and The Space Program.

Thomas, H. (2023) Glencore's pursuit of Teck sends its careful coal message up in smoke. *Financial Times*, 14 April. Available at: https://www.ft.com/conten t/0da5af3e-f4b3-46cb-a3d3-93291544eb7a (accessed 6 June 2023).

Thompson, E.P. (1967) Time, work-discipline, and industrial capitalism. *Past & Present* 38: 56–97. DOI: https://doi.org/10.1093/past/38.1.56.

Thompson, E.P. (1971) The moral economy of the English crowd in the eighteenth century. *Past & Present* 50(1): 76–136. DOI: https://doi.org/10.1093/past/50.1.76.

Thompson, E.P. (1991) *Customs in Common*. London: Penguin.

Thompson, E.P. (2002) *The Making of the English Working Class*. London: Penguin.

Thornton, D.B. (2013) Green accounting and green eyeshades twenty years later. *Critical Perspectives on Accounting* 24(6): 438–442. DOI: https:// doi.org/10.1016/j.cpa.2013.02.004.

Time News (2022) Adidas and New Balance targeted by a complaint for 'green-washing'. Available at: https://time.news/adidas-and-new-balance-targeted-by-a-complaint-for-greenwashing/ (accessed 21 April 2023).

Townsend, S. (2018) 88% of consumers want you to help them make a dif-ference. *Forbes*, 21 November. Available at: https://www.forbes.com/sites/ solitairetownsend/2018/11/21/consumers-want-you-to-help-them-make-a-difference/ (accessed 30 October 2019).

TruValue Labs (n.d.) Raising the bar on ESG data integration. Available at: https:// insights.truvaluelabs.com/wp_raisingbaresgdataint_offer (accessed 22 July 2020).

TruValue Labs (2017) New alpha from ESG2.0 factors – US large cap. TruValue Labs. Available at: https://www.truvaluelabs.com/wp-content/uploads/2017/11/ Sum_PerfTest_SP500.pdf (accessed 22 July 2020).

UBS (2020) Future reimagined: will ESG data and services demand accelerate post-COVID & who will win? Available at: https://www.ubs.com/global/en/ investment-bank/in-focus/covid-19/2020/esg-data-and-services.html (accessed 9 April 2023).

UK National Contact Point (2020) ClientEarth complaint to the UK NCP about BP. Available at: https://www.gov.uk/government/publications/client-earth-complaint-to-the-uk-ncp-about-bp (accessed 21 April 2023).

UK National Contact Point (2022) Group of NGOs complaint to the UK NCP about Drax Group PLC. Available at: https://www.gov.uk/government/publications/group-of-ngos-complaint-to-the-uk-ncp-about-drax-group-plc (accessed 21 April 2023).

UNEP FI (2019) Fiduciary duty for the 21st century. Available at: https:// www.unepfi.org/wordpress/wp-content/uploads/2019/10/Fiduciary-duty-21st-century-final-report.pdf (accessed 18 January 2024).

UNEP FI and Freshfields Bruckhaus Deringer (2005) *A Legal Framework for the Integration of Environmental, Social and Governance Issues into Institutional Investment*. Available at: http://www.unepfi.org/fileadmin/documents/freshfields_ legal_resp_20051123.pdf (accessed 18 January 2024).

UNEP FI and Freshfields Bruckhaus Deringer (2009) *Fiduciary Responsibility – Legal and Practical Aspects of Integrating Environmental, Social and Governance Issues into Institutional Investment.* Available at: http://www.unepfi.org/fileadmin/documents/fiduciaryII.pdf (accessed 18 January 2024).

UNPRI, UNEP FI and The Generation Foundation (2019) *Fiduciary Duty in the 21st Century.* Available at: https://www.unpri.org/download?ac=9792 (accessed 20 April 2020).

UNPRI, UNEP FI, UN Global Compact, et al. (n.d.) *Fiduciary Duty in the 21st Century.* Available at: https://www.unpri.org/download?ac=1378 (accessed 1 July 2020).

US BRT (2019a) Business Roundtable redefines the purpose of a corporation to promote 'an economy that serves all Americans'. Available at: https://www.businessroundtable.org/business-roundtable-redefines-the-purpose-of-a-corporation-to-promote-an-economy-that-serves-all-americans (accessed 18 January 2024).

US BRT (2019b) Our commitment. Available at: https://opportunity.businessroundtable.org/ourcommitment/ (accessed 3 March 2020).

Vallaster, C., Lindgreen, A. and Maon, F. (2012) Strategically leveraging corporate social responsibility: a corporate branding perspective. *California Management Review* 54(3): 34–60. DOI: https://doi.org/10.1525/cmr.2012.54.3.34.

Varsani, H., Menditratta, R. and Katiyar, S. (2021) *ESG and Climate Derivatives in Equity Exposure Management.* MSCI, July. Available at: https://www.msci.com/www/research-report/esg-and-climate-derivatives-in/02631033346 (accessed 2 May 2023).

Verhoef, P.C. and Bijmolt, T.H.A. (2019) Marketing perspectives on digital business models: a framework and overview of the special issue. *International Journal of Research in Marketing* 36(3): 341–349. DOI: https://doi.org/10.1016/j.ijresmar.2019.08.001.

Vermeer, S.A.M., Araujo, T., Bernritter, S.F., et al. (2019) Seeing the wood for the trees: how machine learning can help firms in identifying relevant electronic word-of-mouth in social media. *International Journal of Research in Marketing* 36(3): 492–508. DOI: https://doi.org/10.1016/j.ijresmar.2019.01.010.

Voorveld, H.A.M. (2019) Brand communication in social media: a research agenda. *Journal of Advertising* 48(1): 14–26. DOI: https://doi.org/10.1080/00913367.2019.1588808.

Voorveld, H.A.M., van Noort, G., Muntinga, D.G., et al. (2018) Engagement with social media and social media advertising: the differentiating role of platform type. *Journal of Advertising* 47(1): 38–54. DOI: https://doi.org/10.1080/00913367.2017.1405754.

WBCSD (n.d.a) About us. Available at: https://www.wbcsd.org/Overview/About-us (accessed 26 April 2019).

WBCSD (n.d.b) Redefining value. Available at: https://www.wbcsd.org/Programs/Redefining-Value (accessed 9 January 2024).

WBCSD (n.d.c) What we do. Available at: https://www.wbcsd.org/Overview/Our-approach (accessed 26 April 2019).

Webb, S. and Webb, B. (1909) *The Basis and Policy of Socialism.* London: Fabian Society.

Webb, S. and Webb, B. (1911) *Industrial Democracy*. London: Longmans, Green.

Webb, S. and Webb, B. (1923) *Decay of Capitalist Civilisation*. London: Fabian Society.

Weber, M. (2001) *The Protestant Ethic and the Spirit of Capitalism*. London: Fitzroy, Dearborn.

WEF (1973) Davos Manifesto 1973: a code of ethics for business leaders. Available at: https://www.weforum.org/agenda/2019/12/davos-manifesto-1973-a-code-of-ethics-for-business-leaders/ (accessed 18 January 2024).

WEF (2020) Davos Manifesto 2020: the universal purpose of a company in the fourth industrial revolution. Available at: https://www.weforum.org/agenda/2019/12/davos-manifesto-2020-the-universal-purpose-of-a-company-in-the-fourth-industrial-revolution/ (accessed 18 January 2024).

Wen, H. and Moehrle, S.R. (2016) Accounting for goodwill: an academic literature review and analysis to inform the debate. *Research in Accounting Regulation* 28(1): 11–21. DOI: https://doi.org/10.1016/j.racreg.2016.03.002.

Wexler, M. (2002) Organisational memory and intellectual capital. *Journal of Intellectual Capital* 3(4): 393–414.

Wiencierz, C. and Röttger, U. (2017) The use of big data in corporate communication. *Corporate Communications: An International Journal* 22(3): 258–272. DOI: https://doi.org/10.1108/CCIJ-02-2016-0015.

Wigglesworth, R. (2018) Rating agencies using green criteria suffer from 'inherent biases'. *Financial Times*, 21 July. Available at: https://www.ft.com/content/a5e02050-8ac6-11e8-bf9e-8771d5404543 (accessed 9 January 2024).

Wilf, S. (2008) The making of the post-war paradigm in American intellectual property law. *Columbia Journal of Law and the Arts* 31: 139–207.

Wilkof, N. (2018) 'Strong' trade marks, 'strong' brands: what do we mean? *Journal of Intellectual Property Law & Practice* 13(5): 341–342.

Willmott, H. (2010) Creating 'value' beyond the point of production: branding, financialization and market capitalization. *Organization* 17(5): 517–542.

Yglesias, M. (2018) Elizabeth Warren has a plan to save capitalism. *Vox*, 15 August. Available at: https://www.vox.com/2018/8/15/17683022/elizabeth-warren-accountable-capitalism-corporations (accessed 3 May 2020).

Yuki, T. (2015) What makes brands' social content shareable on Facebook? An analysis that demonstrates the power of online trust and attention. *Journal of Advertising Research* 55(4): 458–470. DOI: https://doi.org/10.2501/JAR-2015-026.

Zelizer, V. (2010) *Economic Lives: How Culture Shapes the Economy*. Princeton, NJ: Princeton University Press.

Zinn, H. (2016) *A People's History of the United States*. London: Boxtree.

Zinn, H. (ed.) (1966) *New Deal Thought*. Indianapolis, IN: Bobbs-Merrill.

Zuboff, S. (2019) *The Age of Surveillance Capitalism: The Fight for a Human Future at the New Frontier of Power*. New York: PublicAffairs.

Index

accounting
  for ethics 97, 103, 116
  frameworks 94, 103, 120
  intangible(s) 97, 98, 100, 108, 115
  practices 13, 61, 94, 96
  social and environmental (SEA) 12,
    94, 95, 97–98, 100–103,
    107–108, 110, 113, 116, 122,
    160
  standards 12, 14, 94, 97, 109, 124,
    137, 159
accountability 1, 2, 12–13, 43, 82, 95,
    98, 101–102, 105, 140
  corporate 1, 43, 140
  environmental 101–102
  social 41

brand 4–5, 12–14, 57, 62–63, 71, 73,
    81, 89, 99, 105, 111, 114–
    115, 119–137, 147, 159–160
Bryan, D. 9–11, 42, 53–56, 69–70,
    76–77, 91

capital
  accumulation 10–11, 26, 69, 71,
    78, 80, 91, 115, 156, 161
  responsible 46, 98
capitalist realist 4
Christophers, B. 10, 28, 51, 53–55, 63,
    69–70, 76–77
commensuration 11, 56, 69, 75, 92,
    96, 107, 112, 116
commodification 12, 22, 54–56, 68,
    103, 107, 160
  of ethics 12, 68, 160
  of risk 12, 54, 56

commodity 4, 11, 22, 69–70, 75–76,
    103, 122, 129, 136
  brands as 122
  ethical capital as 4
  ethics as a 103
consumerism 32, 37
consumption 4, 31, 32, 34, 37–38,
    109, 123, 125–127, 129, 133,
    135, 137
  ethical consumption 4, 126–127
co-production 14, 123, 126
corporate governance 6, 40–42, 47–48,
    51–52, 55–56, 58–59, 81, 98,
    101
corporate social responsibility (CSR)
    35, 42, 44, 90, 102, 126–127
crisis 1, 3, 8, 35, 37, 43–44, 46,
    51–52, 54, 56–57, 129

derivative 4, 8–14, 41–42, 52, 54–57,
    60–61, 63, 77, 82, 86–93,
    120, 127–128, 131, 152, 159,
    161
  logic 8, 10, 54–55, 57, 67, 86, 89,
    93, 128, 131
derivative logic of ethics 10, 12–14,
    52, 57, 67–68, 82, 86–88, 90,
    92, 152, 159, 161

ethical capital assets 57, 116, 159
ethical capital production 14, 120,
    123, 132, 160
ethics-as-risk 5, 12
ESG
  analysts 6, 75–77, 81, 84, 86,
    88–89

Index

information 5, 12–14, 63, 95, 109, 115, 139–140, 143, 146, 148, 150, 159, 160
integration 3, 5, 12, 14, 40–41, 46, 57, 59–63, 67–69, 77–78, 81, 85–93, 95, 98, 100, 139, 149, 159, 161
investing 3, 14, 40, 58, 128, 140, 148, 151–152, 155–157, 162
issues 12, 46, 49–52, 57, 59, 61–62, 87, 89, 91, 107, 111, 113, 116, 125, 137, 143, 147–148, 152, 159
ratings 57, 60, 90, 106, 140–141, 148–150, 156, 160
risks 49–51, 59–63, 67–68, 76–80, 82–85, 87–88, 90–91, 93, 106, 108–109, 112, 114, 126, 128, 137, 139, 142, 151, 156, 160, 162
scores 4, 12, 63, 114, 142, 146–147
externalities 45, 102, 161

Fancy, T. 43, 67, 81
fiduciary capitalism 47, 51, 56, 93, 104
financialisation 41, 54–55, 67, 76, 103, 106, 161
everyday financialisation 54
financialised capitalism 6
Fink, L. 3, 49

governance 1, 6, 40–42, 47–48, 51–52, 55–56, 58–59, 61, 81, 85, 89, 98, 101, 105, 153
corporate 6, 40–42, 47–48, 51–52, 55–56, 58–59, 81, 98, 101
private 47

institutional investors 1, 42, 46–48, 51, 57–58, 63, 84, 87, 141–142, 156
intangible assets 4–5, 10–13, 70, 76, 97–100, 104, 108, 124, 158–159, 160
Integrated Reporting 12, 89, 94, 95, 97–98, 100–101, 103–106, 112, 115–116, 148, 160
intellectual property 6, 13–14, 120–121, 123, 130–132

labour
abstract 55–56, 69, 77
-as-consumer 13–14, 120, 123–124, 129–131, 133–137, 159–160
capital-labour relation 5, 6, 68, 85, 120, 134
concrete 55–56, 69
rights 43, 57, 61, 81, 89, 151
socially necessary 11, 160
as a source of value 12, 69, 74
subordination of 5, 69, 85
liberal 21–24, 38, 40, 55, 86–87, 101, 161
liberalism 8, 20, 22–23, 34, 52

markets
derivative 9, 42, 54
disciplined 36
financial 3, 14, 20, 22, 27, 31–33, 36, 38, 40–42, 50, 52–54, 67, 94, 103, 112–113, 139–140, 146, 153
Martin, R. 4, 8–11, 33, 52–55, 162
Marx, K. 1, 22, 24, 75, 92, 134
measure of value 13, 21, 75–77, 85, 92, 160
monopoly 8, 20, 28–29, 35
moral economy 4–5, 7–8, 10, 12, 17–24, 27–28, 30–39, 100, 105, 158–159
speculative moral economy 4–5, 10, 12, 14, 19, 40–46, 51, 56–57, 62–63, 67–68, 95, 102, 113, 115, 119–120, 125, 128, 132, 158–159

paternalistic 17, 20, 25, 28, 30–31
philanthropy 28, 30
Polanyi, K. 7
private governance 47
probability 2, 8, 79–80

Rafferty, M. 9, 53, 56
reputation 62, 99, 105, 113, 125, 128, 130, 131
resilient 1, 3, 49, 51, 98
responsible corporation 8, 34, 41
responsible capital imaginary 3, 4, 6, 10, 12, 14, 41, 43, 45, 63, 67, 92, 98, 103, 112, 115–116,

125–127, 137, 140, 153, 156–158
and ESG integration 63, 67, 98
responsible investment 1, 4, 12, 14, 58–60, 62–63, 68, 75–76, 79, 84, 87, 89–90, 95, 98, 101, 126, 143, 152
risk
ESG 45, 48–49, 51, 61, 77–86, 89, 91–93, 106, 112, 124, 128, 133, 137, 144–145, 148, 159–160, 162
systemic 47–48, 49–50, 106

SASB *see* Sustainability Accounting Standards Board
shareholder 2, 34, 41–45, 47–48, 58–59, 63, 83, 85, 114
shareholder value 2, 42–43, 59, 63
share ownership 47
social derivative 9
social reproduction 9, 24, 29, 70
speculation 4, 8–10, 13–14, 19–20, 22, 27, 31, 33, 36, 38–41, 45, 54–57, 78, 87, 127, 159–160
speculative moral economy 4–5, 10, 12, 14, 19, 40–46, 51, 56, 57, 62–63, 67–68, 95, 102, 113, 115, 119–120, 125, 128, 132, 158–159
stakeholder capitalism 3, 40
subsumption
of ethics 5
formal 24
of labour in different ways 137

of life and labour 159
real 24, 26
Sustainability Accounting Standards Board (SASB) 12, 60, 88–89, 94–95, 97–98, 100–101, 103, 108–116, 147–148, 160–161
systemic risk 47–48, 49–50, 106

Thompson, E.P. 7, 17–19, 21–22, 25, 158
trademarks 13, 121–123, 128–132

uncertainty 8–9, 20, 53, 55, 96
United Nations (UN) 1, 41, 43, 49, 88, 89, 97–98, 151
universal owner 48–49, 51
universal owners 48, 51

value
Marxian 11, 14, 68–70, 72, 106, 120, 158–159, 162
measure of 13, 21, 75, 77, 85, 92, 160
risk as a 76, 85
relations 4, 56, 68–72, 74, 77, 95
value theory 10–12, 14, 63, 67, 69–73, 77, 107, 132, 162
value theory of labour 11, 72, 77
values
socio-cultural 14, 67, 69–70, 74–77, 85–86, 107
economic 68–69

welfare capitalists 8, 31, 33, 45
World Economic Forum (WEF) 41

Milton Keynes UK
Ingram Content Group UK Ltd.
UKHW021448121124
2786UKWH00006B/27